# PEACE OR WAR? UNDERSTANDING THE PEACE PROCESS IN NORTHERN IRELAND

*To Jim and Geraldine Gilligan, Anita and Connell*

# Peace or War? Understanding the Peace Process in Northern Ireland

*Edited by*
CHRIS GILLIGAN
JON TONGE

LONDON AND NEW YORK

First published 1997 by Ashgate Publishing

Reissued 2018 by Routledge
2 Park Square, Milton Park, Abingdon, Oxon, OX14 4RN
711 Third Avenue, New York, NY 10017, USA

*Routledge is an imprint of the Taylor & Francis Group, an informa business*

Copyright © Chris Gilligan and Jon Tonge 1997

All rights reserved. No part of this book may be reprinted or reproduced or utilised in any form or by any electronic, mechanical, or other means, now known or hereafter invented, including photocopying and recording, or in any information storage or retrieval system, without permission in writing from the publishers.

Notice:
Product or corporate names may be trademarks or registered trademarks, and are used only for identification and explanation without intent to infringe.

Publisher's Note
The publisher has gone to great lengths to ensure the quality of this reprint but points out that some imperfections in the original copies may be apparent.

Disclaimer
The publisher has made every effort to trace copyright holders and welcomes correspondence from those they have been unable to contact.

A Library of Congress record exists under LC control number: 97073871

ISBN 13: 978-0-367-00083-7 (hbk)
ISBN 13: 978-0-367-00086-8 (pbk)
ISBN 13: 978-0-429-44460-9 (ebk)

# Contents

| | |
|---|---|
| List of tables | vii |
| List of figures | viii |
| List of contributors | ix |
| Acknowledgements | xi |
| List of abbreviations | xii |

**Part One: Introduction and overview**     1

1. Introduction     3
   *Chris Gilligan and Jon Tonge*

2. The origins and development of the peace process     5
   *Jon Tonge*

3. Peace or pacification process? A brief critique of the peace process     19
   *Chris Gilligan*

**Part Two: Political perspectives**     35

4. Divided loyalists, divided loyalties: Conflict and continuities in contemporary unionist ideology     37
   *James White McAuley*

5. Unity in diversity? The SDLP and the peace process     54
   *Mark McGovern*

6. From the centre to the margins: The slow death of Irish republicanism     72
   *Mark Ryan*

**Part Three: Issues in the peace process**     85

| | | |
|---|---|---|
| 7 | Cross-border cooperation and the peace process<br>*Alan Greer* | 87 |
| 8 | Security strategies in Northern Ireland: Consolidation or reform?<br>*Paddy Hillyard* | 103 |
| 9 | Education: A panacea for our sectarian ills?<br>*Kevin Rooney* | 119 |
| 10 | The economics of the peace process<br>*Pete Shirlow* | 133 |
| 11 | The Northern Ireland peace process: A gender issue?<br>*Rachel Ward* | 150 |

**Part Four: Conclusion** 163

| | | |
|---|---|---|
| 12 | Conclusion<br>*Chris Gilligan and Jon Tonge* | 165 |

# List of tables

Table 2.1   Parties elected to the Northern Ireland Forum 1996          16

# List of figures

Figure 4.1  Trends within contemporary unionism                49

# List of contributors

**Chris Gilligan** is a Ph.D student in the Department of Politics and Contemporary History, European Studies Research Institute, at the University of Salford. He is a regular book reviewer for *Political Studies* on various aspects of Northern Irish politics. He is currently engaged in research on the way in which 'identity' has become a key category for understanding the conflict, and peace process, in Northern Ireland.

**Alan Greer** is senior lecturer in Politics in the Faculty of Economics and Social Science at the University of the West of England, Bristol. His most recent publications include *Rural Politics in Northern Ireland: Policy Networks and Agricultural Development since Partition*, Avebury, 1996.

**Paddy Hillyard** is Director of Centre for Socio-Legal Studies in the School for Policy Studies at the University of Bristol. He is a member of the editorial board of *Social and Legal Studies: An International Journal*, and a former chair of Liberty (the National Council for Civil Liberties). He has written widely on Northern Ireland particularly in the field of sociology of law and civil liberties. His last book was *Suspect Community: People~s Experience of the Prevention of Terrorism Acts in Britain*, Pluto, 1993.

**James White McAuley** is Reader in Behavioural Sciences at the University of Huddersfield and has written many articles on Northern Irish politics, culture and society. Publications include *The Politics of Identity: a loyalist community in Belfast*, Avebury, 1994.

**Mark McGovern** is a lecturer in Applied Social Sciences at Edge Hill University College, Ormskirk, Dr Mark McGovern is the author of numerous articles on Northern Irish politics and co-editor of *Who Are the People? Unionism, Loyalism and Protestantism in Contemporary Northern Ireland*, Pluto, 1997.

**Kevin Rooney** is a lecturer in Politics and History at West Herts College of Further Education. He is a regular contributor to a range of publications on Irish politics.

**Mark Ryan** is a freelance journalist. He has contributed to a wide range of publications including *The Daily Telegraph*, and *Living Marxism*. He is the author of *War and Peace in Ireland; Britain and the IRA in the New World Order*, Pluto, 1994.

**Pete Shirlow** teaches Geography at the School of Geosciences, Queen~s University, Belfast, where he is also Director of the Socio-Spatial Research Unit. He has written widely on the political economy of Ireland and has recently edited two books for Pluto Press: *Development Ireland; Contemporary Issues* and *Who are the People? Unionism, Loyalism and Protestantism in Northern Ireland*.

**Jon Tonge** is a lecturer in Politics in the Department of Politics and Contemporary History, European Studies Research Institute (ESRI), at the University of Salford, chairing the Irish Studies sub-group within ESRI. He has published various articles and chapters on Northern Ireland, in addition to his most recent publication, *Conflict and Change in Northern Ireland*, Prentice Hall, 1997.

**Rachel Ward** is currently undertaking a Ph.D on the conflict between nationalism and feminism in the context of Ireland, in the Faculty of Economic and Social Science, at the University of the West of England, Bristol. She is a graduate of the University of Salford, where she attained a B.Sc (Hons) in Social Science and an MA in Politics and Contemporary History.

# Acknowledgements

A considerable number of debts have been incurred in the production of this book. We wish to thank Sarah Markham and Anne Keirby at Ashgate for acting so speedily upon our proposal and for their patient help throughout the production of this book. A big thank-you is also due to each author for the prompt submission of their manuscripts. Some of the ideas of the co-editors of this book are influenced by the contributions to the seminar series, Understanding the Peace Process in Ireland, staged by the European Studies Institute at the University of Salford, in 1996. We wish to thank each contributor in addition to those of Dr Alan Greer, Dr Paddy Hillyard and Dr Jim McAuley, whose contributions appear in this book: Professor Steve Bruce Aberdeen); Gregory Campbell (DUP); David Ervine (PUP) Dr Sean Farren (SDLP) Eric Illsley MP (Labour) and Professor Brendan O'Leary (LSE); A thank you is also due to the European Commission and the Ireland Fund of Great Britain for their generous sponsorship of the event and their financial support for a Salford University study tour to Ireland during the same period. In respect of the latter, we wish to thank Alex Attwood (SDLP); Professor Paul Bew (Queens, now Magdalen, Cambridge); Bobby Lavery (Sinn Fein); Nelson McCausland (UUP) and Alex Maskey (Sinn Fein). Considerable debts are also owed to Professor Geoff Harris and Heather Lally for their support and organisation of the seminar series and likewise to Jeff Evans and Rachel Ward in respect of the study tour.

On a personal note, Chris Gilligan wishes to thank Rob, Marcus, Penny, Archie, Neil and Hugh for being a constant source of intellectual stimulation. Simon and Yvonne for their generous hospitality on the many trips to Manchester. Dolores and Katie for helping to make the study trips to Dublin more enjoyable. Louise for helping out on many of the trips to Belfast. And a special thank you to Aisling, whose presence brings brightness to even the gloomiest of days.

Jon Tonge wishes to thank Anita and Connell for all their forebearance and promises substantial compensation.

None of the above should be construed as an attempt to spread blame for any of the contents of the book. Final responsibility rests with the editors.

Chris Gilligan
Jon Tonge

# List of abbreviations

| | |
|---|---|
| APNI | Alliance Party of Northern Ireland |
| CAP | Common Agricultural Policy |
| CCRU | Central Community Relations Unit |
| CLMC | Combined Loyalist Military Command |
| DSD | Downing Street Declaration |
| DUP | (Ulster) Democratic Unionist Party |
| EMU | Education for Mutual Understanding |
| EPA | Emergency Provisions Act |
| EU | European Union |
| GDP | Gross Domestic Product |
| IFA | Irish Farmers' Association |
| IRA | Irish Republican Army |
| JFD | Joint Framework Document |
| LSE | London School of Economics |
| MAFF | Ministry of Agriculture, Food and Fisheries |
| NIAPA | Northern Ireland Producers' Association |
| NICCEA | Northern Ireland Council for Curriculum, Examinations and Assessment |
| NICIE | Northern Ireland Council for Integrated Education |
| NICRC | Northern Ireland Community Relations Council |
| NICVA | Northern Ireland Council of Voluntary Associations |
| NIWC | Northern Ireland Women's Coalition |
| NSB | North-South Body |
| PANI | Police Authority for Northern Ireland |
| PTA | Prevention of Terrorism Act |
| PUP | Progressive Unionist Party |
| RIR | Royal Irish Regiment |
| SDLP | Social Democratic and Labour Party |
| SEM | Single European Market |
| SF | Sinn Fein |
| SWC | Shankill Women's Centre |

| | |
|---|---|
| UDA | Ulster Defence Association |
| UDP | Ulster Democratic Party |
| UUP | Ulster Unionist Party |
| UFU | Ulster Farmers' Union |
| UVF | Ulster Volunteer Force |
| WIN | Women's Information Network |
| WIP | Women Into Politics |
| WSN | Women's Support Network |
| WTFP | Women Together for Peace |

# Part One
# INTRODUCTION AND OVERVIEW

# 1 Introduction

*Chris Gilligan and Jon Tonge*

The peace process of the 1990s appeared to offer the best chance yet of ending violent conflict in Northern Ireland. If a temporary peace did not arrive until 1994, the gestation of the peace process occured from the mid-1980s onwards. The very term 'peace process' is controversial. Critics might argue that the process was a sham, based upon a tactical repositioning of republicanism which proved extremely short-lived. Supporters of the peace process argue, often from different political perspectives, that it provided a framework for reconciliation or even conflict resolution.

This book explores the nature of the peace process, outlining the political changes which allowed it to develop and examining specific themes within the process itself. For this reason, the book is divided into three main sections. The first provides general discussions of the aims and objectives of the peace process. The second section analyses the changing roles of the political parties and party ideology in shaping the peace process and responding to developments within that process. The third section offers discussion of some of the most important themes within the peace process. In carefully selecting these themes, the co-editors are aware that it is impossible to cover in detail every important aspect of the peace process. The book is designed to promote discussion, rather than provide a definitive account of the peace process. *Peace or War?* begins with an overview of the peace process from Jon Tonge in chapter two. When and why did it start? What did it major participants anticipate? Why did it stumble? Following this, Chris Gilligan discusses whether the peace process was genuine attempt at resolving the conflict, or merely an attempt at creating non-violence. Gilligan highlights the seeming contradiction between the stress upon the need for inclusive dialogue and the lack of citizen involvement in the peace process.

In Part two, Jim McAuley assesses the attempt to reconstruct Unionism as a response to the peace process. He suggests that attempts at remodelling have been rendered problematic by the pressure placed upon Unionists not to participate in the peace process. Mark McGovern provides an assessment of how the SDLP's pursuit of internal consociationalism and external intergovernmentalism have shaped the peace process. He examines the tensions within the Party's approach to a lasting settlement.

The SDLP's traditional historical analysis of British responsibility for the problem rests uneasily alongside the Party's beliefs of unity in diversity and parity of esteem. In chapter six, Mark Ryan argues that Irish republicanism has undergone a slow death, masked by a continuing 'armed struggle'. Sinn Fein's recognition of the southern state in 1986 contributed significantly to republicanism's loss of distinctiveness. Concurrently, the pursuit of inclusive dialogue and emphasis upon parity of esteem for the nationalist community have led to greater recognition of the northern state.

Part three's exploration of themes within the peace process begins with an analysis of attempts to promote cross-border cooperation. In exploring different models of cooperation, Alan Greer makes the point that such cooperation is not new, but its attempted extension raises hopes or fears amongst nationalists and unionists. The Framework Documents attempted extensions of cross borderism allied to a limited series of checks upon such activity. In the following chapter Paddy Hillyard provides a critical account of the lack of, reform of policing in Northern Ireland and a similar lack of urgency on the issue of release of prisoners. Following this, Kevin Rooney offers a sceptical view of Education for Mutual Understanding as a vehicle by which community tension might be defused. Rooney suggests that such problems seek only to obfuscate the true nature of the problem. In chapter 10, Peter Shirlow points out that social exclusion and a deprivation amongst the nationalist and unionist working classes have fostered an intra-class war. He urges the establishment of a wide ranging Commission for Economic Reconstruction and Social Inclusion as a remedy. Finally Rachel Ward rejects the idea of women as neutral peacekeepers in the peace process. Whilst welcoming the increased profile of women in politics in Northern Ireland, Ward points to the criticism of the Northern Ireland Women's Coalition by other Women's groups over its lack of policies. As in so many other aspects of the peace process, ambiguity prevails.

# 2 The origins and development of the peace process

*Jon Tonge*

## Introduction

Providing an overview of the peace process presents a number of difficulties. The first problem lies in deciding whether the process was one with a definitive beginning and conclusion. One account suggests that the process 'was a self-contained one with a beginning, a middle and, sadly, an end' (Bew and Gillespie, 1996, p.7). Certainly the IRA bomb at Canary Wharf in February 1996 appeared to end the peace process. Nonetheless much speculation continued that another ceasefire was possible and a limited political process continued. If one accepts that the process ended in February 1996, the origins of the peace process were of considerably longer duration than the period of peace. A second problem is that of labelling. To speak of the Northern Ireland peace process is in a sense misleading. Much of the impetus and some of the ramifications of the process lay outside Northern Ireland. Thirdly, there lie the much broader problems of identifying how and why a peace process developed. Finally, the reasons why that process encountered a series of obstacles require analysis.

### A movable starting line

The start of a peace process has been identified as early as the Papal visit to Ireland in 1979 (Coogan, 1995). After the Pope condemned violence whilst insisting he sought justice, leading elements in Sinn Fein sought dialogue with the Catholic Church concerning interpretations of a just war. Such talks were centred more upon the anxiety of the republicans to justify war rather than engage in peace negotiations. Accordingly, two more conventional starting points for the peace process have been offered.

In 1986 at its ard-fheis, Provisional Sinn Fein voted by a three to one majority to end abstentionism in elections to the Dail. Henceforth, in the unlikely event of Sinn Fein candidates being elected, they would take their seats. If the practical impact of the decision was negligible in terms of the electoral politics of the south, it was of immense importance in respect of Northern Ireland.

The decision was hugely symbolic. It represented a tacit acceptance of the twenty-six county in the state, recognising the legitimacy of its parliament. Previously the southern state was viewed as a neo-colonial British satellite. This volte-face was achieved at astonishing speed. Only one year earlier, the President of Sinn Fein had insisted that the Dail was Irish in name only, amounting to 'a British parliamentary system handed down by ex-colonial rulers' (Adams, 1985, p. 8).

There was considerable irony in the policy reversal. The Provisional IRA had split from what became the ' Official IRA' in 1970 due to the latter's willingness to end abstentionism in t he south, The wheel had come full circle and it was scarcely surprising that the traditionalist wing of the party left to form Republican Sinn Fein, based upon 'purist' republican principles. No longer did Provisional Sinn Fein claim an enduring mandate from its success in the last all-Ireland elections of 1918. Moreover, no longer did Sinn Fein and the IRA see themselves as 'sole liberators' of Ireland. From now, the existing twenty-six county state would be accepted by northern republicans as articulator of the interests of a thirty-two county nation. Pan-nationalism began here.

Not everyone would accept 1986 as the crucial building block in the peace process. There was little change in IRA activity and the Irish Government did not display an immediate willingness to construct an Irish-led peace process. Alternatively therefore, the Hume-Adams dialogue of 1988, revived in 1992, might be seen as the 'kick-starter'. The discussions between the leaders of the SDLP and Sinn Fein were based upon an attempt to convince the latter of three things. Firstly, IRA violence was counter-productive to the nationalist cause. Secondly, the British Government was now neutral on the constitutional future of northern Ireland. It might even be prepared to become a persuader to Unionists of the merits of a united Ireland. Thirdly, Sinn Fein must accept that Unionists had their own identity within the island of Ireland. They were not merely neo-colonial settlers.

Placement of Hume-Adams at the starting point of the peace process depends to some extent upon whether its objectives were achieved. IRA violence was halted, albeit temporarily. Sinn Fein accepted, albeit privately, that Britain was no longer a colonial ruler in Ireland (Mallie and McKittrick, 1996). Against this, Hume-Adams broke up in 1988 and its agreements in 1992-93 were arguably merely a reassertion of a longstanding nationalist principle of self determination i.e. that all the people of Ireland should determine its future. Undoubtedly Hume-Adams was significant in further ending the political isolation of Sinn Fein. By engaging in dialogue with republicans, Hume removed barriers to dialogue confronting others within the 'nationalist family'.

One might argue that the real peace process began with the involvement of the British Government. The opening of a secret line of communication between the British Government and the IRA in 1990 indicated the view of the Secretary of State Peter Brooke that republicans might wish to end the violent pursuit of their goals. This 'Back Channel' of communication was opened against a political backdrop of avowedly increased British neutrality on the constitutional future of Northern Ireland. This was illustrated not merely in the agreements and declarations discussed below, but in the assertion by Brooke that Britain had no 'selfish strategic or economic interest' in Northern Ireland.

Finally, the beginning of the true peace process could be identified as the paramilitary ceasefires. The 'complete cessation' of military operations declared by the IRA in August 1994 deliberately excluded the word permanent. Its omission emphasised that there was no possibility of a surrender by the Provisionals. A plethora of unresolved wrangles over the inclusion if Sinn Fein in all-party dialogue resulted. Six weeks later, the umbrella organisation, the Combined Loyalist Military Command, announced a reciprocal ceasefire. The ceasefires were predicated upon entirely different conclusions; Republicans believed that substantial political progress was possible. Loyalists had devoted the six week interlude to establishing that the Union was safe (Rowan, 1995). A formal peace process was underway, but it appeared extremely fragile.

**British policy: neutrality versus integration**

By the mid-1980s, the British Government had become exasperated by the failure of local politicians to reach agreement in Northern Ireland. The attempted consociationalism of 1974 had been broken by the Ulster Workers Council Strike. Attempts at very weak devolutionary imitations in 1975 and 1982 had foundered. Equally the Conservative Government had realised the limitations of the Ulsterisation and criminalisation approaches of its Labour predecessor as amounting to mere 'keeping the lid on' strategies. The response was to construct arrangements for governance within an intergovernmental framework, predicated upon core assumptions. These were firstly, that a purely internal settlement was impossible in Northern Ireland; secondly, constitutional nationalism should be actively promoted; thirdly, this promotion could only be achieved through concessions to the Republic in return for a bolstering of cross-border security measures.

The Anglo-Irish Agreement of 1985 suggested to some that the British Government was neutral on the future of Northern Ireland. An appearance of neutrality was heightened by the public outrage towards the Agreement generated within Unionist circles. Britain no longer sought to act as a persuader for the Union. Instead, the aim of a united Ireland or support for the retention of Northern Ireland's position within the Union were of equal validity. There was no longer such a thing as disloyalty within Northern Ireland.

For Unionists, the facilitation of a possible united Ireland contained within the Agreement were disingenuous. The desire for a united Ireland had never been prevented, but was now promoted to a status equal with that of the status quo of the Union (Aughey, 1994). Yet the Agreement produced only weak Irish input into decision-making in the North. Its denial of constitutional change without internal consent differed in mechanism only from that provided in the Ireland Act of 1949.

Perceptions of neutrality were aided by the public stance of republicans. Gerry Adams argued that the Agreement 'copper-fastened partition'. A supportive echo was found in the criticism of Charles Haughey, whose Fianna Fail Party led opposition in the Republic. Yet the public utterances of Sinn Fein masked a shift in analysis away from the idea contemporary conflict was essentially colonial. Unsurprisingly, the

British Government was anxious to facilitate this shift. It wished to foster a 'no favoured solution' approach to conflict resolution.

The lasting significance of the Anglo-Irish Government lay more in its framework than its impact. It was imposed above the heads of local politicians. Unionist opposition was ignored. The Agreement placed the Northern Ireland problem within the joint domain of the British and Irish governments. By granting a role for the Republic in the affairs of Northern Ireland through the deliberations of the Anglo-Irish Conference, it placed the government of the twenty-six county state in the vanguard of appeals from other nationalists. It was thus likely to act in future years as a harbinger for nationalist aspirations.

Accordingly, when the peace process began to gather momentum in the 1990s, both the constitutional and ultra strands of northern nationalism bargained with the Irish Government for the most strident expression of self-determination possible to be contained within the Anglo-Irish Joint Declaration for Peace, otherwise known as the Downing Street Declaration (DSD). Issued in December 1993, the Downing Street Declaration was the most overt statement thus far of British neutrality in respect of Northern Ireland. The insistence upon neutrality meant that the British Government would not adopt the persuader role desired by republicans in respect of Unionist consent for a untied Ireland. Nor would existing neutrality lead to the exercise of joint authority over Northern Ireland by the British and Irish Governments. Instead, the British Government would act merely as a facilitator for change in the event of an extraordinary conversion by Unionists to support for a united Ireland, or sufficient change in the demographic balance for a nationalist majority to be achieved.

The Declaration used republican terminology of self-determination. This doctrine was qualified by the insistence that self-determination be exercised on a north and south basis. It was asserted that it was for the people of Ireland alone to achieve Irish unity, via agreement between the two parts. For republicans, the insistence upon a lack of external impediment was, somewhat hollow as the British Government's presence in Northern Ireland would inevitably influence the decision in the north. The Brooke declaration of Britain's lack of selfish strategic or economic interest was restated to 'treat seriously and politely reject' Sinn Fein's belief that a conflict was being fought against British imperialism (McGarry and O'Leary, 1995, p.418).

A further theme of the Declaration was parity of esteem between the two traditions in Northern Ireland. Published in February 1995, the Framework Documents aimed to give practical effect to the principles of the Downing Street Declaration. They attempted to revive a consociational form of internal settlement based upon the establishment of grand elites of local politicians (Lijphart, 1996). The first of the two Documents contained the proposals of the British Government for internal governance within Northern Ireland. These included the election of a 90 seat Assembly by proportional representation; the establishment of departmental committees reflective of party strengths and the creation of a three member panel. The panel would consider contentious legislation. Optimistically, the proposals assumed that this body would be able to reach unanimous (HM Government 1995, p.10). The panel represented the final leg of a series of check and balances, the main element which included weighted majority voting and separate elections to the panel and Assembly.

The second part of the Framework Documents provided the intergovernmental approach to Northern Ireland. Key participants in the Northern Ireland Assembly would not be able to avoid participation in the all-Ireland, north-south body. Part II of the Documents offered a mixture of dynamic cross-borderism and limited attempts at ringfencing of such iniatives. A North-South body would assume a consultative, harmonising or executive role in respect of a wide range of political and economic matters. Delegation of these functions to the cross-border body would occur after approval from the British and Irish parliaments. The British Government insisted that it had 'no limits' to impose on the extent of this delegation in the first instance (HM Government, 1995, p.30). Ringfencing was evident in that subsequent transfer of functions had to be approved by the administration in Northern Ireland.

Thus far it is possible to see Britain's role in the peace process as the promotion of neutrality and the fostering of cross-borderism. Although the British Government continued to insist upon undiluted sovereignty over Northern Ireland, it offered institutional arrangements which straddled the border. Further, the Framework Documents offered the prospect of an all-Ireland dynamic in respect of economic arrangements. Yet the DSD and the Framework Documents were devised whilst the peace process was on an upward curve. A Conservative Government reliant upon Unionist votes in the House of Commons had limited room for manoeuvre. No serious attempt was ever made to sell the Framework Documents. By the time of their issue, Britain's neutral facilitator stance was juxtaposed against the pursuit of integrative policies which resulted in Northern Ireland decision-making and policy scrutiny being more closely in line with that of other regions in the UK since the creation of the state.

The creation of a Northern Ireland Select Committee in 1994 was the first such integrative device. In a rare break with political bipartisanship, the Labour Party derided its establishment as a reward for Unionists for their support for the Conservatives in tight votes on the Maastricht Treaty (Boyce 1996; Kennedy-Pipe 1997). It was denied by Conservatives and Unionists that any deal had been done. If true, it was a situation in which, as Boyce observes, 'Major and James Molyneaux managed to communicate through the means of silence' (Boyce, 1996, p.147). The Select Committee offered the five MP's selected from Northern Ireland the first significant opportunity to study the activities of the Northern Ireland Office since the imposition of direct rule. A second integrative move was the announcement of substantial bolstering of the Northern Ireland Grand Committee in 1996. Previously, legislation was determined by orders in council which could be accepted or rejected in parliament, but not amended (Hazelton, 1995). Legislative proposals would now be subject to much greater debate, signifying a substantial modification of direct rule by decree.

**Towards a new republicanism?**

One of the most dramatic features of the peace process was the manner in which Sinn Fein 'moved from the fringes' (Gibney, 1996, p.14). The construction of a pan-nationalist alliance engaged the Irish Government, SDLP, Sinn Fein and Irish America. There were immediate practical reasons for this development. Sinn Fein had been encouraged by the 'enthusiasm' for debate displayed by Peter Brooke (Adams,

1995). Although the Party had refused to accept the notion of British neutrality suggested by Hume in initial dialogue, it nonetheless sensed that Britain's commitment to Northern Ireland might be weakening. Two justifications existed for Sinn Fein's rejection of the neutrality argument. Firstly, the insistence upon the Unionist consent principle for change provided a proactive defence of the status quo. Secondly, the size of the British subvention to Northern Ireland was so immense as to counter notions of a British neutrality based upon disinterest.

Leading members of Sinn Fein recognised the inadequacy of the Party's 1987 policy document Strategy for Peace as a basis for negotiation with Britain (Sinn Fein 1987; Mallie and McKittrick, 1996). That document amounted to a restatement of fundamental republican principles and prescriptions. Arguably Scenario for Peace, notwithstanding its title, was the crudest fusion of territorial and ethnic nationalism ever undertaken by republicans. It insisted that the struggle to eject Britain was an anti-colonial affair and viewed Unionists as neo-colonial settlers, to be offered repatriation grants if Irish unity could not be accepted. Within five years, there had been a substantial shift in thinking. The 1992 document Towards a Lasting Peace offered a changed approach (Sinn Fein, 1992). It introduced 'pluralist concepts of identity, cultural parity of esteem, and 'Irishness' which soften the harder, more overtly political concepts of reunification' (Bean, 1995, p.2). It acknowledged that Britain could play a positive role in Ireland in a policy of 'constructive disengagement'. Britain should act as a persuader to Unionists, now seen as semi-autonomous actors, that their better interests lay in a united Ireland. Interim demands such as the disbandment of the RUC and proposals for parity of esteem assumed greater importance as the timetable for British withdrawal became vaguer. Two broad perspectives emerged as this change in republican thinking (Tonge 1997). One suggests that the death of republicanism had occurred (Ryan, 1994). In contrast, Unionists have insisted that purely tactical shifts in goal attainment have altered neither the analysis nor prescriptions of republicanism.

The greater flexibility displayed in Towards a Lasting Peace cemented a pan-nationalist alliance based around the desirability of progress towards Irish self-determination. Given the political antecedents of its participants this development might not be seen as surprising. The founding principles of the main actors were that partition was unjust and that politics should centre upon the rectification of this injustice. A pan-nationalist coalition was not difficult to achieve once Sinn Fein and the IRA had abandoned a 'sole liberator' position.

As the new nationalist alliance gathered strength, it attempted to create a dynamic peace process centred upon Anglo-Irish acceptance of the moral and political legitimacy of Irish self-determination. This was most clearly seen in the input to the Downing Street Declaration. This emerged in substantially revised form from the drafts provided by Hume-Adams and the Irish Government. As part of an embryonic process of all-inclusive dialogue, Unionists also had some input into later drafts. The final document provided republicans with a dilemma. Self-determination emerged in neutered form. Constitutional nationalists had allowed it be given a 'new, decidedly softer conceptual content' (Bew et al., 1996 p.229). Separate majorities north and south would be required for the exercise of self-determination.

Such a bi-national means of self-determination was never likely to be acceptable for republicans. Sinn Fein admired the language but rejected the formula. The refusal to accept the DSD was confirmed at Sinn Fein's special Letterkenny conference in 1994. This emphasised that Unionist consent was an 'essential ingredient' for lasting peace in Ireland but pointedly declined to accept it as a prerequisite. Having refused to endorse the DSD, Sinn Fein could not endorse the same principles found ion the Framework Document although again the language of Sinn Fein was conciliatory. The position of Adams on the consent principle was unequivocal, stressing that 'the argument that the consent of a national minority, which has been elevated into an majority in an undemocratic and artificially created state, is necessary before any constitutional change can occur is a nonsense' (Adams, 1995, pp.234-35). Unionists meanwhile insisted that the 'entire (peace) process...boils down to the acceptance of the consent principle' (McGimpsey, 1996, p.46). The peace process was to flounder upon barriers to inclusive dialogue. However, the difficulties of resolving the majority-minority dichotomy within the island would have proved of even greater difficulty in the event of all-party talks taking place.

**Constitutional nationalism unites**

The definitive statement of constitutional Irish nationalism prior to the peace process came in the New Ireland Forum Report in 1984 (New Ireland Forum, 1984). It produced three constitutional models: a unitary state; a confederal state and joint authority. The Report accepted the majority northern consent principle and the existence of two traditions on the island, yet in one of its concluding models veered towards what has been described as the 'ultimate infeasibility of unitary nationalism, predicated upon absolutist sovereignty claims' (Kearney, 1996, p.11). Furthermore, the Report indicated that nationalist Ireland would continue to pursue unity as a logical political outcome. This theme has been echoed by deliberate ambiguity over whether the Republic will repeal articles 2 and 3 of its constitution laying claim to the North of Ireland. Once rid of the ideological purity which challenged the twenty-six county state, it was natural that republicans would seek to build alliances with constitutional supporters of Irish unity, provided that they too engaged in politics beyond that of sterile anti-partitionism.

Potential limitations to a broad nationalist approach were apparent, although some gains were also likely. In siding with fellow nationalists, Sinn Fein's pursuit of new constitutionalism was unlikely to deliver a united Ireland; likely to produce gains for northern nationalists and, if pursued exclusively, risked splitting the republican movement (O'Leary and McGarry 1996). Yet Sinn Fein were encouraged along this path by the leadership of Fianna Fail and the SDLP. As leader of the former, Reynolds engaged in a strategy of pursuing peace as 'an end it itself' (Coogan, 1995, p.368). Leading a Party which carried republican ideological baggage, Reynolds was anxious to lead Sinn Fein towards inclusive dialogue which offered this end, arguing that acknowledgements of Irish self-determination and British neutrality contained within the Downing Street Declaration would provide the means. The DSD was regarded as the 'catalyst for peace' (Mansergh, 1996 p.56). It was the role of Reynolds' coalition government led by Fianna Fail to convert (and dilute) the Hume-Adams principles into an acceptable Anglo-Irish political framework. Overall, the aim of constitutional nationalists was to ease the barriers for republicans towards a fourth and final phase of the evolution of the 'struggle' since 1969; military primacy from 1969-80; parity between the military and political between 1981-88 (the 'armalite and ballot box' approach); primacy of the political from 1988 onwards and now potentially, exclusively political.

Ethnic migrant nationalism had always formed an important aspect of the Irish idea of nation. Sections of the diaspora in America had taken a keen interest in the politics of Northern Ireland. Irish Americans were more heterogenous on the question of Northern Ireland question than their common portrayal in the British press. Under the Clinton administration, a pro-active stance was taken on Northern Ireland. In part this reflected a desire to create a peace process akin to those in South Africa and the Middle East. The circumstances of American involvement were nonetheless substantially different (Guelke, 1994) With Northern Ireland not part of the previous Cold War, Clinton's decision to become involved was more likely to be based upon electoral calculation, allied perhaps to personal interest. It was reflected in a desire to utilise the National Security Council rather than the pro-British state department as his policy vehicle.

Two particular developments arose form American involvement. Firstly, Sinn Fein underwent a 'respectability' process, exemplified by the award of an entry visa to Gerry Adams. The organisation Friends of Sinn Fein embraced a wide spectrum of Irish-American opinion. Ironically, some previous 'friends' were now non-contributors. The traditional main source of Sinn Fein funds, NORAID, began to fragment after the decision to recognise the Irish Republic in 1986. Secondly, the American Government acted as a facilitator. This was symbolised by the deployment of the Democrat Senator George Mitchell to chair a commission of the decommissioning of weapons. It was also illustrated by the visit of President Clinton to Ireland in late 1996 in a vain attempt to shore up a flagging peace process.

**Unionism and the peace process**

Unionists were divided over their approach to the peace process. The Ulster Unionist Party offered a muted response to the Downing Street Declaration. Attached to the actual Declaration, 'Not the Downing Street Declaration' was of greater importance for the UUP. Britain's insistence that it would act on the basis of majority consent and disinclination to act as a persuader to Unionists for a united Ireland appeared to assuage some potential critics.

A far less sanguine attitude was adopted by the DUP. It was particularly resentful over two issues. Firstly, Northern Ireland's place in the United Kingdom had become increasingly conditional. Northern Ireland had always been treated as a palace apart. Now it was treated as a unwanted area of the United Kingdom in which Britain had no particular interest. Secondly, the DSD, like the Anglo-Irish Agreement institutionalised and legitimised the Republic's constitutional territorial claim to the north.

In an attempt by nationalists to defuse such criticism, the political representatives of the loyalist paramilitary groups, the Ulster Democratic Party (UDP) and Progressive Unionist Party (PUP) were given an advance copy of the DSD by the Irish Taoiseach (Bruce 1994). Loyalists valued the affirmation of the consent principle and rejected Ian Paisley's 'knee-jerk rejection' (Bruce 1994, p.94). Indeed the peace process consolidated tension between the DUP and loyalist paramilitaries. The latter regarded the DUP and Paisley in particular, as posture politicians favouring the maintenance of a sectarian band of Unionism. For its part, the DUP regarded the activities and lack of mandate of loyalist paramilitaries with considerable contempt. Hostility was exacerbated by the fact that the UDP and PUP were fishing the DUP's electoral waters.

Given the cautious approach of the UUP to the DSD, the Party's strident criticisms of the Framework Documents were perhaps surprising. Paisley (1997, p.16) argued that it was 'strange to relate those who prepared the womb of the Downing Street Declaration have now rejected its offspring'. Certainly the publication of the Framework documents further increased disquiet within the UUP over Molyneux's leadership. One month later, an unknown challenger, Lee Reynolds, gained 15% of the vote in a leadership contest. Molyneux resigned later that year. The new leader, David Trimble, argued that the framework documents could not be considered a serious blueprint for the future of northern Ireland. The DUP congratulated itself on its consistency in seeing the entire peace process as a 'sell-out', deriding the framework document as one of 'shame and sham' (Democratic Unionist Party, 1995).

After his election, Trimble pledged to construct a progressive unionism. Part of new unionism involved a review of the main Unionist Party's link with the Protestant Orange Order, which continued to enjoy voting rights within the Party. Given that the influence of the Order was declining within the Party and there were members of the Order who wished to loosen ties, it appeared that Trimble might be kicking at an open door. However, the salience of the role of the Order and its importance within Unionism had increased as a consequence of the Siege of Drumcree in 1995. Here, Orangemen insisted upon the right to march down a traditional route. Confrontation was repeated, with the same successful outcome for Orangemen, in 1996. The Spirit of Drumcree group sought a tougher line from the Orange leadership over the question of parades. Equally, the group felt that the Ulster Unionist leadership had equivocated over the rights of the Order and it advocated a severing of relations with the UUP. It was apparent that even if the main Unionist Party moved towards a more liberal unionism, many of its supporters still regarded its cultural base as grounded in the Protestant religion (see Porter 1996).

In many respects the conflicts over parades were sideshows within a peace process which ran into difficulties over the issues of paramilitary violence and an absence of inclusive dialogue. Nonetheless, the 'marching season' offered a barrier to reconciliation. Bans on Orange parades through specified areas represented to nationalists part for the practical equalising process of parity of esteem which permeated recent policy declarations and outlines. To some Unionists, any restrictions upon freedom of expression were unacceptable.

Following the confrontations of 1996, the British Government established the North Committee to examine the question of parades. It concluded that the appropriate means of resolving disputes was through a commission. This would have statutory powers, although certain operational decisions would remain the prerogative of the RUC. To critics the undertone of the North Report was that the RUC could not be seen as a neutral arbiter on the question of consent for parades. By transferring adjudications to a commission, Unionists feared that ease of representation to the commission would create a 'grievance factory'. Almost half of Protestant urged complete rejection of the Report (Irwin et al, in Belfast Telegraph, 8 April 1997). Sinn Fein appeared to lament that North was a toothless watchdog, an interesting argument for greater British regulation in Northern Ireland?

### The collapse of the peace process?

After its bombing of Canary Wharf in February 1996, the IRA referred to the failure of the peace process 'thus far'. It was claimed that this action was designed to win a 'breathing space'; for the IRA (O'Leary and McGarry, p.356). The breathing space did not last long. Four months later the largest bomb ever detonated in England wrecked part of Manchester city centre. Nonetheless, the IRA believed isolated strikes might lead to Sin Fein's inclusion in the all-party talks upon which the ceasefire had been predicated.

Part of the problem with the peace process was that its foundations were so uncertain. Sinn Fein saw inclusive dialogue as the means of conflict resolution. It viewed talks as the gateway to the resolution of an 800 year-old conflict, but its military wing grew impatient with their absence after 18 months. In contrast, representatives of the loyalist paramilitaries believed that the peace process was based upon conflict-management, not resolution (Ervine, 1996). Such loyalists argued for class emancipation as the most appropriate means of breaking down barriers (see Ruane and Todd 1996; Anderson, 1997). The difficulty of developing an emancipatory approach within the constitutional status quo was evident. Such shifts as occurred on the loyalist paramilitary side occurred in respect of identity-perception. A stress upon common identity had always been present, although usually within the proposed political unit if an independent Northern Ireland favoured by the UDA in the 1970s. Now the PUP acknowledged that loyalists were 'Irish, but peculiarly British'. This was reciprocated to some extent by greater republican recognition of the Unionist tradition in policy statements such as Towards a Lasting Peace, although the attempted displays of the Orange aspect of this in nationalist areas was more vehemently opposed as triumphalism than ever previously.

Fundamental difficulties within the peace process were marked by the Clinton visit. Whilst the President insisted that the 'day is over' for terrorists, the IRA was already prepared for a return to violence. The timing of the exercise of that decision would depend upon the British-Unionist barriers preventing Sinn Fein's entry to all-party talks. Certainties are rare in politics in Northern Ireland, but two could be asserted in respect of the IRA ceasefire. One was that the IRA would not surrender its weapons in advance of a peace settlement. The second was that the British would demand a period of 'quarantine' before Sinn Fein's inclusion in all party talks. Mediation between these two positions would be difficult but not impossible, particularly if confidence was built around issues such as the release of prisoners.

For nationalists, British insistence upon IRA decommissioning of weapons was a new precondition. Reynolds insisted that its exclusion from the DSD was deliberate as he would not otherwise have been a signatory. According to the British Government the requirement for decommissioning had been signposted as early as 1993 (Bew, 1995). It was reiterated in March 1995 by the Secretary of State for Northern Ireland, Patrick Mayhew in a speech in Washington. In what became known as Washington 3, Mayhew insisted that the IRA needed to indicate a willingness in principle to disarm; secondly agree a practical methods of disarmament and thirdly begin actual arms decommissioning.

With republicans adamant that prior decommissioning was not on their agenda, the Mitchell Commission was established. It steered a careful path between prior and no decommissioning, advocating that weapons should be dismantled in parallel to talks. To pacify Unionist and British sensitivities over the absence of insistence upon prior decommissioning, Mitchell also stressed that participants in all-party talks must sign up to six principles of non-violence. These were:

1 Peaceful means must be used to resolve political issues.
2 Paramilitary organisations must eventually disarm.
3 Disarmament must be verifiable.
4 The threat or use of force in negotiations must end.
5 Agreements arising from all-party talks must be accepted.
6 Punishment killings and beatings must cease.

Although the Mitchell principles appeared to cause problems for republicans, the main contentions of the Report were overshadowed by a new development. Unionists favoured the creation of an elected body in Northern Ireland as the best means of progress and indicated they would accept the entry of Sinn Fein to all-party talks even without prior IRA decommissioning, provided the party participated in such a contest. The British Government decided in favour of this idea. Nationalists were hostile and Mitchell appeared cool, arguing tentatively for the idea if it attracted a consensus. Given nationalist hostilities, this was clearly not the case.

Elections to a peace forum nonetheless took place in May. Parties elected to the forum, which was devoid of legislative power, would be able to select teams for all party negotiations. Non-participation in the forum did not debar parties from entering their negotiating teams to these talks. Accordingly, nationalists took part on the basis of ad hoc participation in the forum in the SDLP's case. Sinn Fein pledged to boycott the forum, whilst coveting all-party talks, a prospect barred without a renewed ceasefire. The elections were perhaps the most curious ever staged even in Northern Ireland's distinctive political history. The application of the term dog's breakfast slandered canine appetites. Basically the aim was to ensure that representatives of the loyalist paramilitaries, whose fragile ceasefire appeared to generally hold, were included in all-party talks alongside other parties. To this effect, two seats were awarded to each of the top ten parties in the elections to provide an additional twenty members of the four, alongside the ninety elected in constituencies. One result was that the Northern Ireland Women's Coalition, tenth in the poll with a vote of 1 per cent, entered the multi-party peace talks with an equal sized delegation of five to that granted the UUP which polled twenty-four times as many votes (Table 2.1).

| Party | Number of votes | % share of vote | Number elected* |
|---|---|---|---|
| UUP | 181 829 | 24.2 | 28+2 |
| SDLP | 160 786 | 21.4 | 19+2 |
| DUP | 141 413 | 18.8 | 22+2 |
| Sinn Fein | 116 377 | 15.5 | 15+2 |
| Alliance | 49 176 | 6.5 | 5+2 |
| UKUP | 27 774 | 3.7 | 1+2 |
| PUP | 26 082 | 3.5 | 0+2 |
| UDP | 16 715 | 2.2 | 0+2 |
| NIWC | 7 731 | 1.0 | 0+2 |
| Labour | 6 425 | 0.9 | 0+2 |
| Others | 18 083 | 2.3 | 0+0 |

**Table 2.1 Parties elected to the Northern Ireland Forum 1996**

\* The parties listed above were the ten most popular. Two candidates from a Party list submitted by each of the top ten parties were added to those elected within constituencies.

Overall the results appeared merely to confirm a polarisation of opinion. Sinn Fein and the DUP fared well. Sinn Fein's vote created further pressure for the Party's inclusion in talks, but the lack of an IRA ceasefire led to the continuing exclusion. During the British General Election campaign in 1997, the Shadow Northern Ireland Secretary Mo Mowlam reopened the exclusion debate, declaring that Sin Fein's entry to talks could be arrived at within weeks of a renewed IRA ceasefire. It appeared that delays due to quarantine periods and decommissioning might be sidelined. Two-thirds of Catholics opposed the decommissioning prerequisite for entry to talks, whereas 90 per cent of Protestants were supportive (Marsh et al, 1996, p.268).

**Conclusion**

The peace process in Northern Ireland in the 1990s has provided the most sustained attempt thus far at removing violence from he conflict. Different perceptions for the process did not assist its development, as ends and means were confused. The British

Government appeared to view the removal of violence from the conflict as the primary end. In conjunction with the Irish Government, it declared neutrality and offered intergovernmentalism and cross-border political and economic frameworks as the means of consolidating this peace. This might allow an all-Ireland dynamic sufficient to persuade republicans of the futility of continued violence. These do not amount to a mediation of the seemingly irreconcilable ideologies of Ulster Unionism and Irish nationalism. Unionists of all shades of opinion believed these to be irreconcilable. For radical Unionists, the peace process was a useful means of transforming conflict into dialogue, without removing the causes of conflict. For militant Unionists, the peace process merely added to the all-Ireland momentum of any settlement.

The framework in which the aspirations of all were acknowledged was set against an strong integrative undercurrent which owed at least some of its existence to the precarious parliamentary arithmetic which confronted the Conservative Government. This undercurrent was strong enough to yield the only two material gains during the peace process, in the awards of legislative and scrutiny committees. A cynic might argue that the remainder of the peace process amounted to a series of worthy pronouncements, political blueprints and fractured alliances. The rows over decommissioning and the collapse of the IRA ceasefire obscured perhaps the most crucial questions of the process. What would be the 'bottom line' of Sinn Fein if all-party talks took place? Would the party be able to sell a settlement substantially short of traditional republican objectives to its own supporters?

**References**

Adams, G. (1985), in Collins, M. (ed.) *Ireland after Britain*, Pluto:London.
Adams, G. (1995), *Free Ireland: Towards A Lasting Peace*, Brandon:Dingle.
Anderton,J.(1997), 'Transnational emancipation from Irish and British nationalisms?', Paper presented to the Political Studies Annual Conference, University of Ulster, 8-10 April 1997.
Aughey, A. (1994), 'Contemporary Unionist Politics' in Barton, B. and Roche, P.J. (ed.),*The Northern Ireland Question: Perspectives and Policies*, Avebury:Aldershot.
Bean, K. (1995), 'The New Departure? Recent developments in Republican strategy and ideology', *Irish Studies Review*, No. 10.
Bew, P. (1995), 'Seizing the Interval - the Northern Ireland Peace Process, *British Association of Irish Studies Newsletter*, No. 8, pp. 3-5.
Bew, P. and Gillespie, G. (1996), *The Northern Ireland Peace Process 1993-1996: A Chronology*, Serif:London.
Bew, P., Gibbon, P, and Patterson, H. (1996), *Northern Ireland 1921-1996: Political Forces and Social Classes*, Serif:London.
Boyce, D.G. (1996), *The Irish Question and British Politics, 1868-1996*, 2nd edition, Macmillan, London.
Bruce, S. (1994), *At the Edge of the Union: The Ulster Loyalist Political Vision*, Oxford University Press:Oxford.
Coogan, T.P. (1995), *The Troubles: Ireland's Ordeal 1966-1995 and the Search for Peace*, Hutchinson:London.

Democratic Unionist Party (1995), *The Framework of Shame and Sham*, Democratic Unionist Party:Belfast.

Ervine, D. (1996), 'The Progressive Unionist Party and the Peace Process', Presentation to the 'Understanding the Peace Process in Ireland' seminar series, European Studies Research Institute, University of Salford, 20 March.

Gibney, J. (1996), 'From the Collapse of the Peace Process to Real Negotiations', *Irish Reporter*, no.22, pp.13-18.

Guelke, A. (1994), 'The Peace Process in South Africa, Israel and Northern Ireland: a Farewell to Arms? *Irish Studies in International Affairs*, vol. 5, pp. 93-106.

Hazelton, W.A. (1995), 'A Breed Apart? Northern Ireland's MP'S at Westminster', *Journal of Legislative Studies*, Vol.1, No.4, pp. 30-53.

HM Government (1995), *Frameworks for the Future*, HMSO:Belfast.

Irwin, C., Boal ,F. and Hadden,T. (1997),'Drumcree 3?', *Belfast Telegraph*, 8 April..

Kearney, R. (1996), *Postnationalist Ireland*, Routledge:London.

Kennedy-Pipe, C. (1997), *The Origins of the Present Troubles in Northern Ireland*, Longman:Harlow.

Lijphart, A. (1996), 'The 'Framework' Proposal for Northern Ireland and the Theory of Power-Sharing', *Government and Opposition*, Vol. 31, No. 3, pp. 267-74.

McGarry, J. and O'Leary, B. (1995), *Explaining Northern Ireland*,Blackwell, Oxford.

McGimpsey, C. (1996), 'Sinn Fein, Consent and a return to Plan B', *Irish Reporter*, No.21, pp.45-48.

Mallie, E. and McKittrick, D. (1996), *The Fight for Peace: The Secret Story behind the Irish Peace Process*, Heinemann:London.

Mansergh, M. (1996), 'The Future Path of Peace', *Irish Reporter*, No. 21, pp. 49-58.

Marsh, M, Wilford, R, King, S, McElroy, G. (1996), 'Irish Political Data 1995', *Irish Political Studies*, Vol.11, pp.213-308.

New Ireland Forum (1984), *Report*, Dublin.

North Report (1997), *Independent Review of Parades and Marches*, HMSO:Belfast.

O'Leary, B. and McGarry, J. (1996), *The Politics of Antagonism: Understanding Northern Ireland* 2nd edn, Athlone:London.

Paisley, I. (1997), 'Measured and consistent action', *The House magazine*, Vol.22, No.755, pp.16-17.

Porter, N. (1996), *Rethinking Unionism: An Alternative Vision for Northern Ireland*, Blackstaff:Belfast.

Rowan, B. (1995), *Behind the Lines: The Story of the IRA and Loyalist Ceasefires*, Blackstaff:Belfast.

Ruane, J. and Todd, J. (1996), *The dynamics of conflict in Northern Ireland: Power, conflict and emancipation*, Cambridge University Press:Cambridge.

Ryan, M. (1994), *War and Peace in Ireland: Britain and the IRA in the New World Order*, Pluto:London.

Sinn Fein (1987), *Scenario for Peace*, Sinn Fein:Belfast.

Sinn Fein (1992), *Towards a Lasting Peace*, Sinn Fein:Belfast.

Tonge, J. (1997), 'The Political Agenda of Sinn Fein: Change without Change?', in Stanyer, J. and Stoker, G. (eds) *Contemporary Political Studies 1997*, Political Studies Association:Exeter.

# 3 Peace or pacification process? A brief critique of the peace process

Chris Gilligan

## Introduction

The announcement by the Irish Republican Army (IRA) of a complete cessation of military operations in September 1994 was heralded internationally. The declaration confounded many pessimists and appeared to open the way to a lasting settlement of the conflict in the province. The various political shifts and developments which enabled the IRA ceasefire, and six weeks later the Loyalist ceasefire, are commonly referred to as the peace process (Fitzgerald, 1994, pp.12-15; Wilson, 1994, p.5). The peace process has been welcomed as the most significant development in the last quarter of a century of the provinces troubled history, but it did not indicate a final resolution of the conflict. The course of the peace process has not been free of turbulence. Although the ceasefire marked a break from the past, relations between the British government and Irish Republicans have continued to be acrimonious. This acrimony came to a dramatic head with the IRA bombing of Canary Wharf in London's docklands in February 1996.

The peace process has an element of schizophrenia. It has raised hopes of a final resolution of the conflict, yet there is now more emphasis on conflict management than upon conflict resolution. The atmosphere in Northern Ireland appears to oscillate between hope and fear, a sentiment which is captured in the title of David McKittrick's journalistic account of the peace process (McKittrick, 1995). The end of the IRA ceasefire has heightened the fears of a return to the past. This chapter sets out to explain this apparent schizophrenia, and in doing so also argues that there can be no return to the past. This schizophrenia is not a passing phase of the peace process which will be replaced by either a return to the past or a transcending of the conflict.

One of the problems with the concept of peace is that it is a morally loaded one. No reasonable person could possibly object to peace, everyone should desire a peaceful outcome to conflict. Unfortunately this sentiment often prevents any dispassionate analysis of the peace process. In their desire to reach a positive outcome the majority of people do not stop to reflect on the different dimensions of the peace process. This chapter attempts a critical analysis of the peace process. The reader would be justified in groaning at the prospect of another criticism of the peace process. All of the parties to the process have been fulsome in their criticisms, but this chapter differs in that the aim of the criticism is to produce a greater understanding of the peace process. The chapter also differs from most other criticisms in that it does not end in a call for more peace process.

The chapter begins with an examination of two different ideas of peace which feature in the peace process. It then examines the developments which made the IRA ceasefire possible. Through an examination of two ideas of pacification which feature in the peace process, the chapter questions the merits of the calls for more peace process. It points out that an important component of the peace process has been the circumvention of public opinion. This is both a weakness and a strength of the peace process, an argument which is illustrated through an examination of the end of the IRA ceasefire. Finally the chapter concludes that the peace process may actually end up disadvantaging the very people that it is supposed to benefit, the ordinary citizens of Northern Ireland.

**Two ideas of peace**

There are two distinct uses of the term 'peace' in discussions of the peace process. The first is peace as the absence of conflict; the second is peace as the outcome of a process. The first usage was employed by the British Labour Party MP, Harry Barnes, in a statement in response to the end of the IRA ceasefire in February 1996:

> Despair is understandable but ignores the gains of...17 months of peace. [The peace] saved hundreds of lives, thousands of injuries and millions of pounds...Popular resistance to terrorism is now needed. Dublin and Belfast have begun this process with tremendous rallies and vigils for peace (Barnes, 1996, p.17).

This notion of peace has predominated throughout the quarter-century of conflict in Northern Ireland. Since the IRA began its military campaign in 1970, 'terrorism' has been identified as the main problem in the province. Barnes is following a long line of politicians who have condemned the use of violence and appealed to the majority of 'decent' citizens to resist this violence. In the peace process this notion is encapsulated in the principle of non-violence. This usage of the term places the emphasis on an enlightened outcome, *peace*. The second usage of the term places the emphasis on the means to achieve that outcome, the *process*. Sinn Fein's Tom Hartley employed both senses of the term peace when he said:

> [Sinn Fein] want to create a society in which peace is not a mere interlude between wars, but an incentive to the creative and collective energies of all the people who live on this island. There is no other way of achieving that than through talks, inclusive and without preconditions. [R]eal peace [needs to be] built on the solid foundations of the democratic principles of justice and equality (Hartley, 1996, p.16).

Hartley characterises the first usage of the term peace as vacuous, describing only the absence of war. This absence will only be temporary unless the underlying issues which gave rise to conflict are resolved. In this interpretation peace is ephemeral and utopian and it can only be made 'real' by giving it solid foundations. During the peace process this understanding of peace has come into prominence. Where the first usage of the term identifies 'terrorism' as irrational, inflexible and therefore a threat to peace, the second rests on an assumption that the paramilitaries are both rational and adaptable. This involves a recognition that the paramilitaries do have genuine grievances. Furthermore, it endorses the argument that unless there is a two-way process of give and take between the protagonists in the conflict any peace will only be a temporary interlude between wars. This meaning of the term is encapsulated in the principle of inclusion which lies at the core of the peace process.

The growing employment of the second understanding of the term peace is not simply coincidental with the development of the peace process. This highlighting of peace as a process became part of the language employed by Sinn Fein in the late 1980s (Adams, 1988; Hume 1996, pp.93-5) and is indicative of a shift in British government thinking about Republicans. The shift was signalled in an interview with Peter Brooke on the occasion of his first one hundred days in office as Secretary of State for Northern Ireland (Mallie and McKittrick, 1996, pp. 98-100). The second usage has gradually become established as the normative framework through which the conflict and prospects for peace in Northern Ireland are discussed.

### The principle of non-violence

The British and Irish Governments reiterate that the achievement of peace must involve a permanent end to the use of, or support for, paramilitary violence. They confirm that, in these circumstances, democratically mandated parties which establish a commitment to exclusively peaceful methods and which have shown that they abide by the democratic process, are free to participate fully in democratic politics and to join in dialogue in due course between the two Governments and the political parties on the way ahead (Joint Declaration for Peace, 1993, para. 10).

*Support for the principle of non-violence*

As the above paragraph from the Downing Street Declaration (DSD) makes clear, the principle of non-violence is directed towards bringing an end to paramilitary violence. The idea that peace relies on a cessation of paramilitary violence has been around from very early in the current conflict, and enjoys widespread support. Paramilitary violence is considered to be qualitatively different from other forms of violence, so much so that it has been given its own name. 'Terrorism' is distinguished from other forms of violence in that it has no popular endorsement and its primary aim is to terrorise the population which is at the receiving end of the violence (Miller, 1994, pp.4-7; Said, 1988, pp.46-70).

The most vocal opponents of paramilitary violence usually focus on the immediate effects of the violence; the number of people who have died; the often gruesome nature of the deaths, the extent of injuries and the consequences for those affected and the damage to mental health, livelihoods, property and communal relations. Yet the existence of paramilitary violence also has wider effects in Northern Irish society, the presence of armed troops is only one of the most obvious ways in which the existence of paramilitary violence has had an influence on the province. The state has intervened in response to paramilitary violence by introducing no-jury courts, providing massive economic subsidies, and by moulding the human geography of the province (O'Dowd et al, 1980). The human geography has not only been shaped by the state, for example, through a combination of voluntary and involuntary population movements, the province now has high levels of residential segregation (Boyle and Hadden, 1994, p.33-8). To the casual observer it appears self-evident that there can be no peace without an end to violence. However, to focus exclusively on the effects of paramilitary violence is to examine the outcome of a more complex process. Any analysis of the violence needs to go further than the hackneyed observation that the existence of violence has had negative consequences for the people of the province. To gain a greater understanding of the conflict, and the suggested means for ending the violence, we need to examine the different dimensions of the violence.

*Some criticisms of the principle of non-violence*

Paramilitary violence is usually the aspect of Northern Irish society which features most prominently in any discussion of the province. Nonetheless the obvious question begged is whether the violence is an expression of an underlying problem, or the main problem itself? For the purposes of our present investigation it is important to point out that when British troops were first deployed in Northern Ireland in 1969 the IRA did not exist as a military force (Bowyer Bell, 1990, pp.337-366). This point is often forgotten in discussions about peace, the IRA did not initiate the conflict, a conflict already existed. The current conflict arose from the response to the demand for civil rights. In the late 1960s peaceful protestors demanded an end to practices which treated Catholics as second class citizens, these responses were met with repression by the local security forces. British troops were deployed as a 'peace-keeping' force when the ensuing civil disturbances, such as rioting, threatened to destabilise the province. In some instances, most significantly the 'Rape of the Falls', the introduction of internment and 'Bloody Sunday', the actions of the 'peace-keeping' forces actually served to escalate the conflict further, and for some proved critical in moving individuals to a position where they actively supported paramilitary violence. In political terms this represented a shift from questioning the form of rule of a particular regime, the Stormont government, to questioning the right of the state itself to rule (Farrell, 1976, pp.261-290; McCann, 1981, pp.27-104; O'Brien, 1974, pp.229-232). The civil rights movement was demanding reform of the state; Irish Republicans demanded the revolutionary overthrow of the state. The fact that IRA violence re-emerged in response to already existing violence suggests that paramilitary violence is an expression of an underlying problem, rather than the cause of the conflict itself. The principle of non-violence tends to obscure the origins of the IRA's existence as a response to an already existing conflict rather than its cause.

In the paragraph quoted from the DSD the two Governments do not differentiate between violence perpetuated by Republicans and that perpetuated by Loyalist paramilitaries, but in practice British government policy in Northern Ireland has been differential in its application to Loyalists and Republicans. When internment was introduced in 1971 the first dawn raids carried out by British troops were entirely in Republican areas and against Republican suspects. The military operations usually identified as part of a 'shoot-to-kill' policy by the Special Air Services and the Royal Ulster Constabulary were targeted exclusively at Republican paramilitaries. This differential approach towards the paramilitaries has continued throughout the peace process. Loyalist paramilitaries did not come under the same level of public or private pressure to declare a ceasefire. This difference was also evident after the IRA and Loyalist ceasefires. The IRA were prevailed upon to declare their ceasefire permanent, but Loyalists, who explicitly declared their ceasefire to be conditional upon the maintenance of the IRA ceasefire, were not pressed for a similar declaration. This unevenness has been a concern during the peace process since the differential approach to paramilitary violence is taken as an indication by some Irish Nationalists that the British government do not have a commitment to treating Nationalists and Unionists equally.

The British Government refuses to enter into any substantial negotiations with Republicans whilst violent methods are employed, although it has sanctioned the use of violence against the paramilitaries. So, although the principle formally repudiates violence, it is based on an implicit threat of coercion. The British government do not deny that violence has been perpetrated by the state, but they claim that unlike paramilitary violence state violence is legitimate. The British government demand that the IRA repudiate the use of violence for political ends, while upholding their own right to employ violence (Townshend, 1993, pp.167-190). This points to a fundamental issue which underpins the principle of non-violence, the legitimacy of the state. It also indicates a massive imbalance of power which the principle of non-violence disguises. The British state possesses one of the best armed and trained armies in the world, whereas the IRA in comparison has scant personnel and armoury.

Are the effects of violence as detrimental, for individuals and for Northern Irish society as a whole, as the picture presented by the very vocal critics of paramilitary violence suggests? The evidence is more ambiguous than the casual observer is usually led to believe. It is possible to quantify the cost in terms of human lives lost, physical injuries sustained and property damaged. It is more difficult however to measure the wider consequences of the violence. There is evidence from psychological studies on children which suggests that the existence of paramilitary violence has little overall effect on mental health (Cairns and Cairns, 1995, pp.99-102; Whyte, 1990, pp.94-97). There is continuing debate over whether the conflict has had a detrimental impact on the economy or slowed the decline which was already evident before 1969 (Canning et al, 1987, pp. 211-235; Patterson, 1996, pp.124-127; Rowthorn, 1987, pp.111-134; Ryan, 1994, pp.120-121). One author pointed out the ambiguous effects of conflict, when he argued that community action groups and paramilitary groups developed from a 'common root' and that the existence of crisis in the late 1960s and early 1970s 'motivate[d] and mobilise[d] individuals into forming associations for the betterment of their communities' (Griffiths, 1976, pp.169-194).

To sum up so far, the principle of non-violence is widely supported by a range of different groups. Some of the different dimensions of the principle have been questioned by a range of different organisations. It has been criticised for confusing cause and effect, for ignoring state violence, and for being differential in its treatment of Republican and Loyalist violence. Despite these criticisms there has been agreement that there can be no resolution of the conflict as long as paramilitary violence persists. Ironically this places Irish Republicans in a key position as a fulcrum for conflict resolution. In terms of their military power and political influence they have come nowhere near rivalling the British state, but as long as they have the weaponry and determination to wage war there can be no conflict resolution. This suggests three options for a resolution of the conflict: an IRA defeat or surrender, an IRA victory, or a compromise between Republicans and the British government. The peace process has been the process of the British government and Irish Republicans coming to a compromise.

**Preparing the ground for inclusive negotiation**

*Building blocs of cooperation*

On both the Republican and British sides there were developments in the 1980s which helped to prepare the ground for the peace process. The campaign around the hunger-strikes started the Republican involvement in electoral politics and community action. In this respect, this was the beginning of Sinn Fein's ascendency over the IRA. Equally, it brought many Republican activists into closer contact with the more immediate concerns of their core base of support. This was indicative of a shift in emphasis from a primarily military strategy to a primarily political one, and a lowering of the horizon on which the Republican outlook was focused, from the absolute principle of the right of the Irish people as a whole to self-determination towards ensuring that the immediate interests of their core base of support were sufficiently represented in and by British state institutions. The move into party politics was to lead Sinn Fein to drop their commitment to abstain from taking their seats in the Dail, a commitment which had been a key principle for Republicans since the 1920s. In taking their seats in the Irish Parliament and later in local councils in Northern Ireland, Sinn Fein was explicitly recognising institutions set up under partition and thus implicitly recognising the partition of the country itself (McIntyre, 1995, pp.108-118; Ryan, 1994, pp.58-74).

Another process which began in the 1980s was the move to exploratory talks with representatives of 'constitutional' nationalism, initially involving dialogue with John Hume, leader of the SDLP and later with Charles Haughey, then Prime Minister of the Irish Republic. When Republicans did engage in a peace process these contacts were to be important. With the additional support from sections of Irish-America this cooperation with 'constitutional' nationalism became the pan-nationalist alliance. This alliance acted as the amniotic medium through which Republicans were able to ease their movement from a confrontational approach to a conciliatory one. The role of intermediaries was to become very important in the peace process. During the late

1980s contacts were made and a network of connections developed. But at this stage the contacts were largely secret and unfruitful, a reflection of both the pariah status of Republicans and the distance between their stance and that of other political actors (Mallie and McKittrick, 1996, pp.79-90; 133-146).

The British government's negotiation and signing of the Anglo-Irish Agreement with the government of the Republic of Ireland in 1985 marked some developments which were to be important for the peace process. The Agreement brought the British government into closer co-operation with the government of the Republic of Ireland. Unlike previous initiatives, the Agreement was one between the elites of two sovereign states. It bypassed the electorate of Northern Ireland and their political representatives. This closer co-operation was also significant for moving away from viewing Northern Ireland as a purely domestic matter for the British government. In parallel with Republicans building up networks of connections with other groups, the British government developed institutional links with both the Irish government and that of the United States of America. The introduction and maintenance of the Agreement was achieved against the express wishes of Ulster unionists. This was an indication of the declining power of Unionism in Northern Ireland. Unlike the Power-sharing Assembly of 1974, Unionists failed in their attempts to wreck the Agreement. Such a failure also indicated that the British government was prepared to face down Unionist opposition. The Agreement recognised the existence of two distinct communities in Northern Ireland with different traditions and needs. This pointed to an interpretation of the conflict as internal to Northern Ireland and primarily between Irish nationalism and Ulster Unionism, which helped to institute a series of measures ostensibly aimed at overcoming this division (Boyle and Hadden, 1989; O'Leary, 1987).

Many of these elements which were to become important during the peace process. Firstly, the process was built upon the development, by both Republicans and the British government, of closer relations with political groupings which had some common, but not coterminous interests. Secondly, majority opinion in Northern Ireland was circumvented. Thirdly, there was increased concern with local and cultural issues. Despite all of these elements being in place at the end of the 1980s, Republicans and the British government were still diametrically opposed in their political ambitions. Republicans were not interested in negotiating short of a declaration of British intent to withdraw. British initiatives were aimed at defeating 'terrorism'. The thawing of relations between the British government and Republicans began in 1989. In March of that year, the President of Sinn Fein, Gerry Adams, publicly indicated that he sought a 'non-armed political movement' to end partition (Coogan, 1996, p.236). In November Peter Brooke, the new Secretary of State for Northern Ireland, responded by saying that the British government would respond flexibly and imaginatively to an IRA ceasefire (Mallie and McKittrick, 1996, pp.99-100). It was not only events in Northern Ireland, or within 'these two islands', which helped to bring about the peace process. International events, brought about as a consequence of the end of the Cold War, were to provide the catalyst which helped turn a stalemate into a peace process. The national liberation struggles, most notably in the Middle East and South Africa, with which Republicans had allied themselves in the past, now provided models as exemplars of conflict resolution rather than as exemplars of liberation struggles. The conflict in the former Yugoslavia provided a negative model of struggles for self-determination (Ryan, 1994, pp.35-41).

*From confrontation to inclusion*

The re-opening of a line of communication between Republicans and the British government was indicative of this thaw in relations between the two parties to the conflict. In the first phase of these talks the British government actively courted Republicans. It continued to promote the principle of non-violence in their insistence on the need for an IRA ceasefire, whilst stressing that was sought was 'an agreed accommodation, *not* an imposed solution' (Sinn Fein, 1994, p.21, emphasis in original). Sinn Fein's chief negotiator, Martin McGuinness, made a speech to the Sinn Fein Ard Fheis in February 1992 which contained condemnations of British policy in Northern Ireland, but nonetheless passed the initiative to the British by stating that it had a responsibility to 'lead the way by outlining its plan for a final resolution of the problem'. McGuinness also insisted that an essential ingredient of that plan was 'the acceptance of the need for inclusive dialogue as a vehicle towards a final settlement' (Sinn Fein, 1994, p.23). The secret talks ended in November 1993, with public recriminations between the two parties over who had promised what. The ending of the secret talks did not indicate the conclusion of the peace process, rather but instead marked its transfer from secret, private discussions to an open, public process. The peace process was brought into the public domain with the signing of the DSD by the Prime Ministers of the two governments.

It has been suggested that the British government's purpose in entering into secret talks with Republicans was to con Republicans into a surrender (McAlliskey, 1996, pp.23-8). This may have been the initial intention, but such an interpretation underestimates how much has changed in the politics of the province, and overestimates how much control the British government has exercised over the peace process. The British government still uphold the principle of non-violence, but it is now supplemented by the principle of an inclusive negotiated settlement. The British government may have begun to work in closer co-operation with the Irish government and the White House in an attempt to isolate Republicans. The pressure on Republicans may have been further enhanced by the moves to promote cross-community reconciliation. In order to secure the involvement of these other bodies in pressurising Republicans the British government had to give some commitment to the principle of inclusion. Even after the end of the IRA ceasefire the British government was not able to return to promoting a straight 'anti-terrorist' line (Major, 1996, p.6; Mayhew, 1996, p.10).

One consequence of the promotion of the principle of inclusion is that many of the issues which marked a clear dividing line between Republicans and other parties with an interest in the conflict no longer retain their clarity. The border was an issue on which Republicans had a clear agenda, in that there could be no compromise or negotiation on its continuation. Even discussion on a resolution was not possible until the British at least gave a definite commitment to withdraw. In the course of the peace process this issue has become fudged. The border has now become contingent through its future being an open question to be resolved in the process of negotiation. It has become porous through the treatment of the counties which straddle both sides as a region for United States and EU investment. Additionally, it has become ephemeral through the main divide in Ireland now being characterised as the border in peoples minds. This lack of clarity has actually assisted the development of the peace process as various participants, particularly Republicans and the British government, have been able to radically alter their approach while maintaining that their approach has been consistent.

Many of the groups which support the principle of non-violence also support the principle of inclusion. The Irish government, the White House, community reconciliation groups, the churches, the SDLP and some victim support groups. This has altered the substance of the principle of non-violence. The British government can gain acceptance that there should be an IRA ceasefire before any settlement is possible, but if they appear too belligerent or inflexible on the issue they lay themselves open to the accusation of deviating from the principle of inclusion. As a consequence the British government is no longer able to wield the principle of non-violence as an effective device to silence critics. At a very simple level the accusation of 'being soft on terrorism' does not carry weight when the accuser was involved in secret talks with the 'terrorists' before they declared a ceasefire. It is not uncommon now to find the British government being accused of being a barrier to a peaceful resolution of the conflict in the province.

There is still a tendency to view the politics of Northern Ireland as based around a dichotomous conflict. This idea is implicit in the recognition of the rights and identities of the two communities in Northern Ireland. It can be seen in the idea that the two governments should represent the interests of each of these traditions at an intergovernmental level, but rather than seeing the conflict as a fundamentally dichotomous one, it is more useful to characterise politics in the province as consisting of networks of shifting connections (alliance is too strong a word to describe the temporary common stances). Obvious examples of these connections are between Sinn Fein and both the SDLP, and the Irish government, or the connection between Ulster Unionists and the British government. Yet the connections also cross the traditional British/Unionist and Irish/Nationalist divide. There is the obvious intergovernmental co-operation between the British and Irish governments. There have been exploratory talks between Republican and Loyalist paramilitaries. The Ulster Unionist Party (UUP) have appeared to be more conciliatory in their stance towards the government of the Republic of Ireland and Nationalists within Northern Ireland (Nesbitt, 1995, pp.12-15, 21-26).

The openness of the principle of inclusion is widely welcomed as a positive development in the politics of the province and is seen as providing the prospect for a lasting settlement. If inclusion is a positive development which is widely supported in the peace process, why has the peace process been so unstable and why did the IRA ceasefire breakdown? Through an examination of two ideas of pacification which are apparent in the peace process, the next section raises some questions about the merits of the principle of inclusion.

## Two ideas of pacification

There are two distinct ideas of pacification which are employed in the peace process. The first is of pacification as rendering aggressors impotent. This usually entails destroying the capacity of the paramilitaries to wage war. The second is of pacification as pacifism, usually through developing a less confrontational political culture in Northern Ireland. Ian Paisley Jnr of the Democratic Unionist Party (DUP) provided an example of the first idea in a response to the end of the IRA ceasefire, when he said:

> [Sinn Fein/IRA] determined whether 'peace' was on, in crisis or off. Those people who think that peace rallies, telephone polls or whatever else will repossess the peace are sadly deluded...All decent human beings want peace but the reality is that peace has got to be won. If you accept it as a gift from terrorists it is not free - it is enslavement...Now is the time for short sharp shock military tactics against the leadership of IRA/Sinn Fein (Paisley Jnr, 1996, p.16).

According to this outlook Republican paramilitaries and politicians have to be forced into submission. Those who believe that popular expressions in favour of peace will bring about a resolution of the conflict are naive and utopian. Here the use of military tactics is viewed as a means to achieve peace. Paisley also adds a qualification to the term peace. He wants to know under whose terms it is achieved. In viewing peace as the outcome of a process there is a similarity between this understanding of peace and the understanding associated with inclusive negotiations, but the similarity is superficial. The approach of Paisley Jnr and many of those in his party is highly confrontational, whereas the approach associated with the principle of inclusion spurns confrontation. Paisley suggests that there must be winners and losers and that peace is a zero-sum option. His critics argue that everyone stands to benefit from peace.

*From pacifying to pacifist*

The confrontational approach advocated by the DUP is no longer central to government policy in Northern Ireland, but it is still significant to the peace process. This confrontational approach is now highlighted in order to warn of the danger of a return to the past. Confrontation itself is viewed as producing and prolonging the conflict. People who espouse similar views to those of Paisley Jnr are accused of being stuck in the past, repeating well worn phrases that have done nothing to further the search for peace. In the words of the Northern Ireland Women's Coalition they are 'dinosaurs' (O'Neill, 1996; Wilson, 1996, pp.41-57). The one issue on which the idea of emasculation does have a resonance is the decommissioning of paramilitary weapons. Even on this issue the approach is one of seeking mediation, in the form of the Mitchell Commission, rather than confrontation.

There are three aspects of the 'pacifist' approach which we shall outline here; its normative rules; the range and level of support for such an approach and its institutionalised forms. The 'pacifist' approach places an emphasis on mediation as a means of conflict resolution. Throughout the peace process various different individuals and groups have reiterated that any proposed settlement of the conflict cannot be imposed. Instead it must be reached through agreement, in order for it to endure a settlement must command the support of the people across both main communities. The main emphasis is on mediation in cross community relations, but many advocates of a non-confrontational approach promote this as a guide to all human interactions. They claim that democracy depends on trust, but too often people do not show sufficient respect for others with different views. The 'pacifist' approach urges the acknowledgement of fears and urges mutual understanding between individuals and groups. In order to stimulate this more conciliatory approach people and state institutions are urged to think what sacrifice they themselves can make in order to foster the kind of environment where people can live together. During the peace process this is referred to as the creation of 'confidence building measures' (Darby, 1991; Morrow & Wilson, 1995, pp.69-78).

This 'pacifist' approach is widely advocated, from the British and Irish governments through a range of community reconciliation groups to both the Loyalist and Republican paramilitaries. A formal commitment to this approach can be seen in a range of documents, mission statements and manifestos. Support for such an approach can be gauged by the proliferation of mediation bodies and the acceptance of ecumenical services (Dunn, 1995). The level of support for this approach appears to depend on how much the individual or group believes that such an approach will benefit them. The Ulster Unionists, who benefitted from the political institutions which were set up under Stormont and who have experienced changes in those structures as a decline in their power and prestige are unenthusiastic about a 'pacifist' approach. The Loyalist paramilitaries who did not benefit are more enthusiastic (Ervine, 1995, pp.22-24). Nationalists are overwhelmingly in favour of a 'pacifist' approach and they feel that their situation is likely to improve under any new institutional structures. Indeed the 'pacifist' approach has, in part, been a product of the efforts by the British government to incorporate nationalists into the state institutions in Northern Ireland.

The 'restructuring' of the administration of society, is being achieved through a combination of adapting old institutions, revamping existing institutions and creating entirely new ones. An example of the first is the reorganisation of the Northern Ireland Civil Service. The establishment of a Central Community Relations Unit within the Central Secretariat in 1987 signalled a new commitment by the British government to assess and reorganise the administration of the province (Gallagher, 1995, pp.32-41). This has entailed measures like the drawing up of Policy Appraisal and Fair Treatment (PAFT) guidelines designed to ensure that 'issues of equality and equity condition policy-making and action at all levels of Government activity' (CCRU, 1995, p.6). An example of the second is the revamping of the Fair Employment legislation in 1989, which gave more extensive powers to the revamped bodies which have responsibility for 'the promotion of equality of opportunity and the elimination of discrimination' (Edwards, 1995, p.30). An example of an entirely new institution is the Mitchell Commission set up to adjudicate on the issue of the decommissioning of paramilitary weapons.

## Demobilising discontent

It has already been noted that the peace process has come about through an acceptance that Britain bears some responsibility for the divisions in Ireland, an admission which has led to recognition that paramilitary violence is not simply mindless. The peace process has placed an emphasis on people working together to create a lasting peace. What happens to those people who do not see the merits of working together? What about those people who do not agree with a 'pacifist' approach? To gain a full appreciation of the peace process it is also important to remember that there has been a less benevolent side to conflict management measures. The peace process has been made possible through demobilising discontent in the province. This has entailed making concessions to opponents, but it has also meant the different participants having to demobilise potential opposition from among those who were previously their supporters. There are three main ways in which this has been achieved. One is by circumventing the discontent, by excluding the influence of those who might undermine the process. A second way is through diffusing discontent, by, for example, deliberately creating a lack of clarity on core issues. The third is of corralling discontent, by, for example, driving supporters into the process of co-operation and negotiation.

On the British government's side, the circumvention of discontent began with the development of the Anglo-Irish Agreement. The Agreement was successful precisely because it was not vulnerable to pressure from the public mobilisations which brought down the Power-sharing Agreement in 1974. It operates through the governments of Britain and Ireland, not the elected representatives of the people of Northern Ireland. On the republican side the peace process has been pursued by the leadership. During the peace process much of the relationship between the leadership and the grassroots now depends on the level of trust. Republicans have been viewed as resolute defenders of the nationalist ghettos in Northern Ireland. This provides the scope for both diffusing discontent and corralling discontent. Those who are uncomfortable with the peace process are continually told that there has been no sell out and that the IRA still retains its Republican objectives (see Breen, 1995, p.7). Closer supporters are encouraged to work actively to put pressure on the British government to give some substance to their commitment to an inclusive negotiated settlement. Many people still trust the leadership, but the lack of any discernable dividends from the peace process has led to many people in Republican areas becoming cynical and demoralised.

Republican sympathizers are not passive in the sense of inactive, but passive in the sense that they are spectators in the peace process rather than being part of the decision-making process. This has led to a sense of frustration and powerlessness among people in Republican areas (Campbell, 1995, p.10; Hugill & Nelson, 1995, p. 13; Keenan, 1996, pp.36-40; Kelly, 1995, pp.22-23). While the frustrations may be most palpable among existing and former Republican activists, a sense of unease has been more widespread, especially in ghetto areas and among Unionist politicians (Lyttle, 1995, pp.2-3; McKittrick, 1995, p. 1). This sense of frustration and powerlessness has arisen as a result of the 'pacifist' approach, ironically the 'pacifist' approach, in trying to circumvent confrontation, actually ends up rendering people impotent.

## The end of the IRA ceasefire = the end of the peace process?

The end of the IRA ceasefire appeared to mark the end of the peace process. Any explanation of the peace process must be able to take account of the end of the ceasefire. It is an open repudiation of the principle of non-violence and appears to be a return to a confrontational approach. Has the attempt to create a more conciliatory political culture in the province failed?

The IRA statement which announced the end of the ceasefire claimed that the IRA retained 'a total commitment to [their] Republican objectives'. What these objectives were was not made clear. The statement made no direct reference to the withdrawal of British troops, nor to the achievement of a united Ireland, but it did state that the 'resolution of the conflict in our country demands justice, it demands a negotiated settlement'. The statement is vague on the question of Republican objectives, but clear on the IRA's commitment to the principle of inclusion. The IRA blamed its return to violent methods on 'selfish party political and sectional interests in London [which] have been placed before the rights of the people of Ireland' (IRA, 1996, p.6). According to the IRA their ceasefire broke down because of the lack of commitment by the British government to the principle of inclusion. According to the British government the breakdown of the ceasefire is an indication that the IRA were not seriously committed to the principle of non-violence (Major, 1996, p.6).

This difference of interpretation does not indicate a return to a dichotomous conflict. The end of the IRA ceasefire actually demonstrates how both the British government and Republicans are locked into the peace process. The end of the IRA ceasefire was not an attempt to destroy the peace process, but to kick start it. The British government's response has not been to abandon the peace process as an unproductive attempt at rendering the IRA impotent. Instead it has reiterated its commitment to the peace process. The British government has attempted to use the principle of non-violence to exclude Republicans, but the principle of inclusion has infected the process so completely that they find that this is now problematic.

The end of the IRA ceasefire has revealed another aspect of the peace process. Republicans claim that the ceasefire ended because the British government did not provide any substance to the principle of inclusion. Eighteen months after the announcement of its ceasefire, Sinn Fein still awaited entry into cross-party talks. Yet Sinn Fein also claimed that the peace process was not finished. If this is true then the peace process is able to exist in the absence of the principle of inclusion. The British government claim that the break down of the ceasefire vindicated their concern that the IRA were not seriously committed to the principle of non-violence, but they claim that there is still a peace process. If this is true then the peace process is able to exist in the absence of the principle of non-violence. This is an indication that both parties have lost any sense of direction or clear purpose. The peace process has been achieved through the setting aside of purposeful action in preference to negotiating an outcome. One consequence of this is that the process has become more important than the outcome. The British government is most likely to benefit from this situation. It retains control of, or oversees, all of the powerful institutions in society and all the parties to the peace process look to them to play a leading role. In a situation where people have a diminished sense of their own capacity to bring about an objective they are reduced to pleading that others do it for them. It is remarkable that the IRA, who fought for a quarter of a century against the British state, claimed in their statement announcing the end of the ceasefire that 'a negotiated settlement.. is not possible unless the British government faces up to its responsibility'.

## Conclusion

It is ironic that the peace process has been made possible by the development of the principle of inclusion, because the peace process has been founded on the exclusion of the vast majority of people from any influence over it. The exclusion of ordinary people from the peace process is one of its strengths and also one of its weaknesses. The exclusion of ordinary people has given their political representatives greater room to manoeuvre. It has made the renegotiation of long cherished principles possible and it has allowed more time and space for them to negotiate with erstwhile enemies. Yet the exclusion of ordinary people has also meant that the peace process has not established any roots in Northern Irish society. It was noticeable for example that the public demonstrations in Dublin which called for a restoration of the IRA ceasefire were larger than those in Belfast. The exclusion of ordinary people from the peace process has meant that they are not engaged in it. This stands in stark contrast to the 1960s and 1970s when masses of people were engaged in the 'politics on the streets'.

The politicisation of ordinary people brought about massive changes in the early 1970s. Society became completely militarised, governments collapsed, new political parties emerged and the whole administration of society was reorganised. The peace process represents the end of the political cycle which emerged in the late 1960s and in part it has been achieved through the demobilisation of ordinary people. This does not mean that the peace process is insignificant for the politics of the province. The political cycle set in motion by the civil rights movement may not have been taken over by a more energetic movement. Analysis of the peace process suggests it may be characterised by entropy rather than by dynamism, but that does not mean that it is not significant. The politics of the province cannot exist in a vacuum and the peace process has become the mechanism through which new political institutions are being developed. A major concern is that the peace process is being developed at the expense of the population of the province, the very people it is supposed to benefit. If the peace is gained through the pacification of the population of the province it is likely to make the last quarter of a century appear positively liberating by comparison.

## References

Adams, G. (1976), *Peace in Ireland?*, Republican Press:Belfast.
Adams, G. (1988), *A Pathway to Peace*, Mercier:Cork.
Barnes, H. (1996), 'Statement on the end of the IRA ceasefire', *Fortnight*, No.348.
Bowyer Bell, J. (1990), *The Secret Army; the IRA 1916-1979*, Poolbeg: Dublin.
Boyle, K. and Hadden, T. (1994), *Northern Ireland: the choice*, Penguin: London.

Breen, S. (1995), 'Sword in the Stone', *Fortnight*, No. 340.
Cairns and Cairns, (1995), 'Children and Conflict; A psychological perspective', in Dunn, S. (eds), *Facets of the Conflict in Northern Ireland*, Macmillan, London.
Campbell, D. (1995), 'Piece-by-Piece Process', *Scotland on Sunday*, 27 August 1995.
Canning, D., Moore,B. and Rhodes J. (1987), 'Economic Growth in Northern Ireland; Problems and Prospects', in Teague, P. (ed.), *Beyond the Rhetoric;Politics, the Economy and Social Policy in Northern Ireland*, Lawrence and Wishart:London.
Central Community Relations Unit (1994), *Policy Appraisal and Fair Treatment*, CCRU:Belfast.
Coogan, T.P.(1996),*The Troubles*, Arrow: London.
Darby, J. (1991), *What's Wrong with Conflict?*, Occasional Paper No. 3, Centre for the Study of Conflict, Coleraine.
Dunn, S. (ed.) (1995), *Facets of the Conflict in Northern Ireland*, Macmillan:London.
Edwards, J. (1995), *Affirmative Action in a Sectarian Society*, Avebury: Aldershot.
Ervine, D.(1995),'Next Century Unionism?', in Hall, (ed.), *Beyond the Fife and Drum* Island Pamphlets: Newtownabbey.
Farrell, M. (1976), *Northern Ireland; the Orange state*, Pluto:London.
Fitzgerald, G. (1994) 'Still making history', *Fortnight*, No. 332.
Gallagher, A. M. (1995), 'The Approach of Government; Community Relations and Equity', in Dunn, S. (ed.), *Facets of the Conflict in Northern Ireland*, Macmillan:London.
Governments of the United Kingdom and Republic of Ireland (1994) *Joint Declaration for Peace*, HMSO:London.
Griffiths, H. (1978), 'Community Reaction and Voluntary Involvement', in Darby & Williamson (eds), *Violence and the Social Services in Northern Ireland*, Heinemann:London.
Hadden, T. and Boyle, K. (1989), *The Anglo-Irish Agreement; Commentary, Text and Official Review*, Sweet and Maxwell:London.
Hartley, T. (1996), 'Statement on the end of the IRA ceasefire', *Fortnight*, No. 348.
Hughill, B. and Nelson, D. (1995), 'Peace for one year - but the war is still not over', *The Observer*, 27 August 1995.
Hume, J. (1996), *Personal Views: politics peace and reconciliation in Ireland*, Town House:Dublin.
IRA, (1996), *Statement announcing the end of the IRA ceasefire*, 9 February 1996.
Keenan, S. (1996), 'Everybody Knows This Is Nowhere', *Irish Reporter*, No. 21.
Kelly, K. (1995), 'No Champagne Now', *Living Marxism*, No. 82.
Lyttle,J.(1995),'In my home town,even peace is uneasy',*The Independent*, 28 August.
McAlliskey, B. (1996),'Where Are We Now In The Peace Process', *The Irish Reporter* No. 21, pp. 23-28.
McCann, E. (1980), *War and an Irish Town*, Pluto:London.
McIntyre,A.(1995),'Modern Irish Republicanism;the product of British state strategies' *Irish Political Studies*, Vol. 10, pp.97-121.
McKittrick, D. (1995), 'Ulster tiptoes towards a brighter future', *The Independent*, 1 September.

McKittrick, D. (1995), *The Nervous Peace*, Belfast:Blackstaff.

Mallie, E. and McKittrick, D. (1996) *The Fight for Peace: the secret story behind the Irish peace process*, Heinemann: London.

Major, J. (1996), 'Statement to the House of Commons on the Peace Process', *Irish Times*, 13 February 1996.

Mayhew, P. (1996), 'June 10 - A new push for peace', *The House Magazine*, 6 May.

Miller, D. (1994), *Don't Mention the War; Northern Ireland propaganda and the media*, Pluto:London.

Morrow, D. and Wilson, D. (1995), 'Voluntary Action towards Sustainable Peace', in Williamson, A. (ed.), *Beyond Violence*, Community Relations Council/Centre for Voluntary Action Studies, Belfast.

Nesbitt, D. (1995), *Unionism Restated*, UUP:Belfast.

O'Brien, C. C. (1974), *States of Ireland*, Panther, Herts.

O'Dowd et al, (1980), *Northern Ireland; between civil rights and civil war*, CSE, London.

O'Leary, B. (1987), 'The Anglo-Irish Agreement; Meanings, Explanations, Results and a defence', in Teague, P. (ed), *Beyond the Rhetoric; Politics, the Economy and Social Policy in Northern Ireland*, Lawrence and Wishart:London.

O'Neill, B. (1996), 'Democracy is not about the majority', *Living Marxism*, No. 93.

Paisley, I. Jnr.,(1996),'Statement on the end of the IRA ceasefire', *Fortnight*, No. 348.

Patterson, H. (1996), 'Northern Ireland Economy', in Aughey, A. and Morrow, D. (eds), *Northern Ireland Politics*, Longman:Harlow.

Rowthorn, B. (1987), 'Northern Ireland; An economy in crisis', in Teague, P (ed.), *Beyond the Rhetoric: Politics, the Economy and Social Policy in Northern Ireland*, Lawrence and Wishart:London.

Ryan, M. (1994), *War and Peace in Ireland; Britain and the IRA in the New World Order*, Pluto, London.

Said, E. (1988), 'Identity, Negation and Violence', *New Left Review*, No. 171.

Sinn Fein, (1994), *Setting the Record Straight*, Sinn Fein:Belfast.

Thatcher, M. (1993), *The Downing Street Years*, Harper Collins:London.

Townshend, C. (1993), *Making the Peace; public order and public security in modern Britain*, Oxford University Press:Oxford.

Whyte, J. (1990), *Interpreting Northern Ireland*, Clarendon:Oxford.

Williamson, A. (ed.)(1995), *Beyond Violence:the role of the voluntary and community sector in building a sustainable peace in Northern Ireland*, Community Relations Council/Centre for Voluntary Action Studies, Belfast.

Wilson, R. (1994), 'Making the centre hold', *Fortnight*, No. 332.

# Part Two
# POLITICAL PERSPECTIVES

# 4 Divided loyalists, divided loyalties: Conflict and continuities in contemporary unionist ideology

*James White McAuley*

Our fundamental concerns are peace and democracy...The need to decommission derives from the democratic principle...There is no place for guns at the table of democracy...Consent simply means that it is for the people of Northern Ireland as a whole, and for them alone, to determine their constitutional destiny...it is for the people of Northern Ireland to determine to which state they belong. Some say this reflects an old-fashioned view of sovereignty and that the issue of which state you belong to can be blurred or fudged. That is wrong. Sovereignty today is essential to protect the democratic principle. The question is, to whom do you pay your taxes? Who takes decisions concerning your rights and your future? Are those persons elected by you? Do they account to you and can you turn them out if they make the wrong decisions? These are the most fundamental questions that can be asked about the political arrangements of any society. These questions can be answered in a United Kingdom context or a Republic of Ireland context: but they cannot be answered democratically in a condominium or any form of joint British/Irish constitutional fudge (David Trimble MP, 23 March 1996).

The principle of consent for the people of Northern Ireland is fully established. The principle of self-determination and consent must apply in all sets of circumstances so that the people of Northern Ireland have the sole right to determine not just the constitutional issue of the severance of Northern Ireland from the Union, but also any changes in the governance of the Province and the creation of any institutions or structures impacting upon it (DUP Forum election manifesto 1996).

There must be no dilution of the democratic procedure through which the rights of self-determination of the people of Northern Ireland are guaranteed (PUP Forum election manifesto 1996).

The only agenda these negotiations will follow is that of the people. That is what republicans and the Irish government must come to terms with. This process belongs to the people of Northern Ireland (UDP Forum election manifesto 1996)..

## Introduction

The broad aim of this chapter is to analyse the identity and politics of Ulster unionism within the context of its reactions to the contemporary peace process; the paramilitary ceasefires; the publication, in February 1995, of the Joint Framework Documents; the beginning of formal talks and, in early 1996, the breakdown of the IRA ceasefire. It examines the current politics and political discourse of the main political representatives of loyalism and unionism, the Ulster Democratic Party and Progressive Unionist Party, whilst considering the same in respect of the Democratic Unionist Party and the Ulster Unionists. It also suggests some of the major directions in which contemporary unionism is being pulled and the alternatives on offer to unionists. Finally, it considers the direct responses of the Protestant working class and the contemporary roles and political directions of the loyalist paramilitaries.

The starting point for all of this is somewhat difficult to identify. Just what the contemporary peace process involves is clearly a matter for discussion. For many unionists, its origins lie at least as far back as the signing of the Anglo-Irish Agreement of 1985. As Robert McCartney, explains, there is a continuity to contemporary events:

> The process begun by the Anglo-Irish Agreement when the foundation for the transfer of executive power to the Republic was laid, was continued in the Joint Declaration. The political importance of the Declaration was that it transferred the decision as to the political future of Northern Ireland from the British Government to all the people of Ireland (*Belfast Telegraph*, 21 February 1995).

In this chapter, however, I shall largely use the term peace process in a broad and somewhat formal context. In particular, I use it to refer to unionist perceptions and understandings of the events which began with the talks between Gerry Adams, the President of Sinn Fein and John Hume, the leader of the SDLP, which resulted in their joint statement issued in April 1993 and the presentation of these joint proposals to the Irish Government. Following this, partly in response to the Shankill bombing and the Greysteel killings, the two Governments sought to develop their own initiatives. These encountered difficulty when it was discovered that the British Government had been engaged in talks with the IRA. Nonetheless, in December 1993, and with the support of all the major political parties in the UK and Irish Republic, the two Governments issued a joint declaration of principles, which was to become known as the Downing Street Declaration. Later in February 1995, the two Governments published new proposals under the title of *Frameworks For The Future*.

## The 'peace process' and unionism's political responses

Since at least early 1993, the developments sketched out above have produced increasing discontent from within unionism, surrounding the formation of a pan-nationalist front. Many unionists believed that in response to this grouping, which provided the political momentum behind the peace process, the British Government were willing to 'sell out' the Union to a nationalist and republican agenda. Throughout the contemporary period, the political response of unionism to any notions surrounding a peace process has, at best, been ambiguous. Their initial retort was set in the context of the widespread solace and enthusiasm expressed by the unionist population, at the thought that 25 years of violence had ended. Much of the populist expression, supported by national media coverage, suggested that Northern Ireland was, at last, about to enter a new phase of peace.

Behind this, however, many unionists continued to express uncertainty and concern for their future position and indeed the Union itself. There was a prevailing suspicion that the real process was founded on a surreptitious deal between the British Government and the Republican Movement. There were, however, important differences in Unionism's political responses. Some of these will now be examined. The leader of the Ulster Unionist Party, James Molyneaux, insisted to his Party and the public that 'no secret deal had been done'. In contrast, the Democratic Unionist Party (DUP) adopted a rigid stance in defence of the Union. From the outset, according to the DUP, the intention behind the peace process was clear. It was part of a grand plan to weaken, if not destroy, Northern Ireland's constitutional position within the United Kingdom. Hence the DUP immediately dismissed the IRA ceasefire as a tactical change of direction by the Republican Movement, without any change of intent. As one DUP activist put it, 'this is simply a clever manoeuvre to get as much as they can out of the (British) Government and the Brits have fallen head over heels to do it'.[1]

Further, for the DUP, the British Government themselves clearly could no longer be trusted. They had lied about secret contacts with the IRA for years and had formulated a bargain in return for the ceasefire that would ensure the move towards a united Ireland. They sought to betray the Union and the unionist people. This viewpoint was reinforced by Gregory Campbell, who claimed that section 4 of the Joint Declaration for Peace:

> leaves us in no doubt where our Government wants us to go when it talks of the people of Britain extending friendship so that they may live together in harmony and in partnership, with respect for their diverse traditions. We, rather than being a people within the United Kingdom family are regarded as one of the diverse traditions within Ireland. Nothing could be clearer (Campbell, n.d., p.9).

## The loyalist paramilitaries

Initially, both the Ulster Defence Association (UDA) and the Ulster Volunteer Force (UVF) maintained their military campaign. This was demonstrated when the UFF murdered a Catholic in North Belfast, less than 24 hours after the IRA ceasefire was declared. Loyalist spokespersons in Belfast claimed it was in direct response to the British Government's decision to move several IRA prisoners to Northern Ireland from England. As the IRA ceasefire held, however, the loyalist paramilitaries presented a more coherent political response. After much internal debate, some six weeks after the IRA had announced its ceasefire, the Combined Loyalist Military Command (CLMC) said that they too would halt their campaign, declaring that their ceasefire would be permanent unless republican paramilitaries were to resume violence. One of the reasons for the delay in calling a reciprocal ceasefire was that some loyalists believed they had forced republicans into ending their campaign. These loyalists argued for continuation of the campaign to the point of bringing about complete republican submission.

The declaration of a loyalist ceasefire brought to the fore the two loyalist political groupings closest to the paramilitaries, the Ulster Democratic Party (UDP) and the Progressive Unionist Party (PUP). At the heart of the UDP's response remained a document called *Common Sense*. It was first published in the late 1970s and proposed the formation of a devolved government in Northern Ireland, based on a form of power-sharing. More recently, the UDP have begun to promote the notion of a council of the British Isles where political representatives of all the regions would be represented. The PUP's demands in relation to the peace process were structured around six principles; no diminution of Northern Ireland's status as a part of the UK; self-determination for Northern Ireland as a unit; constitutional change achieved by constitutional means; civil rights for all; a written constitution and Bill of Rights for Northern Ireland and support for North-South bodies composed of elected representatives.

**Frameworks for the future - A green bridge too far!**

Unionism clearly has not been homogeneous in its response to the Peace process. In the period following the IRA ceasefire, it appeared that certain sections of the Protestant working-class were no longer content to recognise the DUP as their legitimate representatives. One explicit example of this was the defection by several DUP local councillors to the UDP, largely because they believed the DUP had 'misread the mood' of many loyalists. The conflict between the two groups has ben made overt at several points by Ian Paisley. He has referred to the PUP and UDP as marionettes of the Northern Ireland Office and derided both parties as operating without a mandate. There was, however, almost uniform hostility from within unionism when the Prime Ministers of the United Kingdom and the Republic of Ireland unveiled their joint Framework Document, *Frameworks for the Future*, on 22 February 1995. The Framework Document was designed to form the basis for all-party talks on the future of Northern Ireland. The complex text sought, amongst much else, to lay down proposals to establish a cross-border body of representatives, elected by the Irish parliament and by a new Northern Ireland assembly. Within this, any disputes would be resolved by a directly elected three person panel that would operate by consensus. The North-South body was conceived as having consultative, executive and harmonisation powers in aspects of trade, transport, health, education, and economic policy.

The reaction of unionist politicians to the Framework Document was one of anger, outrage and rejection. On its publication, Ken Maginnis described himself as 'one of the saddest people in the United Kingdom', while Ian Paisley claimed it was 'a one-way road to Dublin'. The next day, the *Belfast Newsletter* recalled the speech made by the late Harold McCusker in 1985, at the release of the Anglo-Irish Agreement. It remains one of the most faithful statements of general unionist dismay at recent events and particularly at the increasingly close relationships developing between the British and Irish Governments. It is still worth quoting, as an example of the impact this dynamic has had upon unionist thinking:

> (I stood) not waving a Union flag - I doubt whether I will ever wave one again - not singing hymns; saying prayers or protesting, but like a dog and asked the Government to put in my hand the document that sold my birthright...everything that I held dear turned to ashes in my mouth (cited in Kenny 1986, p.103).

Ian Paisley immediately damned the Framework Document as concrete evidence of a sell-out. In a statement directed at the British Prime Minister, Ian Paisley made clear his feelings of betrayal when he said, 'You have sold Northern Ireland out. You have sold out the Union' (quoted in *Belfast Newsletter*, 23 February 1995). He was supported in his analysis by Peter Robinson, the DUP deputy leader, when he claimed that 'anyone who opposed the Anglo-Irish Agreement and proposes talks on the Framework Document is a traitor (quoted in *East Belfast Herald and Post*, 2 March 1995). For Robinson and many others, the logic of the Framework Document is evident. The Document had put in place a drip, drip, effect, the result of which would be an all-Ireland state. Elsewhere, Robinson argued: 'This is not a discussion document; it is a declaration of intent - a joint government programme for Irish unity. When the verbal foliage is pruned away, only one central proposition remains and it is an entirely nationalist programme (cited in *Belfast Telegraph*, 22 February 1995).

Further, for Robinson this merely confirmed his broader analysis. In his view, the Document 'like the Downing Street Declaration before it, was framed to buy-off the IRA. The extent to which this succeeded is seen by the IRA's response. They responded to the Joint Declaration by calling a ceasefire. They were satisfied that an endless stream of concessions would flow. The Framework Document was offered to the IRA to show that there was no need for further violence - they are to be given all they demand' (Robinson, 1995, p.37).

The Ulster Unionists also reacted strongly. Their general secretary, Jim Wilson, called it a dangerous recipe for the future. He went on to state that it was 'clear that, if implemented, these proposals would put Northern Ireland on the slippery slope to joint authority (quoted in *Belfast Telegraph*, 22 February 1995). The UUP also had to come to terms with its obvious failure to read the British Governments intentions correctly. John Major's assurances and James Molyneaux's belief in a 'special relationship' now appeared less credible. As Unionist fury intensified, the UUP's 'understanding' with John Major formally ended on 1 March 1995, when the nine UUP MP's, along with the DUP MP'S, voted with the Labour opposition against Conservative European policy.

In contrast to the main political representatives of unionism, the response of the PUP and UDP was more muted. While both criticised the Framework Document as fundamentally anti-unionist, there were some indications that they would welcome the idea of all-party negotiations. Some time later, David Ervine summarised the position as follows:

> The Unionist community is deeply worried by that (Anglo-Irish) relationship. However, I think that many are beginning to recognise that unless we have a hands-on attitude and become involved, we will become steadily worse off. I think that many unionists are prepared to take a pro-active role in terms of monitoring and influencing that relationship, because for many there seems to be a propensity to deal with the relationship North and South, while very much at the exclusion of the relationship East and West (quoted by Hislop, 1996, p.12).

**The Union - slip sliding away ?**

Even before the resumption of the IRA campaign, these were seen as dangerous times by many unionists. Talk of betrayal by Britain has been commonplace. This notion of the peace process putting in place a slippery slope towards Dublin rule is in broad currency within unionism. One of the main problems opposing a solution is that many unionists believe that in broad terms the peace process is merely a form of creeping reunification in direct response to IRA violence. The view is well expressed by Robert McCartney, when he says:

> The British Government has assumed its present position as a response to terrorism. It has obtained the present ceasefire by offering to pan-nationalism an evolving process whereby its shared objective of Irish unity will be obtained, hence the deafening silence of both the SDLP lambs and the IRA wolves. It is now about to mount a propaganda campaign in which it will vilify unionists as being negative and intransigent for failing to agree to their own destruction. It will attempt to foist upon Northern Ireland, terms for a united Ireland that Britain would deem wholly unacceptable for a united Europe (*Belfast Telegraph*, 21 February 1995).

From the unionist gaze, the latest initiatives surrounding the closer workings of the British and Irish Governments mark a perpetuation of Ulster's demise. This includes the Sunningdale Agreement, the Anglo-Irish Agreement, the Joint Declaration and the Framework Proposals. All are seen as part instalments of a larger process, the end of which is the severance of the Union. As a recent edition of the *Orange Standard* (March 1995, p.1) put it, regarding the proposed development of cross-border institutions, 'that would be the slippery slope to a united Ireland and all the honeyed words of Government Ministers in the United Kingdom or Eire will not disguise that fact'.

**Reconstituting unionism - repositioning loyalism ?**

Despite the attitudes expressed above, there has been no unity of ideological thought or political actions between those active in loyalist political organisations. This has been demonstrated by the willingness by some sections of the Protestant working class, largely through the UDP and PUP, to articulate some notion of a distinct response to the peace process beyond that offered by the main political representatives of unionism. That such divisions are manifest can be seen in the fragmented reaction of unionism and the attempt by several different groupings to reconstruct their position around different visions of what constitutes contemporary unionism. This has not, however, resulted in a clear delineation of unionist party politics and in pragmatic terms there clearly is overlap across these sets of ideas and party political groupings. In broad terms, however, four ideological positions are beginning to emerge.

*Reconstructing unionism (1) - voices of the Protestant workers*

Clearly one important question to be asked is whether loyalism has altered its form in the contemporary period? Some of the most important consequences of the peace process have been the changes at the community level. In particular, the effects on loyalist working class districts need to be considered seriously. The consent of the Protestant working class, at least tacitly, has been vital in ensuring any peaceful rejoinder to the issuing of the Framework Document. Obviously their demands, particularly in the light of a renewed IRA campaign, remain crucial.

In political terms, the response of the working class Protestant has been confused. At its most fundamental level their sense of unionism has always rested on a sense of difference, of Britishness and of an identification with Ulster as a political territory. However, reaction to the peace process has highlighted that there is no longer any firm conception of what this means for working class unionism. Certainly, it does not mean accepting the legitimacy or political authority of the British state. This position has been manifest since the signing of the Anglo-Irish Agreement and reinforced throughout the contemporary peace process.

Another manifestation of the peace process has been the opening up of discussion and debate within loyalist communities. This was the experience of those groupings who traditionally have been particularly excluded, such as Protestant women. Whilst recognising that this is a highly diverse grouping, a common experience is that they have been excluded from any visible participation in the public arena (McAuley, 1991, 1994). There is recent evidence, albeit still largely anecdotal, that loyalist women created the opportunity to discuss their own identity and social relations in a more meaningful way, in the absence of overt paramilitary violence.

A fuller flavour of the contemporary debates at the community level can be gleaned from the publication of some of the discussions and debates organised by community activists in loyalist districts, in part documented by Hall (1995) and Hall, *et al* (1994b). These give excellent examples of the types of ideas and material which has been produced from within the Protestant working class. Indeed, in *Ulster's Protestant Working Class*, Hall provides a lucid summary of the dynamics within this section of the community, when he says:

> All that can be said with any certainty is that an energetic reassessment is presently under way within the Protestant working class, except of course among those already so demoralised that they have ceased doubting their eventual fate. Much of

that energy is being channelled into plans for resistance and no-one should be under the misapprehension that the Protestant working class will permit itself to be docilely led into an unacceptable future. But others are directing their energies into a radical reappraisal of where they have come from and where they are going (1994b, p.27).

It is most useful, therefore, to view these events, not necessarily in terms of any end product, but rather of a process which is under way in sections of the Protestant working class. Certainly there are problems with how representative of the wider population are the views of those who did take part. However, what is certain is that ex-prisoners, local councillors, community activists, members of the Ulster Democratic Party and Progressive Unionist Party and local people did demonstrate a degree of self criticism and reflection for which Unionism is hardly noted. The broad contours of the booklet, while always unionist, are also extremely pluralistic, emphasising a shared cultural heritage. Hence at one point it states:

> We are confident that our two communities possess the ability and the willingness to sit down together and negotiate ways in which *all* our traditions and aspirations can be afforded legitimate expression. We further believe that it will be this *inter-community* dialogue which will provide the most realistic basis from which to develop *genuine and purposeful* links between the two parts of our island (1995, p.24, *emphasis in original*).

Much of the above is broadly in line with the approach of those political groupings representing the paramilitaries. The PUP, for example, has argued that, unlike traditional unionists, they are seeking to move unionism away from tribalism and sectarian politics. Indeed some would claim that part of the PUP programme is the redefinition of unionism. This focus was highlighted in an interview with a leading figure within the party, Billy Hutchinson. He expressed his own identity as follows, revealing some of the contradictions currently felt by many working class loyalists:

> I am Irish and I don't see any conflict between that and asserting that I am British. Nor do the Scots, the Welsh and the English have that difficulty; like me, they all retain their cultural identities within the multinational British state. So, I am Irish, culturally speaking, and the language, music and Irish culture generally, are as legitimately mine as of anybody else born on this island, even though Sinn Fein has tried to hijack aspects of that identity. My Britishness is rooted in my sense of belonging to the wider British working class and its struggles and it is from the British working class movement that we take our political philosophy and perspective. If I myself lived on the British mainland I would support the Labour Party. This common British working class identity was forged in the struggles of Belfast's industrial working class which linked them to workers on Clydeside, in Liverpool, Leeds and the other great industrial centres of Britain rather than to the mainly agricultural south. Hence, the political consciousness of our working class base has a much stronger East-West dimension than a North-South one (Hutchinson, 1995, p.4).

*Reconstructing unionism (2) -in its own likeness !*

Other unionists have simply returned to first principles. In particular, those who were extremely sceptical of the entire peace process in the first place and who saw it as a dilution of the unionist position, have sought to reposition along these lines. As Ian Paisley said: 'This is not peace. This is a shameful process of deluding the people while they surrender to the IRA' (cited in Crowley, 1995). This position has been made even more forthright since the end of the IRA ceasefire. Gregory Campbell, security spokesperson of the DUP, writing just before the Canary Wharf bombing restated the position, insisting: 'I don't think the peace process is going anywhere if the end objective is the permanent end of murder and violence. It is not intended to achieve that...The ceasefire was a tactical change by the Provisional IRA movement to gain more concessions by the threat of violence. The price we will have to pay for fewer people being killed is becoming more expensive' (1996, p.44).

Another key discourse around which traditional unionism is restructuring is democracy and the democratic process. Take, for example, this statement from Ken Maginnis. Commentating on the recent meeting between John Hume, Gerry Adams and the IRA leadership, he stated:

> The reiteration of the IRA's commitments to its republican objectives is not a simple restatement of aspirations but an ominous threat that violence will continue so long as it fails to achieve its objectives. With the support of only 4.8% of the total electorate the IRA is not going to achieve its objective of a United Ireland; it knows that and, with its ethos of violence, it is unlikely that it will act in the best interests of society in Northern Ireland (UUP, *News Release*, 29 February 1996).

According to unionist sceptics, the Government's proposals are underpinned by the following three criteria: firstly, a conditional surrender to the IRA; secondly, a denial of democratic control to the majority within Northern Ireland, and finally, the creation of all-Ireland bodies with executive powers to bring about harmonisation of all policies within the island of Ireland until there is an eventual acceptance of a united Ireland and the departure of Northern Ireland from the United Kingdom. Those who take this perspective see the peace process as nothing other than a euphemism for a surrender process. For some unionists the failure of the peace process lie squarely with the British Government who have fallen under the spell of Sinn Fein rhetoric and the politics of the pan-nationalist front. For example, one leading loyalist, Sammy Wilson insisted that 'nationalists want Northern Ireland destroyed and will refuse any proposal which can work...those involved in the pan-nationalist front will risk more bodies on the streets to prove their contention that Northern Ireland is a failed political entity' (cited in Graham, 1995).

*Reconstructing unionism (3) - unionism with a human face*

The forces representing traditional unionist leadership have not, however, completely ossified since 1994. The election of Robert McCartney to Westminster as a prominent, independent, United Kingdom Unionist, was hailed by some as a victory for liberal

Unionism. That said, he too has articulated the clear view that the peace process was part of a conspiracy against Unionists and the Union. Further, a central task of the British Government has been to promote 'propaganda to persuade the pro-Union majority that the benefits of the ceasefire are a fair price for the sacrifice of its British identity'. (*News Letter*, 23 February 1995). For McCartney, the strategy surrounding the proposed political settlement in the Framework Document long pre-dated the IRA ceasefire. The suspension of violence, however, was a necessary precondition for assailing it to Unionists and convincing them of its merits. He, therefore, draws the following conclusions:

> The British Government has, at the least, offered a conditional surrender to the IRA. Peace on these terms could have been obtained at anytime over the past twenty-five years. In the interim the dead have died in vain and the maimed remain mutilated for nothing. In an attempt to stand truth upon its head, the Unionist people who have suffered largely in silence will be castigated by the propaganda machines of both governments as negative obstacles to peace. Those who have bombed, murdered and maimed will he presented as peacemakers while the victims will be blackmailed with a resumption of violence if they do not acquiesce in the destruction of the Union. The good and the great, both lay and clerical, will be called in aid by the British political establishment to lend their voices to a constitutional conspiracy (*Belfast Telegraph*, 19 June 1995).

Having taken this as his starting point, McCartney has offered some important internal criticisms of unionism. Since 1921, for example, he argues that the Unionist Party has relied on two main factors; an inbuilt Unionist majority and the manipulation of pro-Union paranoia about Northern Ireland's place within the United Kingdom. This constitutional anxiety was compensated by an extreme sectarian loyalism. It is this sectarianism, not unionism itself that McCartney challenges. He argues that if the benefits of the Union are to be made clear and the Union is to be preserved, then there must be dramatic changes. This is an expression of Unionism with added social concern.

For McCartney, however, there can now be little doubt that, if the Framework Document proposals are substantially implemented, the fate of the Union is sealed. The best unionism can expect within its parameters is a stay of execution from the Union. He too thinks the traditional unionist leadership has failed, albeit for different reasons from the UDP and the PUP. McCartney believes that unionism has failed to give the decisive leadership, without which the Union will go by default. McCartney argues that this belief amongst unionists 'has engendered fear and anxiety about their future in the hearts and minds of the pro-Union people. Their reaction ranges from hopeless despondency to a mounting resentment at the seeming inability of their political representatives to provide a coherent united policy and positive leadership' (*Belfast News Letter* 7 March 1995).

Elsewhere, McCartney (*Belfast Telegraph*, 21 February 1995) has argued that Britain is seeking to solve her age old dilemma over Ireland by employing social, economic, cultural and educational engineering to force unionists to mutate their political identity into that of the state to whom sovereignty over their territory is intended to be passed. Further, while the Joint Declaration postulated an agreed solution by all the people-of Ireland, the only discernible solution was one of Irish Unity.

If, however, the pro-Union majority in Northern Ireland are placed in a position where the evolution of predetermined events permits no option but to agree, such a process represents nothing but simple coercion. There is thus a continuity to the direction being taken by the British and Irish Governments:

> The process begun by the Anglo-Irish Agreement when the foundation for the transfer of executive power to the Republic was laid, was continued in the Joint Declaration. The political importance of the Declaration was that it transferred the decision as to the political future of Northern Ireland from the British Government to all the people of Ireland. This in turn provided the cornerstone for the forthcoming framework document. The essence of this document is to transfer, so far as possible, the future administration of Northern Ireland away from the United Kingdom. The future governance of Northern Ireland would not be a joint authority in the sense of a division of executive powers between the United Kingdom and the Republic. It would be a joint authority as between a puppet Northern Ireland Assembly and the Republic of Ireland (*Belfast Telegraph*, 12 March 1996).

Although McCartney can be seen as the voice of bourgeois unionism, he has been highly critical of Northern Ireland's middle class for their desire of peace at any price. He claims many from this grouping have accepted the Sinn Fein agenda and the demands that paramilitaries be given a place at the negotiating table, arguing that 'such people are being conditioned by the grant and withdrawal of ceasefire peace to an addiction of peace of any price. The methodology of the IRA is that of the dope peddler; give it free, get them hooked and then make them pay through the nose for it' (*Belfast Telegraph*, 12 March 1996).

*Reconstructing unionism (4) - intellectualising the union*

One recent manifestation within unionism has been the active defence and promotion of the link between Northern Ireland and Great Britain by a grouping of Unionist intellectuals (cf. Cadogan group, 1992, 1994; Aughey 1995; Foster (ed.), 1995; Nesbitt, 1995; Roche and Birnie, 1996). Central to their argument is the view that unionists have been extremely poor ambassadors for their own cause. They reflect, in the main, an inherent belief of the superiority of the Union in political, cultural, social and economic terms. As Foster puts it in his introduction, the grouping whose work he edits seek to:

> repudiate a notion that has been a dogma with Irish republicans since 1920 and that, worrisomely, has lately threatened to take hold among British political parties and media - namely, that the union of Northern Ireland with Great Britain is merely a political arrangement (and an inconvenient and even somewhat bogus one) and therefore rightly vulnerable to manipulation, diminishment and in the end extinction.

> The idea of the Union rests on the proposition that the Union is a social, cultural and economic fabric, with reality and history as its warp and weft. (1995, p.5, emphasis in original).

This approach can also be clearly seen in the works of Patrick Roche and Esmond Birnie. In a recent article, they summarise as their views regarding the peace process, insisting:

> Historians will write about these events as a shameful episode in contemporary British history. The Major government in dealing with Irish nationalism has trampled on the integrity of unionism and has in principle conceded the Union in an attempt to secure and consolidate what was at best a temporary IRA ceasefire...The betrayal of Ulster...was obscured by the professional mendacity of government ministers and justified in parliamentary debates and in the media by the mawkish rhetoric of the so-called peace process. But it was also made possible by the failure of unionists to undermine the intellectual creditability of Irish nationalism...(*Ulster Review*, 1996, p.14).

It is this intellectual challenge, in defence of the Union that this group of writers have set about. For them, there are several fundamental flaws in the Irish nationalist position. Such nationalist ideology is for them, the politics of the absurd, driven by the defective core belief that there is a single nation on the island of Ireland. A central task for these writers is to reveal the weakness of this position. Indeed Roche and Birnie (1996, pp. 13-15) can find no sustainable objective claim to support Irish nationalism. Indeed, they argue that nationalists 'have been reduced to currently using a form of geographical determinism to produce a national identity which would embrace all the inhabitants of the island. The idea is that geographical location of birth determines national identity' (*Ulster Review*, 1996, p.15).

Such arguments have led Roche and Birnie to conclude that Irish nationalism is entirely without validity (1996, p.15). Not only is there little credence in the moral or political arguments put forward by Irish nationalists, but Roche and Birnie also directly challenge the idea that unification would bring about any real economic benefit to the people of Ireland. For them Irish unity would for decades, if not indeed permanently, deprive the inhabitants of the island of an acceptable level of economic well-being (1996, p.15). They dismiss the 'vague expectations of constitutional nationalists on the issue of economic viability and the patent absurdity of Sinn Fein economic policy represent a refusal to face economic reality...there is nothing in either the present situation...or the history of the Irish economy since 1920 to suggest that a unified Irish state could survive at an acceptable level of economic welfare without massive and open-ended external subventions from the British exchequer' (1996, p.43).

Although the above writers have produced a more articulate and certainly more plentiful defence for the Union, they have not really moved the debate forward. Their main claim remains almost a mirror image of that they oppose, namely that those in the north-east of Ireland are a community differing in decisive ways from the people of the rest of the island, in matters such as religion, place of origin and national identity.

**Politics and Ideology of unionism**

One problem in trying to formulate a coherent analysis of unionism is that the core elements in the ideology, such as a distinct British identity, have no straightforward social or political location. Many of the central concepts promoted by Unionism, such as democracy and self-determination for the people of Ulster, are as the opening quotations of this chapter indicate, commonplace within all unionist political discourse. They do not belong to any one social grouping. This is central to an understanding of the politics of Unionist identity. Certain political groupings dominate certain areas of political discourse. This can clearly be seen in the Unionist response to the Framework Document. Unionists have since its publication constantly referred to it as being the first step, or the thin edge of the wedge, to a united Ireland. Such discourse has aroused all the different fears held by all the factions of the Unionist bloc. Such discourse provides a location around which most unionists, irrelevant of their broader orientation, can identify and position.

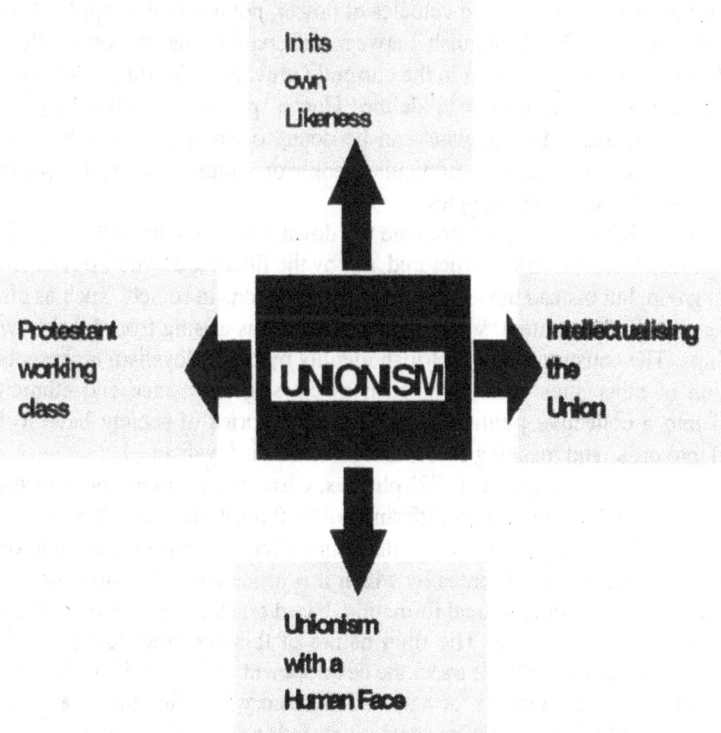

Figure 4.1 Trends within contemporary unionism

It may therefore be useful here to consider unionist political discourse a little more fully. An important entry point into any understanding of the concept are the works of Foucault (1979; 1985). By discourse he means that broad set of ideas, meanings and possible statements about a subject that are dominant at particular times among particular sets of people. This, of course, resembles the Marxist concept of ideology. Foucault, however, rejects the notion that dominant ideas and values can be traced back directly to the particular class whose interests they serve. For Foucault, there is no presumption of necessary power inequality. Those who shape the discourse are also subject to it. Further, the concept of discourse differs from that of ideology, because it does not assume that there is a truth, which ideology conceals. Rather, discourse sets about defining its own truth. It defines what can and cannot be said about a particular subject, what can be seen as the logic of an argument and what are acceptable premises in such arguments.

Foucault's reading of discourse has important consequences for our understanding of power. Foucault disputes this view, arguing that there is no such thing as power, but rather powers. For Foucault, however, power is based on knowledge and, in particular, the ability of discourses to define truth. Knowledge does not constrain; rather, it works by defining certain goals as much more desirable than others. As Foucault argues, individuals are the vehicles of power, not its point of application. Hence, Foucault seeks to distinguish between different forms of power. Power produces knowledge that can be seen in the currently prevailing discourse. Above all, knowledge represents the power to define. Hence, power and knowledge are inseparable. Knowledge decrees what can be done, to whom and by whom. For Foucault, power does not rest with particular people or groups. Rather, it is present in a multiplicity of discursive struggles.

For Foucault, power operates, not from the top down, but, from the bottom up. The lives of individuals are, therefore, structured, not by the filtering down of power from a dominant group, but instead those widespread oppressions in society, such as class and gender and, in this context, sectarianism, are seen as arising from local power relationships. The construction of a British identity by Ulster loyalism represents a proliferation of other sites of identity, such as class, gender, race and ethnicity, organised into a collective political will. These categories of society have to be structured into order and meaning by the discourse that is loyalism.

Hence to rework one of Laclau's (1977) phrases, Ulster unionism has no necessary political belongingness. It can address differing political positions and different social groupings, at differing points in history. Its nature often depends on the traditions, discourses social and political forces by which it is articulated. Unionism seeks to construct a closed social and political formation, based on ethnicity, culture, religion and sometimes notions of race. The fluid nature of this construct has been ably demonstrated by Walker (1996). He traces the development and use of historical myth and suggests that for Unionists, as for nationalists, history has often meant a view of the past influenced by the needs of our late nineteenth-and twentieth-century world (1996, p.14).

## Conclusion

Unionism and loyalism as ideologies are clearly in some state of commotion and repositioning. More important, however, is the question as to whether unionism is in some state of transition. It is important, therefore, to consider the differing perspectives outlined above seriously. The views currently being expressed by the PUP, UDP and those who have acted as spokespersons for the Protestant working class, including the loyalist paramilitaries, must be set against the full range of opinions and options currently on offer. When this is done, it indicates the willingness of sections of the Protestant working class to reassess their own position and perhaps to challenge the authority of the established Unionist political leadership. There is evidence that this process is in operation, even if only to a limited extent. It was directly seen, for example, in the discussions organised recently by community activists throughout Northern Ireland, but particularly in Belfast.

That is not to say there are still not those who wish to fortify the traditional Unionist position. It is here that the DUP's discourse will remain at the fore. The reaction of the DUP has been predictable. That said, their rhetoric is highly seductive to many from a unionist background. Throughout the contemporary period, all those who have been prepared to make any attempt to operate within the parameters of the peace process have been equated with undermining the Northern Irish state itself and of playing the pan-nationalist game. The pressures within Unionism to conform to this perspective are relentless. It has been brought into even sharper relief by the resumption of the IRA's campaign. This has merely strengthened the position of those who seek to reconstruct unionism In its own likeness. As Peter Robinson put it:

> The Peace Process has not ended. It never existed. John Major, and sadly some unionists, were suckered into a surrender process where the IRA exchanged a temporary silencing of its guns for political concessions (*DUP Press Release*, 8 October 1996).

## Note

[1] This, and other non-attributed quotations are from a series of interviews with paramilitary members, community activists and political leaders, which have been carried out, by the author, between August 1994 to December 1995 and between July 1996 to September 1996.

## References

Adamson, I. (1974), *The Cruthin, a History of the Ulster Land and People*, Donard: Dundonald.

Adamson, I. (1982), *The Identity of Ulster, the Land, the Language and the People*, Belfast.

Adamson, I. (1991), *The Ulster People*, Pretani Press:Bangor.

Aughey, A. (1989), *Under Siege, Ulster Unionism and the Anglo-Irish Agreement*,

Hurst: London.

Aughey, A. (1995), 'The End of History, The End of the Union', in *Selling Unionism Home and Away*, Ulster Young Unionist Council:Belfast.

Bowyer-Bell, J. (1996), *Back To The Future: The Protestants and a United Ireland*, Poolbeg:Dublin.

Breen, S.(1996), Part of the political power struggle between unionism and nationalism', Belfast Telegraph, 8 July.

Cadogan Group (1992), *Northern Limits. Boundaries of the Attainable in Northern Ireland Politics*, Cadogan Group:Belfast.

Cadogan Group (1994), *Blurred Vision. Joint Authority and the Northern Ireland Problem*, Cadogan Group:Belfast.

Campbell, G. n.d. *Ulster's Verdict on the Joint Declaration*, publisher not stated.

Campbell, G. (1996), 'Opinions and Doubts', *Irish Reporter*, No. 21, p. 44.

Clayton, P. (1996), *Enemies and Passing Friends*, Pluto:London.

Coulter, C. (1994), Class, Ethnicity and Political Identity in Northern Ireland, *Irish Journal of Sociology*, Vol. 4.

Cranston, S. (ed.) (n.d.) *Framed: A critical Analysis of the Framework Document*, Ulster Unionist Information Institute:Belfast.

Crowley, M. (1995), Paisley says N.Ireland peace is surrender to IRA, Reuters, 25 November 1995.

Dunn, S. (ed.) (1995), *Facets of the Conflict in Northern Ireland*, Macmillan: Basingstoke.

Foster, J. W. (ed.), (1995), *The Idea of the Union*, Belcouver Press:Vancouver.

Foucault, M. (1979), *Discipline and Punish*, Penguin:Harmondsworth.

Foucault, M. (1985), *History of Sexuality*, Penguin:Harmondsworth.

Graham, I. (1995), 'Peace Process Plea to Call Sinn Fein's Bluff', PA News, 24 February.

Hall, M. (1986), *Ulster - The Hidden History*, Pretani:Belfast.

Hall, M. (1994), *The Cruthin Controversy*, Island:Belfast.

Hall, M. (1994), *Ulster's Protestant Working Class: a community exploration*, Island: Belfast.

Hall, M. (1995), *Beyond the Fife and Drum*, Island:Belfast.

Hislop, S. (1996), 'David Ervine - An Interview', *Udders - Student Union Magazine*, Issue 1.

Hutchinson, B. (1995) in *Socialist Voice*, Vol. 5, No. 7.

Kenny, A. (1986), *The Road to Hillsborough*, Macmillan:Basingstoke.

Kerr, A. (1996), *Perceptions Cultures in Conflict*, Guildhall Press, Derry.

Laclau, E. (1977), *Politics and Ideology in Marxist Theory*, New Left:London.

Laclau, E. and Mouffe, C. (1985), *Hegemony and Socialist Strategy. Towards a Radical Democratic Politics* Verso:London.

McAuley, J. W. (1991), 'The Protestant Working Class and the State in Northern Ireland since 1930: a Problematic Relationship', in Hutton, S. and Stewart, P. (eds.), *Ireland's Histories*, Routledge:London.

McAuley, J.W. (1994), *The Politics of Identity: a loyalist community in Belfast*, Avebury: Aldershot.

McCartney, R. (1995), Conditional Surrender, *Belfast Telegraph,* 21 February.

McCartney, R. (1995), Time to face the Crisis, *Belfast News Letter,* 7 March.

McKittrick, D. (1994), *Endgame: The Search for Peace in Northern Ireland,* Blackstaff: Belfast.

Nesbitt, D. (1995), *Unionism Restated. An Analysis of the Ulster Unionist Party's statement of aims,* Ulster Unionist Information Institute:Belfast.

New Ulster Political Research Group, (1979), *Beyond the Religious Divide,* UDA: Belfast.

Progressive Unionist Party (1996), *Manifesto for the Forum Election,* PUP:Belfast.

Robinson, P. (1985), *Ulster in Peril: an Exposure of the Dublin Summit,* DUP: Belfast.

Robinson, P. (1995), *The Union Under Fire: United Ireland Framework Revealed,* published by the author:Belfast.

Roche, P.J. and Birnie, J. E. (n.d.), 'An economics Lesson for Irish Nationalists and Republicans', Ulster Unionist Information Institute:Belfast.

Roche, P.J. and Birnie, J. E.(1996), 'Irish Nationalism - politics of the absurd', *Ulster Review,* No. 20.

Ulster Democratic Unionist Party (1996), *Our Covenant With the Ulster People,* Manifesto for the Forum Election, DUP:Belfast.

Ulster Democratic Party (1996), *Look to the Future,* Manifesto for the Forum Election, UDP:Belfast.

Ulster Unionist Party (1986), *Ulster Must Say No,* UUP:Belfast.

Ulster Unionist Party (1996), *Building Your Future Within the Union,* Manifesto for the Forum Election, UUP:Belfast.

Ulster Political Research Group (1987), *Common Sense,* UPRG:Belfast.

Ulster Society (1986), *Ulster, an Ethnic Nation,* Ulster Society:Belfast.

Ulster Young Unionist Council (1995), *Selling Unionism Home and Away,* UYUC: Belfast.

# 5 Unity in diversity? The SDLP and the peace process

*Mark McGovern*

## Introduction

Irish nationalism created the Irish peace process (Aughey, 1994; Bean, 1995; Mallie and McKittrick, 1996; Patterson, 1995; Rolston, 1994; Ryan, 1994). There has been significant input from other sources, most obviously in the conflict management strategies adopted by the British Government. Indeed, the process could simply not exist if it were merely an all-nationalist affair. However, it is the analyses, strategies, policies and actions adopted by a range of anti-partitionist political forces which have been the ideological and political driving force behind the initiative to break the apparently aspic statis of Northern Irish politics in recent years. The contribution of Irish republicans to the peace process has been huge. However, the role of non-republican nationalists and of the SDLP and its leader John Hume in particular, has also been highly significant (McGovern and Shirlow, 1997). The aim of this paper is to critically examine the conflict resolution strategies of the SDLP in the lead up to and during the peace process.

To understand the SDLP strategy of conflict management and resolution it is necessary to place these within the context of the party's analysis of the Northern Ireland problem and the way in which it reflects the character of northern nationalist political culture (Todd, 1990, pp.31-44). This last point indicates a wider problem that a critical assessment of the SDLP's position must take on board. All nationalist approaches to conflict resolution must define themselves in relation to the concepts which lie at the core of northern nationalist political culture. As Jennifer Todd has argued, northern nationalism is a 'complex, internally differentiated ideology' based upon three core and inter-related concepts which cut across and qualify each other, 'nation, community and justice' (Todd, 1990, p.31). The adoption of a discourse which fails to ameliorate the fears, or meet the aspirations, which find diverse expression in these concepts is doomed to failure. The difficulty is, of course, that these concepts and goals are often perceived (or in actuality are) the antithesis of those current within unionist political culture. A strategy which attempts to fulfil these goals must also be analysed in terms of its likelihood of achieving certain democratic imperatives.

Similarly, to understand the role played by the SDLP it is necessary to see the process not as something which was born blinking into the light with the Hume-Adams declaration of April 1993, but in the context of much longer term developments. John Hume himself has argued that the peace process began with the New Ireland Forum of 1984 and the signing of the Anglo-Irish Agreement in 1985. Hume suggested that the latter was a document from which 'everything that has happened in the past few years stems' (Hume, 1996, p.46). Whilst this is something of an exaggeration and ignores the detrimental impact the Anglo-Irish Agreement had in terms both of Unionist opposition and the continuance of Sinn Fein's political isolation, it does point to the long term strategy of conflict management and control (of which the Anglo-Irish Agreement was a key element) that has helped to create the situation which exists today.

How, then, to understand the SDLP peace strategy? Clearly any strategy for peace must be based upon a particular understanding of the main causes of conflict. There are four basic beliefs which underpin the SDLP's analysis of the conflict and four central platforms to their peace strategy which result. The exigency of changing circumstances dictated each phase of development as much as did any pre-planned blueprint and at any given moment any one of these elements may have taken precedence over the others. However, each element has been a significant component of an overall strategy that has similarly been affected and adapted in the light of events.

The first of these four elements rests upon the belief that the central problem in Ireland today is not so much one of divided states, as of divided peoples; divisions which are ultimately viewed as the historical residue of social, political and cultural separation and antagonism. Given this 'two traditions' approach, the central aim of the peace process must be to 'break down the real border in Ireland, which is in the hearts and minds of our people' (Hume, 1996, p.47).

The 'revisionist' tenor of this 'two traditions' analysis is, however, somewhat qualified by the second element, which adopts a more conventional nationalist conception of the Northern conflict. Although the SDLP argues that the central problem is that of divided communities with contradictory aspirations, the responsibility for the creation of that division rests heavily with the record of British rule in Ireland. In its submissions to the Forum for Peace and Reconciliation in 1995, the SDLP, in similar vein to Fianna Fail, suggested that the divisions and conflict in Ireland are the 'last negative legacy of the ancient quarrel between the people of these islands' (Forum for Peace and Reconciliation, 1995, p.12). The salience of this 'ultimate responsibility' outlook lies in the implications it bears upon policy implementation and the strategy of conflict resolution to be adopted as part of the peace process. The logic is that as Britain is itself part of the problem, it must be part of the solution and should 'join the ranks of the persuaders' for constitutional change.

The third central argument is that Irish nationalism must re-invent and re-articulate itself in such a manner that it emerges as a viable and progressive political philosophy. To do so it must enshrine the key democratic imperatives of equality, justice and liberty. This can only be achieved, it is argued, through the promotion of a secular, inclusive and pluralistic vision, with the rejection of what is seen as the destructive, ethnically exclusive physical force strain of Irish nationalism. However, the party has also adopted an empathetic approach to Republicans as they faced a series of difficulties in moving toward an unarmed strategy. In large part, this empathy has been founded on the belief, shared by all shades of northern nationalist opinion, that the very particular historical circumstances of conflict have created the appeal of physical force nationalism to a significant proportion of the northern catholic population. As a result the attempt to re-invent nationalism has been manifest in a drive for an inclusive nationalist agenda; the so-called 'pan-nationalist consensus'.

Lastly, the SDLP suggests that a central reason why Irish nationalism must change is that the world of the nation-state is gone and that a 'post-nationalist' future requires a new approach to the interdependence of nations in the new global economic order. The political corollary of promoting Irish economic development via the attraction of multi-national capital (particularly from the USA) and supra-national subsidy (via the European Union) is that new international arenas and institutions offer potential alternative avenues of allegiance and influence to create a 'new Ireland'. This approach has also impacted upon the peace process in the direct role played by both the United States and, to a lesser extent, the European Union.

Each of these analytical perspectives and their respective policy imperatives produces concomitant political strategies which have been central to non-republican nationalist approaches to the Northern Ireland conflict during the peace process. Each forms a discrete area of concern. The aim of this paper is to provide critical analysis of each of these elements in turn.

**'The real border'?: The SDLP and the 'two traditions' approach**

Defining both northern and southern nationalist perspectives on the peace process has been a long-term process of re-conceptualising the causes of conflict. Economic and social modernisation in the South, and the embourgeoisement of significant sections of the northern catholic community, paralleling a growing sense of alienation from the armed campaign of militant republicanism, fed into a search for a new explanation for the causes of conflict and a revision of nationalist goals (Bew, 1989; Breen, 1990; Cormack and Osborne, 1994; O'Connor, 1993). While greater cross-border integration still remains the preferred option for nationalists, north and south, the form such re-integration should take, and the means by which it might be best achieved, have gone through something of an epochal shift in the last decade and a half (Cox, 1989; Girvin, 1994). Central to that process, too, has been a re-evaluation of the position of Ulster Unionists and an attempt, which has framed the SDLP approach to conflict resolution, to reconcile what are seen as the 'two traditions' on the island.

Since at least the early 1970s traditional nationalist conceptions of the root causes and nature of the conflict in Northern Ireland have been subject to an intellectual onslaught often characterised as the 'revisionist project'. While the term 'revisionism' is somewhat amorphous, the central premise of the revisionist viewpoint, contrary to that of traditional Irish nationalism, is that the central problem is not so much the British presence, but instead is one of reconciling the goals and aspirations of 'two traditions'; the Irish-Catholic-Nationalist and Ulster-Protestant Unionist communities.

These constitute two separate cultures, if not two distinct national groups (Boyce, 1996; Fitzgerald, 1972; O'Brien, 1972; Whyte, 1991). Partition and the consequent antagonism of the two communities in Northern Ireland were not the result of British involvement but were, to some extent, the product of mutually exclusive ethno-national allegiances and identities.

Arch-revisionists, such as Garret Fitzgerald and Conor Cruise O'Brien, argued that Irish nationalists had therefore to recognise the fears and aspirations of the Unionist population and either remove the causes of those fears, as proposed by the former in his 'Constitutional Crusade' of the early 1980s, or give up the goal of re-integrating the national territory altogether, as the latter continues to vitriolically insist. (Fitzgerald, 1991; O'Brien, 1994). Working in close co-operation with the SDLP in the early 1980s, Fitzgerald became instrumental in re-constituting non-republican nationalism, with the aim of reconciling the 'two traditions' very much in mind. The New Ireland Forum was the result.

While the desire to prevent the seemingly inimitable rise of Sinn Fein in the wake of the 1981 Hunger Strike was undoubtedly the realpolitik context for the creation of the New Ireland Forum, the impetus also drew very much upon a longer term contradiction within Irish political culture (Fitzgerald, 1993; pp.189-202; Rolston, 1988, pp.58-80). That contradiction lay in the complex relationship of a revolutionary, anti-colonial political tradition and the bourgeois nationalism of a liberal-democratic, western capitalist state which seemed, however, to share at least some of the same ideological space. The dilemma for non-republican nationalists and for the SDLP in particular, was how to re-articulate a variant of nationalism which would not alienate the kernel of nationalist sentiment that was clearly evident in the radicalisation of the northern nationalist working class in the aftermath of 1981, whilst pursuing a political agenda that would be amenable to the interests of the modern state and Irish political class.

The New Ireland Forum was the product of this situation and, while the Forum Report was somewhat 'greener' in outlook than some of its instigators would have liked, two key concepts were established that would frame the public debate on the future of the North for nationalists; the cultural distinctiveness of Ulster Protestants, which emerged into the mainstream of nationalist political dialogue, and the 'consent principle'.

Both of these approaches have been important for the SDLP throughout the development of the peace process and have formed a central element of the discourse employed by the party, evidenced in a number of policy documents and statements issued during the late 1980s and early 1990s. Taken together, these concepts of 'two traditions' and the 'principle of consent' represent a shift away from what might be called the assimilationist perspective of traditional nationalism, or of Republicanism, which points towards a transcendent nationalist identity in which the 'division of Catholic, Protestant and Dissenter will be replaced by the common name of Irishman'. The focus now is less upon the elimination of differences between Catholic and Protestant, and towards a strategy of managing difference based far more around the principles of consociationalism (Lijphart, 1977; McGarry and O'Leary, 1993, pp.1-40). McGarry and O'Leary have suggested that consociationalism, in essence power-sharing, rests primarily upon the acceptance of ethnic pluralism (McGarry and

O'Leary, 1993, p.35).

For the SDLP, acknowledging the realities of ethnic differentiation is central to the search for peace. According to John Hume, the real issue at stake 'was not the elimination of diversity, but its accommodation' (Hume, 1996, p.60). Throughout the books, speeches, policy documents and forum submissions issued by the party during the last few years, one strand of the SDLP's analysis has consistently been shaped by this consociational approach, encapsulated in one of Hume's favourite, oft-repeated phrases 'unity through diversity'. For example, at the party's annual conference in November 1995, Hume argued that 'the essence of the SDLP's policies for the past twenty-five years had been to cherish diversity. It must remain the essence of our future' (Clarke, 1995). A consociational approach has been manifest in the power-sharing practices of the SDLP on the local councils where they have either control or the dominating voice. Derry, in particular, is held up as the paragon of a future where 'accommodation' is the order of the day (Pollak, 1993, p.41). This consociationalist perspective also defines a number of the stated policy objectives of the party. The party has proposed that a power-sharing executive should be established as the only governmental structure within Northern Ireland which is likely to deliver stability, albeit allied (significantly) to an all-Ireland institutional framework.

Critics of the SDLP's commitment to consociationalism are not hard to find. From a unionist perspective, the SDLP's perception of Protestants is often seen as 'ignorant, stereotypical and full of post-1921 assumptions' and their commitment to a 'two traditions' approach condemned as the facade for atavistic nationalist demands which mask an assimilationist platform (O'Brien, 1994, p.193; Pollak, 1993, p.340). Similarly their record of practising consociationalism in Derry and elsewhere is viewed as less than perfect by many unionists.

Left critics see the 'accomodationist' avenue as fulfilling a middle class agenda, the philosophical parallel to the emergence of a burgeoning catholic middle class, whose interests lie increasingly in working within the bounds of the current social and political structure. From this perspective 'accommodation' is the ideological *non sequiter* for a new middle ground consensus found among the relatively affluent, whilst the marginalised working class will continue to find themselves excluded from social and political power in the proposed 'agreed Ireland' (McCann, 1995; O'Connor, 1993, p.36). Additionally, the entire 'two traditions' approach has been condemned as more likely to rarefy ethnic division than to destroy it, reducing the potential for cross community class and gender alliances and the realisation of real equality and justice in society. Consociationalism is also elitist, concentrating on the 'high' politics of negotiating institutional arrangements within and between members of the political class as the necessary means to circumvent the cleavages of ethnic division (Lijphart, 1977). Consociationalism can therefore be seen to be anti-egalitarian.

Closely allied to the 'two traditions' approach has been the emphasis placed by the SDLP upon acceptance of the principle of consent for change to the constitutional status of Northern Ireland. Essentially the consent principle means that change to the constitutional position of Northern Ireland must have the expressed agreement of a greater number of the citizens of Northern Ireland. This concept was enshrined in the Anglo-Irish Agreement and has underpinned the non-republican nationalist approach to conflict resolution from that point onward. The consent principle is one that is particularly problematic within the context of a northern nationalist world view and proved deeply contentious during the protracted negotiations which led up to the Hume-Adams joint statement and the subsequent Downing Street Declaration. For Sinn Fein and the IRA a time frame for a British commitment to Irish unity was initially a prerequisite to agreement, but as one of the Dublin government's negotiators argued in respect of the Declaration; 'if you put a time frame in, you abolish consent and consent is one of the pillars of the document' (Mallie and McKittrick, 1996, p.177). For republicans, the consent principle implies an acceptance of partition and the ubiquitous 'unionist veto'. It is, however, the essence of the revisionist nationalism that is synonymous with the standpoint of the SDLP.

To solve the conundrum presented to nationalism by the consent principle, effort has focused upon trying to discover a new language which can circumvent the deadlock of traditional ideological positions. This has formed part of an attempt to re-articulate the core concepts within the political culture in such a way as to allow new political routes to be opened up, whilst suggesting that they represent a continuity with the past. A flexibility in terms of the language used by Sinn Fein was seen as the major breakthrough which would permit a re-focusing of nationalist aspirations without the appearance of a significant shift having taken place (Mallie and McKittrick, 1996, p.174; Hume, 1996, p.93). However, the consent principle is likely to be one of the most difficult obstacles to overcome should genuine all-party talks take place.

The 'two traditions' perspective and the 'consent principle' do provide an 'accomodationist' core to the SDLP's peace strategy, but that strategy is not purely consociational in character. Ultimately the boundary to the SDLP's consociational perspective is set at the point at which it cross-cuts and potentially contravenes the core concepts of northern nationalist political culture. Consociationalism may afford a 'parity of esteem' within Northern Ireland that overcomes both the material reality and the sense of injustice and communal disaffection which lies at the heart of the northern nationalist world view. It will not, however, simply obviate the importance of the 'imagined community' of the nation. As Seamus Mallon has argued, whilst the SDLP's support comes from the broad swathe of northern nationalist opinion which has 'accepted that the route to obtaining nationalist objectives can only be met through the political process' it remains the case that 'these people will not settle for a six-county arrangement' (O'Connor, 1993, p.54).

If stress is placed upon the first rather than the second element of Hume's 'unity in diversity' slogan, the dynamic interaction of those core concepts of northern Irish political culture can be seen to be at work. Similarly the SDLP's conception of the causes of the conflict do not simply revolve around a narrow 'two traditions' perspective, but also include a critical conception of a long-term British involvement which has profound implications for their conflict resolution strategy.

## 'The ranks of the persuaders'?: The SDLP and inter-governmental coercive consociationalism

While the 'two traditions' approach has been important in the SDLP's analysis, it has certainly not seen a complete diminution of the nationalist conception of the role of Britain. The fact that the SDLP lays more stress upon the responsibility of Britain for the conflict in Ireland than any other major political party on the island, with the obvious exception of Sinn Fein, reflects not only the continuing sense of grievance with British government policy felt by northern nationalists, but also the divergence often bubbling just below the surface between northern nationalism and the more tepid waters of its southern mainstream counterpart.

For John Hume the 'real border' in Ireland may indeed be within the 'minds of the people', but what created and perpetuates that division does not have a purely endogenous explanation. It was, argues Hume, the vagaries of British policy in Ireland, both before and after partition, which fed the sectarian rivalries of Northern Ireland and the reactive policies of crisis management which did little but heighten those rivalries during the last twenty five years. John Hume identifies the British guarantee of the current constitutional status of Northern Ireland as *the* barrier to meaningful political dialogue: 'As I see it the two greatest problems in Northern Ireland are the British guarantee and the Unionist dependence on it' (Hume, 1996, p.57).

The British constitutional guarantee, suggests Hume, ensures that there is no advantage for unionism in changing its political outlook and as a consequence it is the traditional policy of the British government which creates the conditions for ongoing sectarian division:

> It [British policy] guarantees the integrity of 'their quarrel'. While this guarantee exists there is no incentive for unionists to enter into a genuine dialogue with those with whom they share the island...That is the nub of the political deadlock in Northern Ireland. Only when the 'Orange Card' of threat, violence and sectarianism is denied political currency can that deadlock be broken. This requires an alternative approach by Britain (Hume, 1996, pp.37-39).

The 'British culpability' perspective sees unionism as ultimately and inevitably dependent upon Britain. As such this belief defines the second element of the peace strategy of the SDLP; 'intergovernmental coercion'. This essentially means that the British government, in co-operation with the Irish government, should 'force'(coerce); 'persuade' or 'facilitate' constitutional change by removing the British guarantee of the constitutional status quo. The belief that the British role as guarantor precludes a political settlement legitimates an approach which, whilst having consociational goals, seeks to achieve them through the application of non-violent pressure upon unionism as the necessary means of removing the problem of the 'Orange Card'. It also suggests that there is only one party to the conflict who can apply such pressure; the British. To achieve a lasting settlement, suggests Hume, 'the responsibility of Britain [must be] realised and acknowledged' and that it is only the British who can 'create the conditions in which unionists can perceive their true interests' (Hume, 1996, p.48). It was this 'coercive consociational' approach which underpinned the Anglo-Irish Agreement, Hume's 'brainchild'. The conception of a 'coercive', 'persuasive', or 'facilitating' role for the British government has continued to underwrite the SDLP's strategy ever since.

The Anglo-Irish Agreement, conceived 'not [as] a solution, but [as] a framework for a solution', was designed to create a new middle ground consensus by providing unionists with an incentive to change (McGarry and O'Leary, 1995). Whether consciously or not this conception of the British government's role undoubtedly tapped into a long-standing discourse within unionist political culture enshrined within Protestant myths of betrayal, siege and deliverance. As an ethico-political discourse, loyalty is central to unionism. Its negative corollary is betrayal wherein the 'fickle English' are regarded as an unreliable source of deliverance (McGovern, 1994; Todd, 1987). In a sense the SDLP philosophy has attempted to play on this fear of betrayal, whilst re-directing it away from its traditional reactionary course towards an accomodationist road. This continues to be very much part of the SDLP approach. When Hume argues that Unionists need 'trust no-one but themselves' and that they should be 'their own guarantors' it is precisely this 'Lundy' myth that is conjured (Hume, 1996, p.53).

The Anglo-Irish Agreement did not, however, prove particularly successful in this regard, as the wholesale unionist opposition and the re-emergence of loyalist paramilitarism in the late 1980s and early 1990s demonstrated. Whilst the coercive stick of the Anglo-Irish Agreement undoubtedly helped to bring unionists to the negotiating table by the early 1990s, it became clear that it was not going to push them towards anything other than an internal settlement. The SDLP approach did have significant ramifications for the position and policy of the British government. The Anglo-Irish Agreement represented a partial shift from the traditional British guarantor role. This was further signalled in 1989 when, largely in response to the SDLP-Sinn Fein dialogue of 1987-88, the then Secretary of State for Northern Ireland, Peter Brooke, stated for the first time that Britain had 'no selfish strategic or economic interest in Northern Ireland' (Catterall and McDougall, 1996, p.5). While this may not have represented a real change in the British government's implicit position, its explicit public declaration was something new.

The intergovernmental framework was similarly utilised throughout the period immediately prior to the declaration of the IRA ceasefire as a means to publicly indicate what was in essence a pan-nationalist initiative. As Mallie and McKittrick have shown the Downing Street Declaration was, to all intents and purposes, the product of negotiations between various strands of Irish nationalism which then utilised the intergovernmental mechanisms to construct the public discourse of the peace initiative. It would be wrong to suggest that the British government had no part to play in this, but its role was largely reactive and defined by the parameters of the facilitator role.

During the peace process the position of the British Government has often been criticised by nationalists precisely because it has not shifted from the 'guarantor' role as much or as swiftly as they would wish. The wave of optimism which greeted the 'window of opportunity' opened by the IRA ceasefire in August 1994 soon foundered and for the SDLP, as for most nationalists, it was the unwillingness of the British government to adopt a more dynamic strategy, to move away from the holding operation of crisis management and, in particular, the reluctance to join 'the ranks of the persuaders' for change, which threw the process into intermittent crisis and which led to the ending of the IRA ceasefire in February 1996. The sense that the British government continues to be unwilling to end its guarantor role, largely for narrow and short-term political ends, continues to cast a gloom on the prospects for a settlement from an SDLP perspective.

The SDLP's attitude toward unionism, as it is reflected in the intergovernmental coercion approach is again defined by the mobilisation of the core elements of northern nationalist political culture. The understanding of unionism contained within the 'British culpability' perspective has been severely criticised by revisionists, for while there is indeed a recognition of the autonomy of a unionist identity, unionism's political agenda and aspirations are seen as invariably dependent upon the British presence. While Hume writes that he admires the fact that Irish Protestants have always sought to maintain their distinctiveness, he adds that the 'exclusive' character of that distinctiveness is something fostered by Britain, 'events showed the way and principal among them was the consistent encouragement given be centuries of British policy to maintain a separate and exclusive existence (Hume, 1996, p.54).

This is undoubtedly a perspective born out of northern nationalist world view which, in both its collective historical consciousness and in terms of it's lived experience, finds it absurd to suggest that Britain has not had a major part to play in defining the parameters of unionist politics. Yet it is clear that there has been an attempt by the SDLP and for that matter by Sinn Fein, to re-negotiate and re-articulate northern nationalism in such a way that 'British culpability' becomes 'British responsibility' and therefore forms part of a conflict resolution strategy which eschews political violence. The reluctance of the British government to adopt a 'persuasive' role toward unionism emphasises the limits of intergovernmental coercion'. It certainly led to nationalist disillusionment with the Anglo-Irish Agreement and as a result helped pave the way for what appeared the real catalyst to the peace process, the Hume-Adams Initiative. With the emergence of Hume-Adams, the implicit approach of the Anglo-Irish Agreement strategy of achievement of a new pan-community middle ground consensus before achieving peace, was reversed. What was needed, in the words of an Irish government memorandum to the British, was a 'period of stability' which would then create a different atmosphere, in which an all-Irish dimension might become more acceptable to a sufficient spectrum of unionist opinion (Mallie and McKittrick, 1996). The persuasive potential of intergovernmental co-operation was therefore itself subject to a pressure for change from a different source; the pan-nationalist alliance.

**A new departure? : The SDLP and pan-nationalist consensus**

The limits of the Anglo-Irish Agreement, the failure of the Brooke-Mayhew talks and, very significantly, the re-thinking which occurred within the Republican movement from the mid-1980s onward, all saw a 'new departure' in the search for a political settlement during the early 1990s. This came to fruition in the Hume-Adams Initiative. The search for a common nationalist agenda which could be adhered to by the SDLP, Sinn Fein, the southern Irish government, major parties in the south and international opinion, particularly in the USA, was the most vital political development of the last decade. It was also an approach that owed more to changing circumstances than to a pre-conceived strategy on the part of the SDLP. However, whilst the quest for this pan-nationalist consensus and the Hume-Adams dialogue in particular, represented something of a departure from the strategy enshrined in the Anglo-Irish Agreement, the seeming contradictions in the SDLP's position were more apparent than real.

Undoubtedly the emphasis on isolating Sinn Fein and the attempt to construct a new consensus with mainstream unionism was far less to the fore with the emergence of Hume-Adams. However, it is also important to recognise that the 'pan-nationalist consensus' strategy did not simply emerge as an alternative after other avenues were blocked but was being pursued in parallel to inter-governmental coercive consociationalism from the late 1980s. As early as 1987, talks were taking place between Sinn Fein and the SDLP following the first hesitant steps of the republican leadership toward an overhaul of their whole strategy. Although these talks formally came to an end in 1988 with no agreement reached, discussion between key figures in the two parties (and between Hume and Adams in particular) continued in private thereafter. Similarly, whilst the public debate appeared to end in acrimonious failure, the clarification of the relative positions of the two parties and their areas of disagreement certainly fed into the development of the peace initiative.

Two crucial areas of disagreement were identified (Adams, 1995, p.197; Hume, 1996, p.94; McGovern and Shirlow, 1997). Firstly, there was dispute over whether the continued presence of the British in Ireland was due to their own social, economic and strategic interests, as republicans had traditionally argued, or whether, as the SDLP suggested, it was merely the residue of a responsibility felt by the British toward the unionists. In the last few years some republicans have begun to suggest that the main reason for Britain remaining in Ireland is neither due to economic nor strategic interest, but rather for political and ideological ends; that the British could not be seen to be forced to leave as this would undermine the legitimacy of the state itself (McGovern and Shirlow, 1997). Such republican re-thinking was a major stepping stone on the road to the IRA ceasefire and toward the construction of a common northern nationalist agenda.

The second major point of difference identified during the Sinn Fein-SDLP negotiations was the apparent contradiction between the principle of consent and the principle of Irish rights to self-determination. For the republican movement, the principle of national self-determination was the fundamental plank of its political philosophy. The insistence that this had to be the basis of any future constitutional arrangement appeared to preclude any acceptance of the consent principle which had become central to the perspective of the SDLP, although a shared belief in the ideal of national self-determination was agreed between the parties as early as 1988 (Hume, 1996, p.94).

Through protracted contacts and rethinking within both parties, space for a consensus began to emerge in the early 1990s. It became increasingly clear that the republican interpretation of what would constitute the expression of national self-determination was being redefined. The achievement of a thirty two county unitary Irish Republic, whilst remaining the formal goal of the party, was being supplemented by the idea that the expressed will of the whole of the people of the island would represent the existence of national democracy. The increasing flexibility of republican language and the shift in perspective which this represented clearly allowed for the possibility of common ground to be found with non-republican nationalism.

It was also clear that republicans, in seeking an alternative strategy, had to be offered the means to enter the political arena whilst maintaining the integrity of their own movement (McGovern and Shirlow, 1997). This necessitated something of a moratorium on the politicking for the nationalist vote which was the normal nature of things between two parties competing for the same constituency. It also required a more careful and thoughtful expression on the part of non-republican nationalists as to the causes of political violence. While an opposition to the use of force was always maintained, the SDLP did adopt a more ameliorating voice in regard to the reasons why people may have been involved in the IRA's campaign. Such steps represented an effort to heal moral, social and political rifts which had opened up within the Catholic community as a result of the conflict. The adoption of certain aspects of republican language and political agenda into the shared discourse of a pan-nationalist consensus was also an inevitable consequence of a process predicated on the need to re-constitute communal solidarity.

However, of equal, if not greater, significance has been the diminution of the radical and revolutionary element of Irish nationalist ideology that 'pan-nationalism' has involved. The politics of revisionism have clearly been at work in this context. One commentator went so far as to suggest that the declaration of the IRA's ceasefire represented 'the ultimate proof of the strength of the revisionist intellectual assault on Irish nationalism' (Patterson, 1995). Certainly the attempt to find a common agenda for northern nationalists required some fundamental ideological re-thinking on the part of Irish Republicans and the ditching of socialist and radical aspects of their programme.

Given these developments it was clear that the Hume-Adams Initiative also represented a critical juncture for the development of Irish nationalism and nationalist ideology, exemplified in the two critical areas of debate between Sinn Fein and the SDLP. Discussion of whether or not the British might be willing to disengage from the north without the necessity of force and alternative means by which the right of Irish national self-determination might be exercised, were again defined by the nexus of discursive concepts which constitute northern nationalist political culture.

While there is more than a hint of anti-republican revisionism in the oft-heard suggestion that Hume and Adams had more in common with each other than either had with anyone else on the Irish political scene (Coakley, 1993), certainly the Hume-Adams Initiative was, again, an expression of the distinctive inter-related core of concepts that are the essence of northern nationalist political culture and which, as Jennifer Todd contends, 'both republicans and constitutional nationalists share...although they articulate them in different ways' (Todd, 1990, p.31). The very idea of developing a peace strategy on the basis of a pan-nationalist consensus emphasises the importance of both the imagined community of the 'Irish nation' and the binds of communal solidarity within northern nationalism. The trick was to re-conceive these in such a manner to which both the SDLP and Sinn Fein could subscribe.

Undoubtedly the pan-nationalist approach became the dominant element in the SDLP's strategy in the early 1990s on largely pragmatic grounds. Combining the political and diplomatic influence of the nationalist parties of the north with that of the southern government and international opinion was also a means to further the goals which the SDLP espoused. Even more importantly, the opportunity of a permanent cessation to the IRA's armed campaign, given the re-thinking taking place within Sinn Fein, was an opportunity which appeared too good to miss. However, the way in which that opportunity was seized does say a great deal about the character of northern nationalism and of the continued relevance of the nationalist goals that remain central to the SDLP's perspective. The phrase, 'unity in diversity', does not simply refer to the recognition of two traditions. It also places them within a re-defined pluralistic concept of national self-determination. If Hume no longer explicitly argues, *a la* Tone or Adams, for the substitution of 'Catholic, Protestant and Dissenter' by the common name of Irishman, he still at least hopes that they might 'come together on our small island' (Hume, 1996, p.156). It was upon that terrain that a rapprochement with republicanism was feasible. The national territory continues to define the context for accommodation.

## Ireland in a new world: The SDLP and the international dimension

The national territory may have defined much of the pan-nationalist approach of the SDLP to the peace process, but the party has also tried to argue that the 'realities' of a 'post-nationalist' world need to be taken on board in Irish political life (SDLP, 1991, pp.5-6). An avowedly pro-European perspective, combined with a concerted campaign to mobilise the Irish-American lobby and involve the US administration in the search for a settlement in Ireland, have given shape to the international outlook of the SDLP in recent years. For the SDLP, the international arena has three roles to play in regard to conflict resolution in Ireland. First, in terms of the development of the peace process itself, the party has sought a role for international arbitration. Second, the attraction of transnational capital is viewed as a necessary springboard toward a peaceful resolution of the conflict and as a means to alleviate economic stagnation. Last, the supra-national bodies of the European Union are seen to offer Ireland a way out of the clash of ethnic identities. All three elements are defined by this idea that a re-imagining of Ireland's international context can deconstruct what are regarded as the destructive competition of the two traditions exclusionary claims.

The SDLP have sought to involve non-Irish and non-British groups and bodies in the search for a political settlement. Arbitration has not been seen as central to their strategy of conflict resolution, but as a useful additional influence (McGarry and O'Leary, 1993, pp.1-40). In particular they have been keen to engage successive governments in the United States as an alternative source of international influence to counter-balance that of Britain. As a result the party developed links with various powerful Irish-American political figures (Guelke, 1988, pp.128-152; Holland, 1987, pp.114-151; Wilson, 1995, pp.226-284). In part this was designed to counter republican influence in the US, but it was also intended that such links might be employed both to attract US investment and to impact upon the US government's policy toward Ireland. The presidency of Bill Clinton, who had been obliged to woo the Irish-American lobby within the Democratic party during his campaign for the party's nomination with a commitment to adopt a more pro-active policy on Ireland, afforded the opportunity for these networks of influence to be brought into play. This fact was also very much in the minds of republican leaders as they developed their unarmed strategy (Adams, 1995, p.210).

From 1993 onward the slow steps toward inclusive dialogue were often taken on the 'neutral ground' of the United States. The US government also emerged as a loci of diplomatic pressure. Very often such pressure was more concerned with appearance than substance; the visit of Clinton to Ireland at the end of 1995, which in material terms was utterly meaningless, but which had a great deal of political currency, being an obvious case in point. However, the selection of the US senator George Mitchell as the chair of the multi-party talks emphasised the desire to include the US as an international arbitrator within the peace process. The SDLP's position in regard to US involvement may be couched in the idealised image of the peoples of Ireland working 'in unity with Irish descendants across the world [to develop] a whole new concept of identity', but there is a more immediate and hard edged pragmatism involved; for a settlement to emerge the British must be 'persuaded' to 'persuade' the unionists, and the US is more likely to 'persuade' the British than anyone else (Hume, 1996).

The much vaunted 'peace dividend' is also predicated on the role which both the US and the European Union are supposed to play in the search for a lasting political settlement. The SDLP argues that taking advantage of European structural and regional funds and attracting US and European foreign capital investment will not only promote economic growth, but will also reduce economic deprivation and injustice, so removing another cause of conflict. The 'war economy' of the North will make the transition to a 'peace economy' far easier if the economic dependence which is the inevitable consequence of Ireland's position in the global economy is not denied but developed.

Alongside the practicalities of arbitration and economic regeneration, the international dimension is envisaged as having a more obtuse, but no less important, ideological role to fulfil. The SDLP has probably been the most consistently pro-European party of any in Ireland and, while the eminently practical part which European subsidies play in propping up the 'workhouse economy' of Northern Ireland provide the material basis for this policy, it is overlaid with a veritable cacophony of ethico-political rhetoric.

For Hume, Europe offers not merely a route to economic regeneration, but a model for dealing with ethnic difference through international co-operation; the very essence of 'unity in diversity'. This is, of course, an exemplar which Ireland could follow. The double bind of Ireland's competing territorial allegiances, with the zero-sum politics which this produces, could be unwound, it is suggested, by offering alternative spatial and institutional arenas through which people could construct a non-conflictual and non-exclusionary sense of belonging. 'The new European scene', John Hume writes, 'offers a psychological framework in which such issues [of sovereignty and national identity] can no longer be pursued in absolutist terms' (Hume, 1996, p.230). Given the belief that ethnic enmity defines the Northern Ireland problem, the institutions of the European Union can reduce the divisiveness of the 'two traditions', without in any way diluting their cultural distinctiveness, by breaking the link between collective identity and territorial aspirations. Not independence but 'interdependence', the political corollary of global capitalism creates the circumstances where a combination of supranational and regional political institutions can take Ireland into a 'post-nationalist' world.

While the attempt to engage the US as an ally or arbitrator in Ireland's affairs has undoubtedly borne fruit, the relatively limited role which Britain will allow any third party to play in the North has restricted quite significantly this particular avenue of conflict resolution. Similarly, whilst there has been a great deal made of the supposed economic benefits of peace, the level of new investment which has so far been forthcoming has been relatively limited. In addition, the totally uncritical view that the SDLP adopts toward the supposed economic benefits of attracting multi-national capital as the best means of stimulating growth takes no account of the peripheral, vulnerable and dependent position into which this places the Irish economy. Nor are substantial benefits likely to accrue to a working class community whose engagement with the branch plant economy of trans-national capitalism tends to be in low paid, part-time and de-regulated labour markets.

Allegiance to the institutions of the European Union may offer an avenue out of the conflicting national identities which exist in Ireland, but the proof that Europe is capable of superseding the nation-state is a case not yet made. Certainly there is very little reason to believe that Europe offers a realistic alternative place of shared belonging to either community in the North. The ideal of a democratised 'Europe of Regions' is as remote to most people in Northern Ireland as it is from reality. This particular attempt to redefine the concepts of northern nationalism has not proven particularly efficacious.

**Conclusion: the limits of the peace process**

The apparent intractability of the conflict in Ireland has been evidenced by the slow pace of the peace process. Unionist intransigence and British prevarication has ensured that nationalist and republican energies have been consumed with trying to create a forum for inclusive dialogue that has, to date, met with little success. The problems of creating a *process* of conflict resolution has also tended to overshadow debate on the *substance* of any future settlement. In fact the SDLP has argued, as a deliberate policy, that discussion of what an 'agreed Ireland' might look like should be deferred till after the structure for talks has been put in place. This has tended to obscure the fact that their strategy to the process implies certain substantive outcomes. Similarly, although shelving the debate may appear tactically astute, it is indicative of two further problems with their strategy to conflict resolution. First, the reification of sectarian division which the management of difference, rather than its eradication, may bring in its wake and second, the essentially managerial and undemocratic nature of consociationalism.

The four beliefs and elements that have been identified as constituting the SDLP's understanding of the Northern Ireland conflict and their conflict resolution strategy also contain within them the seeds of what the party envisages as the likely shape of an 'agreed Ireland'. Once again four aspects may be discerned. First, an internal settlement constituted on consociationalist principles. Second, the creation of North-South institutions which would be designed to facilitate a gradual process of cooperation and integration, if not unification. Third, the re-constitution of Irish nationalist political culture so as to make it more amenable to the unionist community and fourth, the attraction of European Union and multi-national capital investment as the basis for future economic growth and as a consequence of political stability.

The SDLP has issued detailed suggestions for a future power-sharing regime. While these proposals have met with opposition, there is a greater likelihood of agreement on such arrangements than with their implicit proposals for North-South relations. As the Brooke and Mayhew talks showed, whilst the major parties of the North may find grounds for an understanding on an internal settlement, it is the North-South relationship which will prove the most difficult and contentious stream of any future negotiations. That is why the strategy of inter-governmental coercion has been so focused on this area, as the Joint-Framework document showed. Nationalists have wanted Britain to apply pressure on Unionists to accept all-Ireland institutions as the necessary corollary to an internal settlement, arguing that only in this way can the 'parity of esteem' of the 'two traditions' be realised. It is likely too that nationalists and republicans do see cross border institutions as a stepping stone toward some form of unification. For the SDLP this is envisaged within the framework of the consent principle. Unionists, it is believed, will come to see over time that their fears over unification are unfounded and that their interests really do lie with those who share the island. The question of course arises, what if consent is not given? What, in other words, will be the balance between consensus and coercion in achieving a lasting settlement? The SDLP's policy in the face of this dilemma is far from clear.

The age-old difficulty for nationalism remains the opposition of unionists to any move toward an all-Ireland settlement. The attempt to salve Unionist trepidation by redefining the character of nationalist political culture has met with little success. It has certainly not led to a political rapprochement in which unionists see anything other than a co-operative role for the southern government. Nor do unionists appear to recognise that any significant shift in republican thinking has taken place. In fact the attempt to re-orientate nationalism by developing the 'pan-nationalist consensus' is interpreted by unionism as yet another sally by the traditional enemy in new guise. The pre-existent siege world view that frames unionist ideology sees a conspiracy of irredentism behind the mask of accommodation. Whatever its intent, the pan-nationalist strategy has in many ways reinforced the unionist intent to reject the creation of meaningful North-South institutions.

The SDLP's attitude to future economic development signals an acceptance of Ireland's dependent role within the new global order of multi-national capital. As such, it is very much in line with the consensus in southern Irish political circles and their promotion of the 'Celtic tiger' image of the Irish economy. This perspective raises a number of issues. It gives assent to the growing class disparity and labour market dualism that has proved to be part and parcel of such an agenda. Further, growing disparity may engender even greater marginalisation and alienation within the very sections of the community who have been most actively engaged in the conflict; the Protestant and Catholic working classes. There is a potential, therefore, that whilst conflict may become contained or changed in character, it may be sustained and fuelled by an ever more acute competition for scarce resources amongst a sectarianised 'underclass'. Whilst the SDLP may argue for the advantages of development through US investment and empowerment through Europeanisation, the capitulation to geo-political and economic norms which that agenda enshrines may only serve to change the nature, rather than the fact of division.

The acceptance of existing external social and economic conditions as the basis for a future settlement is mirrored internally by the attitude toward ethnic difference within the SDLP's analysis. Here again their realpolitik logic has an appeal of lowering expectations to what appears realisable. However, it may also create as many problems as it solves. It could be argued that 'managing difference' reinforces the sectarianisation of Northern Irish politics. Both communities (and their politicians) have a vested interest in preserving and intensifying their differences within a zero-sum political game of ethnic competition. This is certainly one interpretation of the Forum election results of May 1996. It may also be seen in the failure to make any political headway by any of the more obviously 'non-sectarian' parties, such as the Alliance or Workers' parties). In many ways, the last few years have actually witnessed a heightening, rather than a diminution of sectarian tensions and the shape and nature of the peace process itself may have contributed directly to this.

As critics have noted, consociationalism is an intrinsically elitist approach to conflict resolution (Todd and Ruane, 1996). Its focus upon the political class tends to foster a distrust of public negotiation and participation. Certainly the peace process in Northern Ireland has often been characterised by an intense secrecy which has been lauded as statesmanship. Secrecy may, at times, have been necessary. However, it has certainly done little to rectify the democratic deficit of northern Irish politics. The essentially anti-democratic tenor of managerial consociationalism has also helped to feed a climate of doubt and suspicion. The disillusionment felt by many people throughout the process is because they believe there is a constant attempt to convince them that what they know is being done or said is not being done or said, because someone decides to call it something else, or to pretend that it has not really happened, or been said at all. Again, such distrust is only likely to breed future discord rather than provide a platform for agreement.

The SDLP's peace strategy has undoubtedly been well intended and has not been without successes. Rooted on a coherent, if flawed, analysis of the conflict, it has attempted to mobilise a series of powerful political forces, through the various elements of its modus operandi, in a meaningful effort at conflict resolution. While peace is still some way off there has been a significant de-escalation of the conflict and the SDLP has undoubtedly been instrumental in creating the 'windows of opportunity' which have been opened. However, there are problems with its approach to the business of bringing peace. The SDLP's agenda does not seek to challenge, but merely to re-define the ethnic differentiation that is sectarian division in the North; it creates a mirage of plurality when bourgeois nationalism remains central to its position; it acquiesces to the dominant geo-political and economic character of the 'new world order' and global capitalism, seeking, through re-definition, to represent it as an empowering phenomenon. In a number of ways it sets limits to the liberating potential of a peace process which may have to aim at more thorough and radical social and political change if peace is truly to be achieved.

# References

Adams, G. (1995), *Free Ireland: Towards a Lasting Peace*, Brandon:Kerry.

Aughey, A. (1994), 'The Downing Street Declaration: A Clarification', *Talking Politics*, Vol. 7, No. 1.

Bean, K. (1995), 'Recent Departures in Republican Strategy and Ideology', *Irish Studies Review*, No.10, pp. 2-7.

Bew, P. (1989), *The Dynamics of Irish Politics*, Lawrence and Wishart:London.

Boyce, D. G. (1996),'Past and Present:Revisionism and the Northern Ireland Troubles' in Boyce, D. G. and O'Day, A. (eds) *The Making of Modern Irish History: Revisionism and the Revisionist Controversy*, Routledge: London.

Breen, R. (1990), *Understanding Contemporary Ireland*, Gill MacMillan: Dublin.

Catterall, P. and McDougall, S. (1996), *Northern Ireland in British Politics*, Mac Millan: London.

Clarke, (1995), 'Time for Peace, Time to Go' Sunday Times, 19 November.

Coakley, J. (1993), 'Three Factors Pushing the North's Two Traditions Towards New Attitudes', *Irish Times*, 11 October.

Cormack,R.J. and Osborne, R.(1991)*Discrimination and Public Policy in Northern Ireland*, Clarendon:Oxford.

Cox, H. (1985) 'Who Wants a United Ireland?', *Government and Opposition*, Vol. 20, No. 1, pp. 29-47.

Fitzgerald, G. (1993), 'The Origin and Rationale of the Anglo-Irish Agreement of 1985', in Keogh, D. and Haltzel, M. (eds), *Northern Ireland and the Politics of Reconciliation*, Cambridge University Press:Cambridge.

Fitzgerald, G. (1991), *All in a Life*, Gill and MacMillan:Dublin.

Fitzgerald, G. (1972), *Towards a New Ireland*, Gill and MacMillan:Dublin.

Forum for Peace And Reconciliation (1995), *Paths to a Political Settlement in Ireland*, Belfast:Blackstaff.

Girvin, B. (1994), 'Constitutional Nationalism and Northern Ireland', in Barton, B. and Roche, P.J. (eds) *The Northern Ireland Question: Perspectives and Policies*, Avebury:Aldershot.

Guelke, A. (1988), *Northern Ireland: The International Perspective*, Gill and Mac Millan: Dublin.

Holland, J. (1987), *The American Connection: US Gun, Money and Influence in Northern Ireland*, Poolbeg:Dublin.

Hume, J. (1996), *Personal Views: Politics, Peace and Reconciliation in Ireland*, Town House:Dublin.

Lijphart,A.(1977)*Democracy in Plural Societies*,Yale University Press:New Haven.

Mallie, E. and McKittrick, D.(1996), *The Fight for Peace: The Secret Story Behind the Irish Peace Process*, Heinemann:London.

McCann, E. (1995), *War and an Irish Town*, Pluto:London.

McGarry, J. and O'Leary, B. (1993), 'The Macro-Political Regulation of Ethnic Conflict' in McGarry, J. and O'Leary, B. (eds), *The Politics of Ethnic Conflict Regulation: Case Studies of Protracted ethnic Conflict*, Routledge:London.

McGovern, M. and Shirlow,P.(1997),'Language, Discourse and Dialogue: Sinn Fein and the Irish Peace Process, *Political Geography*, Vol. 16, No. 7.

O'Brien,C.C.(1994), *Ancestral Voices:Religion and Nationalism in Ireland*,Poolbeg Dublin.

O'Brien, C.C. (1972), *States of Ireland*, Hutchinson: London.

O'Connor, F.(1993), *In Search of a State:Catholics in Northern Ireland*, Blackstaff: Belfast.

Patterson, H.(1995), 'The Disarming of Sinn Fein's Critics', *Northern Ireland Brief*, Spring.

Pollak, A.(ed.)(1993), *A Citizen's Inquiry:The Opsahl Report on Northern Ireland*, Lilliput:Dublin.

Rolston, B. (1994), 'Ceasefire: The IRA cashes in its Chips', *Irish Reporter*, No.16.

Rolston, B. (1988),'Alienation of Political Awareness: The Battle for the Hearts and Minds of Northern Nationalists', in Teague, P. (ed.), *Beyond the Rhetoric: Politics, Economy and Social Policy in Northern Ireland*, Lawrence and Wishart:London.

Ruane, J. and Todd, J. (1996), *The Dynamics of Conflict in Northern Ireland*, Cambridge University Press: Cambridge.

Ryan, M. (1994), *War and Peace in Ireland: Britain and the IRA in the New World Order*, Pluto:London.

Social Democratic and Labour Party(1991),*The SDLP Analysis of the Nature of the Problem*, SDLP Discussion Document:Belfast.

Todd, J.(1990),'Northern Irish Nationalist Political Culture', *Irish Political Studies*, Vol. 5.

Todd, J.(1987),'Two Traditions in Ulster Protestant Political Culture',*Irish Political Studies*, Vol. 2.

Whyte, J.H. (1991) *Interpreting Northern Ireland*, Clarendon:Oxford.

Wilson, A. (1995), *Irish-America and the Ulster Conflict, 1968-1995*, Blackstaff Press:Belfast.

# 6 From the centre to the margins: The slow death of Irish republicanism

*Mark Ryan*

**Introduction**

The greatest problem besetting the study of Irish republicanism is the tendency to see the movement in isolation from broader currents of both international and Irish politics. An iron curtain appears to exist in the minds of observers which precludes the possibility of mutual influence between republicanism and the rest of the world. Just as the media present the IRA as an organisation driven by internal and often irrational forces, so too more reflective and academic studies have tried to analyse the IRA solely in terms of its own history and its own experience of confrontation with the British state.

For a movement which has existed for nearly 80 years and which has had no small impact on the politics of this century, it is surprising how little the politics and experience of republicanism have been examined from an international perspective. There is no study of the impact of republicanism on de-colonisation, despite the influence the years from 1916-23 had on the evolution of anti-colonial politics in Africa and Asia. Equally neglected is the political and military repercussions the war against the IRA had on subsequent British colonial policy. A number of writers have examined the effects of conflict on Britain's evolving counter-insurgency strategies (Townshend, 1986; Wilkinson, 1981) although the links between military and broader colonial policy are generally neglected. The coincidence between the re-emergence of the IRA and the last great international upsurge of left-wing militancy in the late sixties and early seventies has also received scant attention. While the civil rights movement is often placed in the context of the student rebellions of the late sixties, the emergence of the Provisionals has largely been treated as a reversal into more tribal and inward-looking preoccupations on the part of the Catholic community.

The result is that Irish republicanism, particularly in its post-1969 form, has been studied by and large as a peculiarity, something divorced from the world around it and following a purely internal dynamic. This approach is perhaps best exemplified by Conor Cruise O'Brien, who presents the IRA as an organisation wholly subordinate to its past, arguing that 'within the republican movement...the mandate from the dead always outweighs the mandate from the living.' (1994, p.179). In a similar vein, if less eloquently, J Bowyer Bell Jr, describes the IRA's enslavement to history: '...the republicans are used to the denial *(sic)* of the Irish people and the failure of nerve. They answer only to Irish history and to the patriot dead' (1995, p.167). Even more considered analyses which take account of evolving republican strategy tend to see that evolution both as following an inner logic and at the same time preserving the essentials of republican politics despite tactical shifts. Brendan O'Brien for example maintains that by investing its hopes in the peace process, 'the Republican Movement had moved to an unarmed strategy with the same goal [of a united Ireland] in mind' (O'Brien, 1995, p.13).

The view that republicans operate within a logical and moral space all of their own has become more entrenched as the experience of modern republicanism has diverged more and more from that of the rest of Irish society. The result is that in recent years commentary on the IRA has tended to depart from the realm of political motivation altogether and has turned instead to psychology in its attempt to fathom the inner recesses of the IRA mind. The title of Kevin Toolis's work *Rebel hearts: Journeys within the IRA's Soul* (1995) sums up the approach adopted in countless newspaper and magazine articles. Paradoxically, the more the 'IRA mind' becomes the narrow focus of inquiry, the more it loses any distinctive features. This is particularly obvious in the case of the doctrine of 'conflict resolution', now so popular in understanding and offering solutions to the Northern problem. One writer offers this profound insight into what motivates groups such as the IRA: '...conflict is often caused by a group's need for identity, recognition, security and other similar societal values' (Dunnigan, 1995, p.8). Much the same could be said of any group which has ever entered into conflict at any time and at any place in human history, a fact which makes the insight worthless.

The hermetic view of Irish republicanism has seriously hindered an understanding of its evolution in the last 30 years. This chapter argues an entirely different point of view. Rather than having some intrinsic power of its own derived from the past, Irish republicanism has always been deeply influenced by the changes taking place in world politics. This is as true of republicanism in 1916 as it is in 1996. Without this sensitivity to the interaction between republicanism and broader politics, the most important features of the peace process and the Sinn Fein and IRA involvement in it, remain obscured. As will be shown, even the growing isolation of the movement is a product of its relations with the world at large.

Having placed the emphasis on the broader influences shaping republicanism, it is not true to say, as McIntyre does, that the past is of little relevance in understanding the predicament of Sinn Fein/IRA today. McIntyre argues that the modern republican movement is the product of British state strategy (1995). While it is useful to stress the dynamic side of the interaction between the British state and the republican movement, McIntyre wrongly excludes the influence of republican doctrine and the experience of 70 years of striving for a united Ireland. It may be true, as he claims, that republicanism is now geared towards overcoming the structural exclusion of nationalists within the North of Ireland' (p.98). That, however, is the endpoint of a long process of development in the course of which the movement gradually came to terms with its isolation. Projecting the present low expectations onto the past misses out on the crucial developments which can put the present situation in context. McIntyre objectifies republicanism to the point where he deprives it of any political dynamic and coherence of its own.

Both objectifying and psychologising republicanism have the effect of reducing its coherence as a political doctrine. Yet if we look at Irish history this century we find that even in its weakest phases, republicanism exerted a powerful influence on every aspect of Irish politics. Nearly every political party in the Republic came out of the IRA at some point in its history. Even today, becoming a republican means acquiring a world-view through which political events both in Ireland and internationally are assimilated. Those who joined the IRA or Sinn Fein over the years in Northern Ireland might have done so for a variety of personal reasons, mainly as a result of their direct experience of British rule, but what they joined was a movement with a history, an understanding of Ireland's predicament and a remedy for the future. For the leadership of the republican movement, as for any political leadership, the challenge was how to reconcile the day-to-day experience of the movement as a whole with the aims and principles it fought for over the years.

The dynamic interplay between this political tradition, the way in which it responds to the changing world around it and the experiences of its members and supporters, should constitute the main elements in any analysis of Irish republicanism. It is against this background that we should examine changes in republican strategy since the onset of the peace process. The significance of the peace process for the politics of republicanism is that for the first time in its history, the movement has adapted to, rather than fought to overcome, its marginal position within Irish politics. This adaptation has led to a lowering of its entire political horizons and an accommodation to British rule which is of quite a different character to the compromises made by sections of the movement in the past. This accommodation to its lowly position is something which was taking place long before the peace process got under way. It is only in recent years, however, that the development has accelerated to the point where it has effected a fundamental change in republican thinking. What is not important, or at least not the defining feature of new thinking, is the repudiation of the military option, a repudiation which is thoroughly contingent in any case. Nor is the readiness to make terms with the British government such a novel idea. All this we have seen before. Supposed divisions, whether the tags be 'realists' versus 'fundamentalists, or 'hawks' versus 'doves', miss the point that what has taken place is a total reorientation of the *entire* republican movement.

### The novelty of inclusive dialogue

'If we are going to resolve the conflict in Ireland what is required is a genuine peace settlement brought about through inclusive negotiations without preconditions' (IRA spokesperson, *An Phoblact*, 7 March 1996).

The acceptance of a more marginal place within a new Ireland is expressed most clearly in the calls for 'inclusive dialogue'. Hardly a single communique from Sinn Fein, or indeed from the IRA, is complete without a call for inclusive dialogue and an acceptance of Sinn Fein's electoral mandate. The call for inclusiveness is a fundamental departure from traditional republican beliefs. At a purely legalistic level, it undermines the authority which the IRA claims to have inherited from the past. The IRA's manual, The Green Book, states that Oglaigh na hEireann is the Army of the Republic declared in arms at Easter 1916 and subsequently ratified by the first and only all-Ireland parliament, the 1918 Dail Eireann. The arcane ritual whereby the survivors of the 1921 Dail Executive handed legitimacy to various IRA Army Councils over the years testifies to the importance which was attached to this historic title. It is this mandate which allowed the republican movement to lay sole claim to the authority of 1916, and also to be the sole representatives of what they say was the only body that was ever freely elected by all the people of Ireland.

Demanding therefore that Sinn Fein be allowed to enter talks with other parties and reach an agreement with those parties to bring about a new Ireland in effect disestablishes the Republic proclaimed in 1916 and strips the IRA of the executive power which was invested in it in the years 1916-21. More substantially, the call for inclusive dialogue is a tacit recognition of the fact that Sinn Fein/IRA is nothing more than a community organisation representing between 10 and 15 per cent of the electorate of Northern Ireland. When Gerry Adams and Martin McGuinness demand that the British Government recognise Sinn Fein's electoral mandate and include the party in talks, what they are doing, wittingly or unwittingly, is detaching republicanism from the goal of national independence and attaching it to the defence of one community within the existing framework. The call for inclusive dialogue is a tacit recognition of the fact that republicanism can no longer connect with the aspirations of the Irish people as a whole and that survival lies in consolidating its hold at least on one of the outer margins of Irish society. It is possible to trace the evolution of this process of accommodation through, firstly, a brief examination of the longer historical time frame and, secondly, from the narrower perspective of the peace process.

**The long decline of republicanism**

By the early 1960s it was already apparent that republicanism was losing its commanding position as the ideological cornerstone of Irish society. The abandonment of economic autarky in the late 1950s and the opening of the economy to foreign capital weakened many of the assumptions on which republicanism was based. The IRA itself was showing signs of entering a state of terminal decline. De Valera's suppression of the organisation in the late 1930s, not to mention his success in wooing the bulk of the movement into Fianna Fail had drained the organisation of almost its entire membership. The IRA was turning into a parody of itself, summed up in Brendan Behan's joke of the three IRA men meeting to elect a Chief of Staff, only to split in the process. The disastrous Border Campaign of 1956-62 only compounded the loss of direction. The drift towards the left in the late sixties with the apparent willingness on the part of large sections of the movement to consider renouncing some of the key tenets of republican policy shows how the IRA was on the verge of meltdown just as the troubles broke out in Northern Ireland (Cronin, 1980, p. 185-91).

The republican movement was badly caught off guard by the events of 1969. The proposal from the leadership around Cathal Goulding and Tomas MacGiolla to abandon abstentionism and enter both the Dublin and Stormont parliaments at the very time when the latter was seen to be organising a pogrom against nationalists in the North must go down in Irish history as one of the worst ever cases of bad timing. The actions of the leadership led to a split at the General Army Convention of January 1970 and the formation of the Provisionals.

At the time it appeared as if the birth of the Provisionals was a simple resurgence of republicanism after a long hibernation. That is certainly how the Provisionals themselves saw events. However in retrospect it looks more like the downward spiral was arrested or even just slowed, rather than reversed. The fundamental difficulties the movement had in making its politics relevant to a new Ireland were simply obscured by the intensity of the conflict in the North and by the new-found support which the movement received in working class Catholic areas. The military renewal was so spectacular that it hid the degree of political exhaustion.

Military strength, political weakness: this imbalance would bedevil republicanism for the next 25 years. The weakness is revealed by the narrow base of support from which the struggle resumed. The North, which had been largely quiescent during the Tan War and Civil War now became the centre of conflict, whereas in the South, where the great struggles of the 1920s took place, decline continued apace and even accelerated as public opinion grew more hostile to the Provisionals' campaign. Despite many efforts, the republican movement failed to broaden its base of support beyond a minority section of the Catholic population of the North. This is a striking contrast from the years after 1916 when Sinn Fein won an all-Ireland election by a landslide and where both passive and active support for the IRA throughout the country (except the North) was considerable.

The narrowness of the IRA's support base was the source both of its strengths and its weaknesses. It helped the organisation in the sense that it now had a very coherent and, for a nationalist movement, extremely homogeneous, social base. Unlike the twenties and thirties, republican leaders were now less troubled with the problem of trying to reconcile conflicting class interests within the one movement. Almost every republican activist, whether in the IRA or Sinn Fein, came from much the same working class background in Belfast or Derry, or from poor rural areas. The social world inhabited by republican activists from the North is a far cry from the social circuits followed by earlier leaders. Patrick Pearse was a respected figure of Dublin middle class society in his time. Sean McBride, Chief of Staff from 1936 to 1939 never lost the accent he acquired at his French private school, while Cathal Goulding, appointed Chief of Staff in September 1962, was a familiar figure on the bohemian circuit in Dublin. It is difficult at times not to suspect a class edge to the bitter animosity between the predominantly-Southern Officials and the Provisionals, despite the former's self-proclaimed orientation towards the working class.

The social homogeneity of the Provisionals was one of the keys to the organisation's military tenacity. There was never any pressure on the leadership to accept some deal which fell far short of national independence, but which would have been attractive to a more middle class constituency. That is not to say there was no war weariness, but that weariness was never articulated into a demand for a constitutional settlement. The homogeneity of the movement must also explain the difficulty the security forces always had in trying to penetrate the IRA. There were none of the usual divisions found in an organisation made up of people from different class backgrounds, while the changes in lifestyle, in habits and so on which are inevitable in the life of an informer would be immediately noticeable to friends and neighbours. The solidity of the Provisionals' support explains why the Provisionals were one of the most successful guerilla army of modern times.

The success of the armed struggle explains its almost sacred place within republican thinking. It was the armed struggle which constantly saved the movement from its political failings. The split of 1970 and the emergence of the Provisionals saved the IRA from ignominy in Belfast. Until 1972, the intensity of the war meant that the political difficulties which the movement had got itself into in the first place could be ignored in the belief that victory was just around the corner. Following the ceasefire of 1975, when the British Government duped the republican leadership into thinking that withdrawal was on the cards, it was the armed struggle which again came to the rescue. As Adams notes, 'the resumption of military struggle by the IRA prevented the successful implementation of th[e British government's] timetable' (Adams, 1995, p. 103-4). The 'ballot-box and armalite' strategy of the 1980s was a continuation of this tradition. The armalite side of the formula was an insurance policy against the failure of the ballot box, as well as an assurance to supporters that the armed struggle would continue irrespective of whatever political strategy Sinn Fein chose to follow. Finally the breaking of the ceasefire in February 1996 was a desperate attempt by the IRA to rescue Sinn Fein from the humiliations it had suffered as a result of its 'peace strategy'.

However the very intensity of the war in the North and the unwavering commitment of a substantial section of the Catholic population to both the IRA and Sinn Fein often obscured the real problem; the failure to connect with the rest of Irish society. Unlike the republican movement of the 1920s, which could justly lay claim to being a national movement, the Provisionals never managed to broaden their appeal beyond the Catholic working class in the North. In effect, although they espoused national ideals, they never developed from being a community-based movement. The contradiction between espousing national ideals while in practice relying on a community to realise those ideals was the fatal flaw which the republican movement never succeeded in overcoming. It was their misfortune that just as they experienced an unexpected and dramatic rebirth in the North where they were traditionally at their weakest, they were losing forever their support elsewhere in the country. Hence the claim to being a national movement was undermined from the beginning.

## Breaking the impasse

During the early years of the war little attention was paid to the restricted base of republican support. The prevailing doctrine up to 1974 was the 'one last push' strategy proclaimed in the 'Year of Victory' headlines on the first issue of Republican News every January. It was only after the reverses suffered at the hands of the Labour Governments of Harold Wilson and James Callaghan that the movement began to address the problem of how to win broader support. The need to break out of the ghettoes was the theme of the Bodenstown address of 1977 given by veteran republican Jimmy Drumm, who argued that 'the isolation of socialist republicans around the armed struggle is dangerous and has produced the reformist notion that Ulster alone is the issue, without the mobilisation of the working class in the Twenty-Six Counties' (Republican News, 15 June 1977).

Yet it was only after the hunger strikes of 1980-81 that the movement began to see how it could begin to give Drumm's exhortation some practical meaning. The electoral strategy, formulated by Danny Morrison at the 1981 ard-fheis as the 'armalite and ballot box' strategy was something which the movement stumbled upon by accident in the course of the hunger strikes, when Bobby Sands won 30,000 votes in the Fermanagh and South Tyrone by-election. The boost Sands' victory gave to the hunger-strikers' campaign convinced some republicans that electoral politics could be turned to their advantage.

The electoral strategy as it developed was the one serious attempt by Sinn Fein to broaden its base of support beyond the Catholic working class in the North. Initially Sinn Fein focused its energies on Northern Ireland, hoping to displace the SDLP as the leading nationalist party there. The early results gave cause for hope, with Owen Carron, Bobby Sands' election agent, retaining Fermanagh and South Tyrone after Sands' death and Sinn Fein as a whole doing well in the Assembly elections of 1982. However the static nature of the party's vote soon became clear, reflecting as it did the support it had in the core working class areas. By the mid 1980s the few inroads it had made elsewhere were rolled back in the face of renewed support for the SDLP following the Anglo-Irish Agreement.

In response to the electoral impasse in the North, Sinn Fein decided to develop the strategy in the South. At the 1986 ard-fheis the party voted to abandon the old principle of abstaining from what it once considered the 'puppet parliament' at Leinster House. Sinn Fein TDs, if elected, would now enter the Dublin parliament (Sinn Fein, 1986). The strategy backfired disastrously. No Sinn Fein TDs were elected. At the 1987 general election in the Republic the party polled a pitiful 1.9 per cent of the vote, while in 1989, that figure dropped even further to 1.2 per cent. Paradoxically, the dropping of abstentionism and the attempt to make inroads in the South had the opposite effect of weakening further the Southern component of the movement through the departure of the old leadership around Ruairi O'Bradaigh. The only effect of trying to turn Sinn Fein into a normal political party in the South was that it lost its distinctiveness as the only party which regarded the state itself as illegitimate. With that went many of its old-time supporters.

By the late 1980s there was no escaping the fact that the republican movement was at a dead-end. Not only had the electoral strategy come to nothing, but the military struggle was also beginning to take a turn for the worse. The Loughgall attack in May 1987 in which eight IRA men from the East Tyrone brigade were shot dead by undercover special forces began a period of serious reverses for the IRA, despite the arrival of a number of massive arms shipments from Libya (Mallie and McKittrick, p.44-8). As a result, the traditional military fall back which had saved the movement so often in the past was becoming less effective. In addition, the Thatcher government had intensified the propaganda war against Sinn Fein by instituting a broadcasting ban on its representatives similar to that already in force in the Irish Republic.

To the leadership of the republican movement, it was becoming apparent that the 'long war' was not getting the movement any closer to the goal of a united Ireland and that something would have to change. As republicans saw it, a fortuitous combination of internal and external factors had, by the late 1980s, started to change the map of Irish politics.

**The road to Stormont**

We now know that the private republican response to the Anglo-Irish Agreement of 1985 was less hostile than public pronouncements at the time might have suggested. An internal paper written by Mitchell McLaughlin shortly after the signing of the Hillsborough agreement suggested that 'republicans should welcome many aspects of the Agreement as steps along the road to what they wanted, a constructive and progressive reduction of the British presence' (Mallie and McKittrick, p.36). It was around the same time that Adams opened up a secret line of communication through Fr. Alec Reid, at Clonard Monastery in West Belfast, to Fianna Fail leader Charles Haughey, then in opposition (Mallie and McKittrick, p.70-72).

By the late 1980s the world had begun to change. The decline of the old Soviet empire which led to a rapprochement with the West, the fall of the Berlin Wall and perhaps most importantly, the way that national liberation movements around the world were forced to come to terms with their old opponents, were all seen by Sinn Fein and the IRA as positive developments which opened the way to a negotiated settlement of the Anglo-Irish conflict. The lesson Sinn Fein leaders drew from the experience of South Africa and the Middle East was that the old confrontational politics based on rival and mutually exclusive claims to national sovereignty were exhausted and that a negotiated settlement was now the way forward (Ryan, p.19-43).

Thus by the early 1990s the republican movement was openly looking for peace. This was certainly the conclusion drawn by the British government which resumed contact with the republican leadership in October 1990. What is important for an understanding of the present state of the republican movement is the *form* that search for peace would take. The IRA could have simply called a halt to the armed struggle in the recognition that it was achieving nothing, something they had done in the past. In pressing for inclusive dialogue however, they were not only looking for peace. In return for political survival as the representatives of a section of the Catholic community in Northern Ireland, they were also forsaking the prospect of ever bringing about the old vision of the Republic.

Inclusive dialogue finally resolved the tension between claiming on the one hand to be a national movement while on the other relying almost exclusively for its support on the Catholic working class in Northern Ireland. It resolved the tension in favour of representing the Catholic community while effectively relegating a united Ireland to the level of an aspiration which might one day be achieved with the help of the SDLP, the Dublin government and a sympathetic United States administration and without the opposition of the British government and the unionists, a concatenation of circumstances which must lie beyond the hopes of even the most unreasonable optimist. With inclusive dialogue, the transformative element in republican thinking, of transcending division by creating a unified nation, is dropped in favour of representing one of those communities within a divided nation.

The question of how such a fundamental change to republican policy could be achieved with so little dissent deserves some consideration. Republicans are rightly known for their rigid adherence to doctrine and their alertness to the betrayals of the past. Yet such a profound change in policy as the call for inclusiveness is now accepted as a defining feature of republican policy. To assess the reasons for the smoothness of this policy change, we must examine developments both within and outside the republican movement.

## The narrowing ground

One reason the policy change was effected so smoothly was the persistence of the armed struggle. The way in which the armed struggle has become such a defining feature of republicanism since 1969 has served to protect the leadership from the charge of betrayal. The continued military effectiveness of the IRA and its spectacular return to active service in February 1996 preserved the appearance of continuity and adherence to principles. Ironically, the importance of the armed struggle as a symbol of republican resistance meant that more profound political changes could be pushed through with very little opposition.

Another reason for the lack of opposition to the new turn was the decline and eventual departure of the southern old guard around Ruairi O' Bradaigh following the abandonment of abstentionism in the Republic in 1986. As suggested earlier, republicanism was historically a southern phenomenon. Figures such as O'Bradaigh, Daithi O'Connail and Sean MacStiofain were republicanism's living link with those southern roots, with all the splits and the persecution they suffered at the hands of constitutional nationalists. Their departure had the effect of tilting the experience of the movement in an exclusively northern direction.

This had a number of important political consequences. For a start it tightened the grip of the Adams leadership over the movement as a whole and made it difficult for any centres of dissent to form. Also, it concentrated the experience of nearly the entire membership in a very small world, geographically, socially and politically. Most importantly of all it inevitably led to a closer identification of the republican movement with its core base of support within Northern Ireland.

This identification was reinforced by the other side of the electoral strategy, community politics. Much attention has been given to Sinn Fein's efforts to secure seats at Westminster and at Irish elections, but what was more influential in transforming the day-to-day thinking of the movement was its more lowly involvement in community politics. While the extensive aspect of electoralism, based upon encroachment on constitutional nationalism North and South, was unsuccessful, what we might call the intensive aspect of deepening the relationship with the existing base of support continued unhindered. The setting up of Sinn Fein advice centres, which attended to local problems on everything from drug dealing to drainage repairs, not only diverted substantial resources away from the main political focus of the movement, but also brought Sinn Fein into a closer relationship with the northern state. Although he was critical of the local councils, Adams for example, could state that 'there has been some success in making the councils more accountable to local people' (Adams, 1988). Evidently he saw no contradiction between overthrowing the existing state while at the same time making it more accountable.

The significance of the electoral strategy can be seen in a clearer light now. What was originally a tactic aimed at breaking out of the ghettoes and of becoming a genuinely national movement in fact as well as in principle, ended up having precisely the opposite effect, namely of confirming to republicans both their isolation from the rest of Ireland and the strength of the link with the core base of support. What began as a realisation of the need to transcend the limits of locality ended up making a virtue of that local rootedness.

The trend towards the localisation of republicanism can be seen in the language that Adams in particular started to use from the late 1980s. Phrases such as 'the republican family', or 'the republican community', began to creep into his speech. This showed the extent to which the idea of the Republic was becoming detached from any broader conception of political association such as the nation, and coming to refer instead to one particular community. The essence of republicanism up until then was the stress it laid upon the Republic being the whole nation, irrespective of creed or community. Now the Republic was coming to mean, quite casually and without any conscious political battle taking place over the issue, something else entirely, namely one community among many.

**Republicanism and the politics of identity**

The drift towards community politics takes on an added significance when seen against the background of the changes taking place in political thinking throughout Ireland from the early 1980s. The development of pluralism, or what might be more loosely termed 'the politics of identity', has been well charted in relation to mainstream politics in Ireland (Ryan, 1994, p.98-112; Hussey, 1993; Kearney, 1988). Because the politics of identity developed in explicit opposition to the majoritarian claims of republicanism, it is often assumed that the former had no influence on the latter. This is not the case. Neither Sinn Fein nor the IRA ever embraced or rejected identity politics. Although they were hostile to the way many exponents of pluralism used their ideas to justify partition, republicans remained strangely agnostic on the more substantive case advanced by pluralists - that diverse identities should be cherished and promoted. Instead of confronting pluralism, republicans adapted to it. Instead of rejecting the concept of identity itself, republicans ended up asking the more limited question, 'what about our identity?'.

The early evolution of the politics of identity in relation to Northern Ireland has been ably charted by the late John Whyte (1990, p.138-40, 197-99). Its basic proposition, that equal respect should be accorded both 'traditions' or 'identities' permeated institutional arrangements such as the Anglo-Irish Agreement of 1985 and the Joint Framework document of 1995. The notion of equal respect was a direct response to the republican claim to national unity and effectively made that unity a practical impossibility.

While Sinn Fein spokesmen were highly critical of the political consequences of pluralism, Adams for example charging that the Anglo-Irish Agreement 'copper-fastened partition', the proposition that all identities should be cherished equally created less difficulty because it chimed so well with the movement's experience of representing a deprived and disenfranchised community. Instead of rejecting the politics of identity, Sinn Fein developed its own variant. This stressed the dynamic cultural life of the nationalist community which the movement represented, particularly in its strongholds. The initiation of the West Belfast Festival in 1988 was an important landmark, while the promotion of the Irish language and 'community art' such as the murals which adorn the gable ends of nationalist areas were important elements in the creation of a community culture.

In the course of the peace process, republicans began to adopt the language and ideas so closely bound with mainstream identity politics. Looking at the republican movement today, it sometimes seems like the most ardent devotee of identity politics. Its spokesmen argue the need for cultural diversity and the recognition of different traditions and identities, especially their own. Leading Sinn Fein spokesman Tom Hartley argued in his 'Charter for Justice and Peace' that self-determination must respect 'the rich cultural and religious diversity of the Irish people', called for a period of 'national reconciliation' prior to the 'harmonious exercise of self-determination' and outlined a new Ireland committed to cultural pluralism which would allow 'the flourishing of local and national cultural practices' (Hartley, 1995). Such pronouncements show the extent to which traditional republican ideas such as self-determination have been emptied of all meaning through the adoption of identity politics.

In 1994, twelve years after then Irish Prime Minister Garret Fitzgerald first used the term and two years after it became popular through the Report of the Opsahl Commission (Pollak, 1993), Sinn Fein spoke of the need for 'parity of esteem' as an area of immediate practical concern to the Nationalist community (Adams, 1996). It is worth remembering that a similar, if less opaque, idea of equality within the Northern state was first put forward by the Official IRA and violently rejected by the Provisionals 25 years earlier.

Of all the historic and much-reported handshakes which took place in Ireland in the course of the peace process, that between Gerry Adams and Mary Robinson in June 1993 was the most richly symbolic. At the time, the handshake was seen as a gesture aimed at enticing the republican movement away from physical force and towards constitutional politics, which of course it was. The gesture went beyond such short-term considerations however. Adams was received by the Irish President, an illegitimate title according to traditional republican doctrine, not as the head of a movement committed to the overthrow of British rule in Ireland, but as one humble West Belfast community representative among 30 others. In conferring a handshake on Adams, Robinson was indicating to the wider republican movement that in return for dropping the broader claim to national leadership and accepting community status, Sinn Fein could at last become part of the mainstream. Republicans found themselves in a paradoxical position. If they asserted their claim to be the centre of Irish politics, the more isolated and marginalised they found themselves, while the more they accepted their marginal role, the more they were accepted in the mainstream.

## Conclusion

It can be seen that the experience of failure in broadening its appeal to the rest of Ireland, primarily through the electoral strategy, left the republican movement politically exhausted and only too willing to pursue a strategy which played to the one strength it knew it could rely on - its local and community support. Whereas republicans were shunned and vilified for as long as they tried to drive the British out of Ireland, they were treated quite differently when acting simply as the representatives of one community within the existing framework.

The turn to community politics may preserve both Sinn Fein and the IRA as viable organisations. Given the fractiousness and resentment which exist between the communities in Northern Ireland, community politics can only thrive. Policing the nationalist community itself appears to be the main concern of the IRA in areas such as West Belfast. IRA involvement in the Direct Action Against Drugs organisation is accepted as a fact of life. Ensuring that the Catholic community is accorded respect has also taken Sinn Fein and the IRA into more explicit sectarian confrontation with Protestants. The three main residents' associations involved in confrontations with Protestant parades over the summers of 1995 and 1996 - Garvaghy Road, Lower Ormeau and the Bogside - all are chaired by former IRA Volunteers and are little more than republican front organisations. Meanwhile the promotion of community culture through events such as the West Belfast Festival has brought republicans into very direct contact with the labyrinthine funding mechanisms of a state whose destruction the movement was once foresworn to achieve.

The organisational continuity of republicanism has helped disguise the political break from the past. To date, there has been no surrender of arms, no murderous feuds and no acknowledgement that historic aspirations are being quietly shelved. However if we concentrate more on the substance of republicanism and a little bit less on the form, then it might be more obvious that we have come to the end of a very long era in Irish politics. An Ireland without traditional republicanism is difficult to imagine. Yet that is what we will have to get used to in the years to come.

## References

Adams, G. (1988), Interview, *Living Marxism*, No. 3, pp.26-30.
Adams, G. (1995), *Free Ireland: Towards a Lasting Peace*, Brandon:Dingle.
Adams, G. (1996), 'Collective Efforts to Find a Lasting Solution', *The Irish Reporter*, No. 21, pp. 13-18.
Bowyer Bell, J.(1995),'The Irish Republican Army Enters an Endgame: An Overview', *Studies in Conflict and Terrorism*, Vol. 18, No. 3.
Cronin, S. (1980), *Irish Nationalism: A History of its Roots and Ideology*, Academy: Dublin.
Dunnigan, J. P. (1995), *Deep-rooted conflict and the IRA Ceasefire*, University Press

of America:Maryland.

Hartley, T. (1995), 'Charter for Justice and Peace', An Phoblacht/Republican News, 9 March 1995.

Hussey, G. (1993), *Ireland Today: Anatomy of a Changing State*, Viking:London.

Kearney, R. (1988), *Across the Frontiers: Ireland in the 1990s*, Wolfhound:Dublin.

Mallie, E. and McKittrick, D, (1996),*The Fight for Peace:The Secret Story behind the Irish Peace Process*, Heineman:London.

McIntyre, A. (1995), 'Modern Irish Republicanism: the Product of British State Strategies', *Irish Political Studies*, Vol. 10, pp. 97-121.

O'Brien, B, (1995), *The Long War. The IRA and Sinn Fein from Armed Struggle to Peace Talks*. 2nd edn, O'Brien: Dublin.

O'Brien, C. C. (1994), *Ancestral Voices: Religion and Nationalism in Ireland*. Poolbeg: Dublin.

Pollak, A. (ed.) (1993), *A Citizen's Inquiry. The Opsahl Report on Northern Ireland*, Lilliput: Dublin.

Ryan, M. (1994), *War and Peace in Ireland: Britain and the IRA in the New World Order*, Pluto:London.

Sinn Fein. (1986), *The Politics of Revolution: Main Speeches and Debates from the 1986 Ard Fheis*, Sinn Fein:Dublin.

Toolis, K. (1995), *Rebel Hearts: Journeys within the IRA's Soul*, Picador:London.

Townshend, C. (1986), *Britain's Civil Wars: Counterinsurgency in the Twentieth Century*, Faber and Faber:London.

Whyte, J.H. (1990), *Interpreting Northern Ireland*, Oxford University Press:Oxford.

Wilkinson, P. (ed.) (1981), *British Perspectives on Terrorism*, Allen and Unwin: London.

# Part Three
# ISSUES IN THE PEACE PROCESS

# 7 Cross-border cooperation and the peace process

*Alan Greer*

**Introduction**

This chapter assesses the importance of cooperation across the Irish border for attempts to find a political accommodation in Northern Ireland. If historical precedents are any guide, consensus on the nature and scope of cross-border linkages is likely to be very difficult to achieve, perhaps even more difficult than the decommissioning of paramilitary arsenals. Some of the most controversial proposals in both the 1920 Government of Ireland Act and the 1973 Sunningdale Agreement were for the creation of Councils of Ireland to give institutional underpinning to the development of relationships between north and south. More recently the British and Irish governments have promoted collaboration between Northern Ireland and the Irish Republic in the Anglo-Irish Agreement (1985), the Downing Street Declaration (1993) and a Joint Framework for Agreement (1995).

The central assumption which underlies such initiatives is that cross-border cooperation is essentially a positive-sum game in which nobody loses. The problem, however, is that the issue of cross-border cooperation is not value neutral, nor simply a matter of technocratic management. The desirability or otherwise of north-south arrangements has always been viewed through the traditional conceptual lens of national sovereignty. Thus for many nationalists cross-border cooperation, particularly the need for institutional structures of coordination, is simply another route to the holy grail of a united Ireland. Unionists, whilst not averse to a good neighbourly relationship with the Irish Republic, typically see cross-border institutions in terms of a 'slippery slope', 'Trojan horse' or 'embryo united Ireland'.

## Civil Society approaches

Cooperation across the Irish border exists in many areas, to a greater or lesser extent, having developed over a longer or shorter time frame depending on the sector concerned. Three main approaches to the question of cross-border cooperation can be identified: civil society, economic and institutional. These are not exclusive and can be combined in a variety of ways.

Recently there has been an increasing tendency to view the problems of Northern Ireland from the perspective of civil society. This bottom-up approach focuses on the practical activities of citizens and argues for popular mobilisation. Reconciliation is promoted by building trust through the development of grass roots economic, social and cultural networks amongst ordinary people. As such it is:

> optimistic about contact between ethno-national groups as a means of promoting reconciliation. By accelerating certain types of contact between groups it is hoped that barriers and stereotypes are broken down and mutual understanding promoted, thereby facilitating the negotiation of a settlement by the elites (Dixon, 1996, p.138).

Whilst a civil society approach is usually linked to the promotion of better community relations within Northern Ireland, it also stresses the importance of developing cross-border contacts between individuals, communities and voluntary organisations. For example the agricultural cooperation organisations on both sides of the border told the New Ireland Forum that cooperation 'could be developed to good effect in the search for reconciliation between the two communities in Northern Ireland and between them and the people of the Republic' through a programme of education including residential courses with participants drawn from both jurisdictions (Belfast Telegraph, 1 March 1984).

Although some commentators bemoan the poverty of north-south links, there has always been a great variety of such contacts. Historically cross-border cooperation has been largely private and associational. In a little known study, John Whyte surveyed the extent to which the border was ignored by private organisations such as churches, youth and sporting bodies, cultural and scientific bodies, charitable and welfare groups, professional associations, trade associations and trade unions (Whyte, 1983). Whilst most of the 900 organisations surveyed observed the frontier and confined their activities to one side or the other of it, some 116 or 13 per cent organised on an all-Ireland basis and a further 58 (6 per cent) were organised on an all-archipelago basis. Three quarters of the churches and church related bodies organised on an all-Ireland and a further 20 per cent on an all-archipelago basis. Around a quarter of youth/sporting and cultural/scientific bodies were also organised on an all-Ireland basis, including those for Gaelic games, rugby and hockey. Of the professional associations, 10 per cent organised on an all-Ireland basis and 15 per cent all-archipelago; for the trade unions the figures were 3 per cent and 11 per cent respectively.

The study of formal organisational structures can both understate and overstate the extent of cross-border contacts, because the existence of a unified or separate administration tells us little about the cooperation within or between organisations. For example, although rugby union is formally an all-Ireland sport, the branch structure meant that competitions were traditionally organised on a partitioned basis with separate provincial competitions. Undoubtedly there were many friendly fixtures, but it is only comparatively recently that an all-Ireland league competition has been inaugurated. Secondly, focusing on formal administrative structures is likely to underestimate the extent of cross-border activity. For example, in practice many bodies accepted members from outside their jurisdiction, there were many cross-border linkages and affiliation arrangements and the largest organisations tended to be the ones most likely to cross the frontier (Whyte, 1983, p.3).

There are and have always been, therefore, a myriad of north-south linkages of differing intensity and significance. The political implications of this are more difficult to assess. Some envisage a type of civic functionalism, in which state boundaries and allegiances will gradually be eroded by the development of a multiplicity of socio-economic, political and cultural contacts, perhaps coordinated by overarching institutions. Certainly, as Whyte noted, practical cross-border cooperation is often a question of:

> self-interest or self-esteem overriding wider national preferences. Nationalists join British-based trade unions or professional associations; unionists accept selection for all-Ireland sporting teams or cultural bodies. People are more flexible than their political ideologies might lead one to expect; they are willing to accept different territorial frameworks for different activities' (Whyte, 1983, p.14).

Civil society accounts are open to a number of objections. Firstly, the focus on bottom-up contacts ignores the fact that many north-south links are often promoted by the elite leaderships of organisations, for example in the business and agricultural sectors. Secondly, they are imprecise about the nature of the future civil society. Is the ideal a common Irish civil society or a more minimalist conception of friendly cooperation between two Irish civil societies? Thirdly, civil society accounts place too much faith in the capacity for conflict resolution of bottom-up contacts. Politics and political preference cannot be wished away. As Whyte has astutely commented:

> other things being equal, nationalists prefer to belong to an all-Ireland body, and unionists to a United Kingdom or Northern Ireland one...Because people accept co-operation in a non-political field, that does not mean that they will agree to it in the political. For instance, it would be a great mistake to assume that because unionists can cheer the Irish rugby team, they might therefore accept Irish unity in politics (Whyte, 1983, pp.14-15).

Moreover the individual and associational contacts beloved of advocates of civil society approaches have existed for many years *alongside* fundamental constitutional and political conflict. Indeed the existence in many respects of a much more cohesive and common Irish civil society before 1920 failed to prevent political conflict and partition. Similarly the thaw in north-south relations in the 1960s did little to ameliorate the viciousness of the subsequent outbreak of sectarian violence within Northern Ireland. Robin Wilson recognises that cross-border contacts may not have the impact which some civil society accounts suggest when he remarks that:

> the tragedy is that, given the example of President Robinson, the years of work by bodies like the Irish Association and Co-operation North in undermining enemy images, the increasingly organic relationships between the social partners (including the voluntary sector) north and south, and the neutral framework offered by European integration, the establishment and enhancement of north-south relationships ought to be much *less* forbidding than in 1974 (Wilson, 1994, p.18).

**Economic approaches**

The debate about the constitutional position of Northern Ireland has always been informed by economic perspectives. For unionists the economic prosperity of Northern Ireland can best be promoted through its attachment to the United Kingdom. Protestants 'have always been worried that reunification would wreck the economy of the north and greatly impoverish them' (Rowthorn and Wayne, 1988, p.152). Conversely many nationalists see increased cross-border cooperation as a step towards Irish unity and have long tried to persuade Protestants of the 'economic merits of a united Ireland, on the supposition that economic anxieties or interests must lie at the heart of unionism' (McGarry and O'Leary, 1995, p.277). What Lyne refers to as 'technocratic anti-partitionism...Ireland's homegrown specimen of neo-functionalism' can be traced back at least to the Lemass reforms of the 1950s when the breakdown of economic barriers between north and south were seen as conducive to securing Protestant support for a united Ireland (Lyne, 1990, p.418).

Most economic accounts are grounded in the assertion that increased cross-border linkages will bring mutual benefits to both Irish economies, not least because partition resulted 'in a much lower level of trade and general economic integration between north and south than might otherwise have been expected' (Boyle and Hadden, 1994, pp.186-7). Similar considerations, added to fears of peripheralisation and increased competition within the single market, underpin Quigley's proposal for an integrated 'island economy' and a Belfast-Dublin economic corridor (Pollak, 1993, pp.289-92). As Anderson and Shuttleworth comment, there are 'real fears that if the two parts of Ireland don't swim together they may sink separately' (Anderson and Shuttleworth, 1992, p.19; see also Pollak, 1993, p.292).

Central to most analyses of economic integration is the conviction that European Union (EU) membership provides an impetus for cross-border cooperation. For example Tannam argues that the single market has:

> provided strong economic incentives for actors in Northern Ireland and the Republic of Ireland to co-operate with each other, not only by increasing trade, but also by encouraging actors to develop business links so as to combat the SEM's threat and to avail of EU money (Tannam, 1996, p.107).

Although there is only mixed evidence of increased cross-border co-operation between business elites overall, it was nonetheless apparent that:

> even before the announcement of the cease-fires, cross-border co-operation was becoming less hindered by unionist perceptions of 'unity through the back door'. Where perceived benefits exceeded costs co-operation began to increase. The EU has been significant in altering this cost-benefit calculation for business communities on both sides of the border (Tannam, 1996, pp.103;127).

In economic explanations of conflict, different national identities are embedded in different material interests. Adherents of such views 'often credit functional cross-border economic co-operation and especially European integration, with great conflict terminating potential. They believe that economic change will erode the material foundations of national differences' (McGarry and O'Leary, 1995, p.267). Political and ethnic conflict is thus reduced to economic causes and can therefore be overcome by economic cooperation. This process will 'create a transcendent identity which will overcome the current national divisions. National and ethnic conflict will dissolve through functional co-operation and the balm of shared economic interests and threats' (McGarry and O'Leary, 1995, p.275).

There are a number of problems with economic accounts. Lyne for example has identified four types of barriers to technocratic anti-partitionism: difficulties in creating a truly single market; doubts about the economic viability of cross-border cooperation; doubts about the capacities of respective governmental machines for administrative cooperation and questions concerning the extent to which cross-border cooperation can undermine the political and cultural roots of partition (Lyne, 1990, p.423).

Firstly, the rationale for extensive north-south economic cooperation, especially in the form of an 'island economy', has by no means been demonstrated convincingly. Advocates of increased cooperation provide little reliable evidence to support their argument that major benefits to both north and south will accrue. Indeed the whole debate tends to be conducted in terms of general assertions which seem to owe more to a normative political account than dispassionate economic analysis. Some argue that partition imposes significant economic costs, such as duplication of effort, lack of sectoral coordination and the creation of economically marginal border areas. The New Ireland Forum (1983) commissioned reports which argued that the economic consequences of partition had been negative for both jurisdictions, particularly in terms of competition for inward investment and the problems of smuggling resulting from different treatment under the Common Agricultural Policy (CAP). This however was a response to a controversial submission by Sir Charles Carter and Louden Ryan who argued that as 'partition had little significance in economic terms, therefore its end could not be expected to be economically significant either' (Lyne, 1990, p.425). Hitchens et al. also conclude that the 'weakness of the indigenous sector in both parts of Ireland limit the gains which might be expected from increased economic co-operation across the Border' (Hitchens et al., 1990, p.261). Although economies of scale could justify treating the island as a single economic unit in some cases, 'these are unlikely to be large enough to make a critical difference to economic performance on either side of the Border...' (Hitchens et al., 1990, p.261).

In the desire to identify the comparative advantages to be gained from cooperation, the economic *competition* between north and south in sectors such as economic development and tourism is often overlooked. The agricultural sector, for example, is seen as a prime candidate for north-south cooperation, not least because of common membership of the CAP and the general acceptance that the agricultural economies of north and south 'are very similar and have important linkages. In many respects the island of Ireland still functions like a single economy today despite partition' (Sheehy et al., 1981, p.68). Significantly, however, the fact that both industries have small domestic markets and are export oriented undermines some of the rationale for north-south cooperation. Indeed they often compete in overseas markets. Moreover there is relatively little north-south trade. In 1989 the north accounted for a mere 5 per cent of the Republic's export markets whilst only 4% of the latter's imports came from Northern Ireland (Lyne, 1990, p.426).

There is also the substantial British subvention to Northern Ireland. Munck and Hamilton argue that whilst breaking the financial link with Britain would entail substantial adjustment costs it is:

> misleading and erroneous to suggest living standards would automatically fall intolerably. A wide range of economic factors would come into play, many with substantial benefits not currently enjoyed because of the divided state of the [Irish] economy. Analysis which just focuses on the subvention is partial and tendentious. The heavily dependent nature of the north's economy on Britain, and the role of the subvention in particular, has been far from beneficial over the long term (Munck & Hamilton, 1994, p.26).

However there is little consensus amongst economists on the subvention question. John Simpson has questioned the *economic* gains of linking Northern Ireland to the faster growing economy of the Republic when both were members of the EU and when 'the main economic benefit of the existing framework was and is the continuing large scale government financial transfers to Northern Ireland from the United Kingdom Exchequer which would be difficult to sustain in an all-Ireland setting' (Simpson, 1983, p.109).

Functional accounts of economic cooperation are also dangerously reductionist. There is scant evidence to show that economic cooperation can successfully ameliorate conflict of the type which disfigures Northern Ireland. For example, over at least forty years the Ulster and Irish Farmers' associations (UFU and IFA) have developed machinery to facilitate consultation and the regular exchange of views, but this appears to have had little impact on the political preferences of farmers (see Greer, 1996, ch.8). Moreover cooperation, such as the decision of both organisations to make a joint submission to the Forum for Peace and Reconciliation, often provokes political controversy.

In Northern Ireland political, cultural and economic differences are reflected in the structure of the associational world and in patterns of cross-border cooperation. Thus the Northern Ireland Agricultural Producers' Association (NIAPA, founded 1975) has no reservations about cross border links because 'public and frequent contact with counterparts in the Republic helps it to define its position both with its predominantly nationalist membership and the wider coalition of radical "farm family" orientated unions with which it is associated' (Collins, 1995, p.678). Indeed NIAPA has seriously considered merger with southern based organisations to be better able to meet the expenses of lobbying in the EC.

The UFU on the other hand, historically an organisation with close links with unionism, has always had to proceed with the utmost caution in the area of cross-border contacts. Whilst the UFU's relations with the south are 'frequent, friendly and pragmatic' there is a limit to the extent of cooperative activity as 'public links with the Republic are open to misinterpretation by UFU members and could cause embarrassment' (Collins, 1995, p.678). The UFU has had to strike a balance between north-south cooperation in the best interests of regional agriculture and the need not to alienate its many unionist members. Thus in 1984 the UFU refused to attend a north-south conference in Drogheda because it was 'too politically sensitive'. As Michael Drake, the Belfast Telegraph's agriculture correspondent noted, the UFU had refused to send 'even a lone representative to keep a watching brief at this meeting on the green grassy slopes of the Boyne' (Belfast Telegraph, 19 January 1984).

Enthusiasts for increased cross-border cooperation in business and farming tend to assume 'that it is best, wherever possible, to pursue this kind of cooperation on a strictly non-political basis' (Boyle and Hadden, 1994, p.187). Thus Quigley has remarked that 'making a reality of the island economy is dependent on there being no political agendas, overt or hidden' (as quoted in Pollak, 1993, p.290). However, cross-border economic cooperation clearly cannot be isolated from political considerations. Whilst the Quigley proposals were warmly welcomed by nationalists, unionists were invariably hostile. As Boyle and Hadden note, 'the development of formal institutions for economic or other forms of cooperation between Northern Ireland and the Republic nonetheless has a political dimension that cannot realistically be ignored' (Boyle and Hadden, 1994, p.188). Similarly Anderson argues that the 'biggest obstacle to economic integration is the lack of an adequate institutional framework and political programme' and that, contrary to Quigley's assertions, making a reality of the island economy is 'precisely dependent on their being "political agendas"' (Pollak, 1993, p.293).

The history of cross-border cooperation in agriculture and other spheres supports the contention that there is 'little substantive proof that increased economic transactions, or increased economic interdependence between warring national or ethnic factions dramatically softens their rivalries' (McGarry and O'Leary, 1995, p.302). Even if a convincing economic case could be made for either the maintenance of the union or reunification this is unlikely to alter the political preferences of unionists or nationalists. Enthusiasm for the union exists autonomously of economic considerations and it is unlikely that 'even a very significant improvement in the Republic's economic performance will persuade a critical mass of unionists to convert to nationalism' (McGarry and O'Leary, 1995, p.300). For Lyne, 'any successful anti-partitionist strategy will also have to address itself to the political and cultural reasons for the division of Ireland' (Lyne, 1990, p.432) and Tannam comments that whilst the 'existence of increased co-operation in certain areas and the rhetoric of the unionist business community indicate that economic incentives can carve an avenue of cooperation between conflicting communities by cross-cutting conflicts of identity and political differences' there is little evidence to suggest that this 'gradually leads to peace and the end of sovereignty as a salient political issue' (Tannam, 1996, pp.123-4). Any project for economic cooperation must therefore embody realistic and attainable goals. As Teague remarks:

> North-south economic cooperation or all-Ireland economic strategies would not involve taking the province out of an economic union with Britain and establishing a similar arrangement in Ireland. The economic and political conditions do not exist for such a strategy. Rather, the project is about forging more intimate and symbiotic relationships between companies, institutions and social partners on both sides of the border so that a new commercial environment can be established (Pollak, 1993, p.288).

**Institutional approaches**

In institutional approaches the primary focus is on formal governmental policy and organisational structures of cross-border cooperation. This perspective can also be linked with economic and civil society approaches. For example, some argue that economic cooperation cannot develop properly unless given a political push. Thus:

> private business interests cannot achieve economic integration on their own, and it is too important to be left to them. It requires executive institutions to give it coherence, to involve the large public sectors, and to provide democratic accountability in north-south policy-making (Anderson and Goodman, 1996, p.17).

Great claims are often made for north-south institutions. For some they are intended to overarch political, economic, and social elements, in order to:

> diffuse the deadlocked conflict over "national sovereignty", to meet the threat of economic peripheralisation in the Single European Market, to facilitate the cross-border links of social, community and campaigning groups, and to democratise the growing connections between the two parts of the island (Anderson and Goodman, 1996, p.16).

However, suggestions for institutional cooperation have a long history. The framers of the Government of Ireland Act, for example, envisaged friendly cooperation between the northern and southern jurisdictions in areas such as transport and agriculture. The Council of Ireland, which the British Government hoped would act as a bridge between the two parliaments and facilitate reunification, would have been able to discuss matters of mutual interest and consider what services ought to be administered on an all Ireland basis, although it had no executive powers.

In the 1920s the balance of political forces enabled the unionist dominated regional parliament to use its transferred powers to develop a policy based on parity with Great Britain and frustrate hopes of extensive cross-border cooperation. Significant political and governmental cross-border cooperation was rare for most of the Stormont period. Indeed hostility and mutual suspicion characterised the relationship between Belfast and Dublin. Nonetheless official contacts developed in the post war period, especially in the agricultural sector. It was recognised that issues which posed a common problem such as animal disease and the management of the River Foyle could benefit from north-south cooperation. For example, the Foyle Fisheries Commission was jointly established by the Dáil and Northern Ireland Parliament in 1952. The unionist Minister of Agriculture, Harry West, also spoke of the 'closest possible consultation with the Department of Agriculture in Eire on animal disease generally. We keep very close contact and this is one of the things in which we have complete co-operation with that Department' (NIHC Deb.66, c.432). The prime ministerial meetings between O'Neill and Lemass were parallelled at the agricultural level by contacts between Harry West and his opposite number Charles Haughey. However, whilst the Unionist government could justify cross-border cooperation on the 'good neighbour' principle of friendly relations on matters of common interest, suggestions for institutionalised north-south arrangements were implacably resisted.

Direct rule, EU membership and the need to find an agreed political solution to the Northern Ireland problem have undoubtedly given renewed impetus to cross-border cooperation. In some cases, for example the EU common sheepmeat regime, the trend has been for Ireland to be treated as a single entity. After nearly twenty five years of direct rule, Collins found very good social and business relations between senior officials in the agricultural departments in Belfast and Dublin. Nevertheless political realities continue to constrain cross-border cooperation and still frequently outweigh considerations of administrative or economic advantage. So despite the perceived benefits of cooperation most civil servants in the Northern Ireland Department of Agriculture have 'very little contact with any part of the agricultural network in the Republic. The links with MAFF are the most important outside Northern Ireland although informal direct links with DG VI are increasing' (Collins, 1995, p.678).

For nationalists the development of closer ties with the Irish Republic has always been seen as a way to weaken the linkages between Northern Ireland and Britain. In the 1960s, for example, Cahir Healy advocated the resuscitation of the Council of Ireland to help formulate policies in those areas such as agriculture where the conditions in both countries were very similar and different to those prevailing in Great Britain. More recently, during the controversies on milk quotas and BSE, nationalists frequently claimed that farmers in Northern Ireland would benefit from a single agricultural policy for Ireland as a whole, not least because of the much more sensitive agricultural and rural policy followed by the Irish Government. On quotas, SDLP agriculture spokesman Denis Haughey complained that it was Mrs Thatcher, with her demands for cuts in the agriculture budget, who was the main opponent of Irish farmers north and south: 'What a pity that in these negotiations which are vital for NI...we are misrepresented in Brussels by Mrs Thatcher...It is only in the context of the European Community that Irish agriculture can escape the stranglehold of Britain' (Irish News, 22 March 1984). Similarly, during the BSE crisis, when Northern Ireland cattle were included in the ban on exports of UK beef, nationalists claimed that farmers in Northern Ireland were being disadvantaged by the policy link with Britain.

The perception that farmers in Northern Ireland were disadvantaged by British government policies gave greater credence to nationalist arguments for the development of an all Ireland agricultural policy. In 1984, for example, John Hume spoke of 'a remarkable and growing unanimity across party lines in the North that the same agricultural arrangements should apply North and South' and argued that all agricultural interests in the island of Ireland should aim to establish 'a common agricultural regime for farmers in Ireland within the overall framework of European agricultural policy' (Belfast Telegraph, 3 April 1984). Such a proposal is likely to meet severe practical difficulties. For example, whilst the authors of a 1981 Co-operation North report identified considerable benefits from a uniform implementation of CAP throughout Ireland, they added that the problems which would arise 'in respect of the North's trade with Great Britain would have to be resolved in any such arrangement and these problems could be so complex that a mutually acceptable solution might be very difficult to achieve' (Sheehy et al., 1981, p.69).

Politically, the claim that the interests of Northern Ireland farmers could be better protected by the Irish Government created difficulties for unionists who could less easily point to benefits of the link with Britain. During the BSE crisis, for example, the seeming irony of unionists pointing to the vital significance of the Irish Sea was not lost on nationalists. However this is entirely consistent with the traditional unionist claim for different policies for Northern Ireland where justified by regional conditions (Greer, 1996). This does not imply the development of an all-Ireland policy, but rather a more sympathetic policy for farmers in the United Kingdom as a whole. Thus unionist reaction to calls for all-Ireland policies has invariably been hostile and they also reject the nationalist claim that all-Ireland policies can be politically neutral. During the milk quotas controversy, Jim Nicholson warned that an all-Ireland agricultural economy would have serious ramifications for the constitutional position of Northern Ireland and accused the European Community, John Hume, the Dublin Government and the IFA of attempting to make political capital out of the difficulties of Northern Ireland producers. The proper solution was to press the British Government to ensure that the region's dependency on agriculture received special recognition (Belfast Telegraph, 24 April 1984). Whilst the Ulster Unionist Party recognized the advantages of cross border cooperation they would not countenance any attempt to evolve an all Ireland system. Roy Thompson of the DUP also strongly condemned the suggestion:

> It is nothing new, but Denis Haughey's purpose in resurrecting it now has nothing to do with the best interests of the farmers of Northern Ireland. He is out to promote wherever possible the merger of North and South for purely political motives (Belfast Telegraph, 24 January 1985).

The fact that north and south shared certain interests in agriculture was 'an entirely different thing from saying that North and South should always be treated as one unit for agriculture' (Belfast Telegraph, 24 January 1985).

## Conclusion: Cross-border cooperation and political accommodation

What lessons for the search for peace in Northern Ireland can be drawn from these different approaches to cross-border cooperation? Implicit in civil society accounts is the idea that bottom-up contacts can at least make a small contribution to facilitating agreement, if not solve the problem. Similarly economic cooperation only becomes controversial when linked to a normative political project. A rational economic calculation may demonstrate the benefits of the union or unity, but this ignores all the other intangibles which also help to shape individual preferences, such as religion, culture and national identity. The problem with both civil society and economic accounts is that at root they do not solve nor manage the political conflict, but try to circumvent it, either by creating an alternative identity or by dissolving ethnic identity. Economic and civil society cooperation across the Irish border may indeed be desirable and mutually beneficial, but neither can solve what are essentially political problems within Northern Ireland itself. The most that can be hoped is that cross border contacts can help to facilitate a political settlement. As Whyte commented about the Anglo-Irish process in 1983:

> the existence of so many connections across the border, in both a north-south and an east-west direction, can do the process no harm, and may possibly help to lubricate it. The unusual degree to which the Anglo-Irish border is already permeated by private organisations may prove to have some, if limited, political significance (Whyte, 1983, p.16).

The importance of cross-border cooperation lies in the political sphere. The 'bringing the political back in' which characterises institutional approaches challenges the neo-functionalist assumption that increased economic cooperation itself generates demands for political cooperation amongst elites. The question of the shape of any political Irish dimension has been pivotal in all previous negotiations. For example, Hadden and Boyle argue that the 'almost all-party talks process failed in 1992 when the Irish government and the SDLP failed to meet the unionists half way on Articles 2 and 3 and cross-border bodies' (Fortnight 348, March 1996, p.20). The Council of Ireland proposed at the Sunningdale Conference in 1973, the Anglo-Irish Joint Studies and Intergovernmental Council initiated after the summit in 1981 and the Anglo-Irish Agreement, have all been designed to create the conditions for increased cross-border political and institutional cooperation. However the most clearly delineated proposals for north-south cooperation, coordinated by institutional structures, were outlined in the framework documents of February 1995. In *A New Framework for Agreement* the British and Irish Governments agreed on the need to establish 'new institutions and structures to take account of the totality of relationships and to enable the people of Ireland to work together in all areas of common interest while fully respecting their diversity' (*Frameworks for the Future* Part II, 1995, para.5).

The pivotal role would be assumed by a North-South Body (NSB), drawn from the Irish Government and new democratic institutions in Northern Ireland, which would carry out delegated functions over a range of designated matters. The designation of NSB functions, initially by both governments, would take account of, for example, the extent of common interest in issues between north and south, the mutual benefits of political and administrative cooperation, the achievement of economies of scale and the avoidance of unnecessary duplication of effort. In principle any responsibilities transferred to a Northern Ireland assembly could be designated to the NSB. Moreover relevant EU matters could be considered by the NSB which would also have an important role in developing 'an agreed approach for the whole island in respect of the challenges and opportunities of the European Union' (Frameworks for the Future Part II, 1995, para.26).

The prime candidates for designation to the NSB are sectors such as tourism, economic development, and agriculture. Three broad categories of designated functions are identified in the document. On *executive* matters drawn from several broad categories, including sectors involving a natural or physical all Ireland framework and EU programmes, the NSB would be directly responsible for the formulation and implementation of agreed policies. Clearly this opens the way for the joint implementation of a CAP regime for Ireland. On *harmonising* matters, for example agricultural research, animal welfare, transport, energy, trade, health, social welfare, education and economic policy, both sides would be obliged to seek agreement on common policy although implementation might be undertaken separately. Thirdly the NSB would be a *consultative* forum with a duty to consult about policy and exchange information, but no formal requirement for agreement, policy harmonisation or joint implementation.

Clearly both the British and Irish governments hope that the proposals outlined in A New Framework for Agreement will command widespread support and provide the basis for political accommodation. However there is so far little sign that mainstream unionist politicians are ready to sign up to a settlement which involves the creation of executive all-Ireland bodies, particularly if these are to be dynamic. The problem is how to find middle ground between two conceptions of cross-border cooperation, neither of which are likely to command widespread support.

Unionists view cross-border cooperation as essentially one of 'good neighbours', a minimalist building on existing associational, economic and governmental links. It is possible for unionists to support cross-border cooperation without being committed to political integration. Indeed some unionists see the need to engage in cross-border cooperation 'precisely for protecting the constitutional status of the province and to avoid reunification by stealth' (Lyne, 1990, p.431). Teague comments that whilst many unionists are:

> quite open and amenable to close linkages with the republic, these can only be established after an internal settlement has been reached...The vision is of civil servants, politicians and independent experts from both jurisdictions coming together in *ad hoc* and informal policy networks to set up collaborative projects, in such areas as transport, energy and economic development. But, crucially, there is no place for any overarching economic and political bodies to connect north and south institutionally. Certainly, cross-border institutions with executive powers are flatly ruled out by this model (Teague, 1994, p.31).

On the other hand many nationalists advocate a joint authority/sovereignty approach in which formal responsibility for Northern Ireland would in some way be shared between the British and Irish states. In its crude form this has been described as a system 'under which "the London and Dublin governments would have equal responsibility for the government of Northern Ireland" so as to accord equal validity to the two traditions there and thus to reflect the reality of their divided allegiances' (Boyle & Hadden, 1994, p.165). However, even if such arrangements were economically and administratively feasible, unionists would 'react to the creation of joint authority in the same way as they would respond to the establishment of a united Ireland' (Teague, 1994, p.32). The most significant disadvantage therefore 'may be the continuing resistance by the major unionist parties to any direct involvement by the Irish government in internal Northern Ireland affairs' (Boyle and Hadden, 1994, p.171).

What sort of compromise can be found between these opposing positions? Teague argues that any future cross-border arrangements are likely to approximate to one of two models. Rolling integration is about 'setting in train a process through which Northern Ireland's economic and political connections with Britain would atrophy and there would be a hypertrophy of its linkages with the south, culminating in a new Ireland' (Teague, 1994, p.33). Such a strategy, however, may not herald a new dawn but 'may simply create new arenas for the fighting out of old antagonisms. Every move towards closer integration between the two parts of the island would meet strong unionist resistance' (Teague, 1994, p. 33). Alternatively consensual integration stresses not the 'transcending of constitutional borders, but peaceful co-existence between different nations - softening fanatical loyalties to particular political movements or mistrust between citizens of different states' (Teague, 1994, p.33). The aim is not to dissolve existing national political structures but to 'create deep interactions between peoples and territories, whilst respecting existing political loyalties and systems' (Teague, 1994, p.34). Overall the consensual integration project is about 'creating a Northern Ireland with an Irish orientation' (Teague, 1994, p.34).

In the Irish context this would involve creating all-Ireland institutions, some with executive powers, which straddled two separate constitutional entities. A technocratic or democratic Council of Ireland might be established to promote networks and develop collaboration. Now clearly the consensual integration project is likely to be more palatable to unionists than rolling integration. Nationalists, on the other hand, seem to require north-south institutions which are both executive and dynamic, something most mainstream unionist thinking still seems to regard as a step too far. What many unionists most object to is the proposal for cross-border institutions 'with clear identity and purpose' to 'cater adequately for present and future political, social and economic inter-connections on the island of Ireland, enabling representatives of the main traditions, North and South, to enter agreed dynamic, new, co-operative and constructive relationships' (Frameworks for the Future Part II, 1995, para. 24). Whilst the document makes it clear that the executive and harmonising functions of the NSB would be 'clearly defined in scope' the general tenor of the proposals seems to contradict this wish. Indeed the proposals appear to represent a thinly disguised move towards rolling integration rather than a sophisticated consensual integration package. Thus designated matters could be moved on the scale between consultation, harmonisation and executive action. It is unlikely, however, that 'downgrading' is envisaged given the express intention that the 'remit of the body should be dynamic, enabling progressive extension by agreement of its functions to new areas. Its role should develop to keep pace with the growth of harmonisation and with greater integration between the two economies' (Frameworks for the Future, 1995, para.38). For many unionists the apparent open-ended nature of the proposals indicates a clear embodiment of an anti-partitionist strategy and, like the Councils of Ireland before it, the NSB is seen as yet another embryonic all-Ireland parliament. For Jeffrey Donaldson the framework documents provide a blueprint which:

> once again shifts the balance in favour of a united Ireland. The purpose of these documents is to create a framework within which it will be possible to bring about the unification of Ireland, over a period, without the necessity of requiring the consent of the greater number in Northern Ireland. This is to be achieved through harmonisation between the two parts, a process overseen by an all-Ireland body with limitless executive powers. In effect the framework documents propose a third government in Ireland, with the new assembly, hamstrung by a complex web of checks and balances, gradually becoming subservient to its authority in a federal Ireland...Since the documents propose structures which would take Northern Ireland out of the union, they are hardly a sound basis on which unionists could enter negotiations (Donaldson, 1995, p.20).

Inevitably the language of the framework documents reflects the tortuous process of negotiation and compromise between two governments. Ambiguity, however, is precisely part of the problem. Significantly the Opsahl Report spoke of 'the problem of language itself: what Protestants perceive to be Catholic indirectness versus Protestant directness, and hence the Protestant propensity always to think in terms of the hidden agenda' (Pollak, 1993, p.37). What is required is certainty and clarity. There may well be a settlement in which cross-border bodies provide recognition of the validity of both traditions in Ireland, but there will have to be much more clarity about just how the nature, role, powers and scope of such cross-border bodies will be specifically constrained. This will require explicit and strict limits on the extent to which cross-border bodies can be dynamic. As Teague remarks, such cross-border institutions need to be 'well-defined and ringfenced so they cannot grow' (Teague, 1994, p.34). Similarly McGarry and O'Leary see the need for a meaningful institutional cross-border link which guarantees parity of esteem to nationalists whilst at the same time reassuring unionists that such institutions do not guarantee 'any creeping political reunification of Ireland' (McGarry and O'Leary, 1995, p.379).

This is easier said than done. The essential task facing participants in political negotiations will be to construct proposals which can meet these two objectives. However, the threat that cross-border bodies might be imposed on unwilling unionists does little to provide the guarantees required. Most speculation has centred on the extent to which unionists will be willing (or can be persuaded) to compromise. For McGarry and O'Leary it will 'be an essential task of political leadership to persuade the unionist population that the establishment of these agencies will not imply any direct erosion of either state's sovereignty...that such delimited bodies will represent a considerable compromise on the part of the nationalist population' (McGarry and O'Leary, 1995, p.380). The point, however, is that unionists are unlikely to be persuaded that the proposals in the framework documents represent nationalist compromise or sufficiently delimit the powers of cross-border bodies. Unionists need to be convinced that these bodies are going to be effectively delimited in practice, a task in which both governments have so far failed. Agreement requires that nationalists also compromise on the nature of cross-border institutions. Nationalists must be prepared to agree to well-defined limits on the dynamism of cross-border institutions if unionists are to be convinced that they are not a trojan horse for a united Ireland.

## References

Anderson, J. and Goodman, J.(1996),'Border Crossings', *Fortnight*, Vol. 350, pp. 16-17.
Anderson, J. and Shuttleworth, I. (1992), 'Currency of co-operation', *Fortnight*, Vol. 312, pp. 18-19.
Boyle, K. And Hadden, T. (1994), *Northern Ireland: The Choice*, Penguin: Harmondsworth.
Collins, N. (1995), 'Agricultural Policy Networks of the Republic of Ireland and Northern Ireland', *Political Studies*, Vol. 43, pp. 664-682.
Collins, N. and Mack, N. (1995), 'Farm household participation in agricultural policy decision making', *Irish Political Studies*, Vol. 10, pp. 1-26.
Dixon, P. (1996), 'The Politics of Antagonism: Explaining McGarry and Donaldson J (1995), 'Practising politics', *Fortnight*, Vol. 338, p. 20.
Greer, A. (1996), *Rural Politics in Northern Ireland: Policy Networks and Agricultural Development Since Partition*, Avebury:Aldershot.
Hitchens, D.M., Wagner, K. and Birnie J.E. (1990), *Closing the Productivity Gap: A Comparison of Northern Ireland, the Republic of Ireland, Britain and West Germany*, Avebury:Aldershot.
HM Government (1995) *Frameworks for the Future*, Belfast:HMSO.
Lyne, T. (1990), 'Ireland, Northern Ireland and 1992: The Barriers to Technocratic Anti-Partitionism', *Public Administration*, Vol. 68, pp. 417-433.
McGarry, J. And O'Leary, B. (1995), *Explaining Northern Ireland*, Blackwell: Oxford.
Munck, R. and Hamilton, D. (1994), 'A disintegrated economy', *Fortnight*, Vol. 324.
New Ireland Forum (1983), *A Comparative Description of the Economic Structure and Situation, North and South*, New Ireland Forum:Dublin.
Pollak, A. (ed.) (1993), *A Citizens' Inquiry: The Opsahl Report on Northern Ireland*, Initiative '92/Lilliput Press:Dublin.
Rowthorn, B. and Wayne, N. (1988), *Northern Ireland: The Political Economy of Conflict*, Polity:Cambridge.
Sheehy, S.J., O'Brien, J.T. and McClelland, S.D. (1981), *Agriculture in the Republic of Ireland and Northern Ireland*, Co-operation North: Dublin and Belfast.

Simpson, J. (1983), 'Economic Development: Cause or Effect in the Northern Ireland Conflict?' in Darby, J. (ed.) *Northern Ireland: the Background to the Conflict*, Appletree:Belfast.

Tannam, E. (1996), 'The European Union and Business Cross-Border Co-operation: The Case of Northern Ireland and the Republic of Ireland', *Irish Political Studies*, Vol. 11, pp. 103-129.

Teague, P. (1994), 'Approved border road', *Fortnight*, Vol. 332, pp. 31-4.

Whyte, J. H. (1983), 'The Permeability of the United Kingdom-Irish Border: A Preliminary Reconnaissance' (paper prepared for the ECPR Workshop on the Politics of Frontiers and Boundaries, Freiburg-in-Breisgau, March 1983, and the Conference of the Political Studies Association of Ireland, Dublin, May 1983).

Wilson, R. (1994), '(Dis)solving the border', *Fortnight*, Vol. 330, pp. 18-19.

# 8 Security strategies in Northern Ireland: Consolidation or reform?

*Paddy Hillyard*

**Introduction**

On the 9 February 1996 a massive bomb exploded near Canary Wharf, killing two people and creating over £2 million damage. Shortly before the bomb detonated, the IRA announced that its ceasefire had ended. The impact on security both in Ireland and Britain was immediate. Soldiers are once again on the streets of Belfast, port and airport procedures are back in place and familiar warnings against left luggage are made at regular intervals in public places. It looks increasingly likely that the whole security apparatus will be re-engaged to try and deal with political violence. At the same time, the problem of insecurity is again at the forefront of everyone's mind as they go about their daily business. The cease-fire provided seventeen months and nine days of peace, apart from an occasional act of violence. It also provided an opportunity to reflect upon a range of security issues: the methods, style and organisation of policing, the form of the criminal justice system; mechanisms for the protection of human of rights; and the treatment, release and transfer of political prisoners.

The aim of this chapter is to consider these four main security issues in greater depth and explore what progress has been made in addressing them. The chapter is structured into a number of different sections. In the first section there is a brief overview of the extent of political violence in Northern Ireland in the last 25 years and the impact that this has had on people's lives. The second describes the security apparatus which has been developed to deal with the political violence. The third examines some of the many problems with the existing security apparatus. The fourth considers the British Government's position on security and shows how it has consistently denied that there is any major problem in this area. The fifth and final section analyses the prospect of radical reform to the security apparatus emerging from the peace process.

**Political violence in Northern Ireland**

Between July 1969 and 31 December 1993 there were 3,285 deaths directly linked with the conflict in Northern Ireland. These have been subject to a detailed analysis by Sutton (1994). He shows that over 3,000 of the deaths have occurred in Northern Ireland, 91 in the Irish Republic, 118 in Britain and 17 elsewhere in Europe. Republican groups have been responsible for nearly 2,000 of the deaths, of which over 1,000 have been members of the security services killed by the IRA. Loyalist groups have killed nearly 1,000 people of which 713 have involved the deliberate killing of Catholic civilians or Protestant civilians who were mistaken for Catholics. In addition, the security forces have killed 357 people of whom 141 have been republican military activists, 13 loyalist military activists and 194 civilians. Over 33,000 people have suffered serious injuries, nearly one in fifty of the population.

As well as the deaths and the injuries there has been widespread intimidation both within and between communities. Ethnic cleansing has taken place in some parts of Northern Ireland in the period, but mainly in Belfast with people being driven out of their homes through fire-bombings, death threats and other methods. Another form of intimidation, principally carried out by the Protestant community and which has been on the increase in recent years, is to organise public marches through Catholic areas. In 1988 there were 2,055 parades but these increased to 2,792 in 1994, of which over 90 per cent were loyalist (RUC, 1990, 1995). In addition, people have been intimidated through various forms of 'popular justice' carried out in both communities.

There has been an ongoing debate about how this level of violence should be interrupted. In 1990 the Northern Ireland Office compared the overall homicide rate in Northern Ireland of 6 per 100,000 with that of 31 per 100,000 in Washington DC. The RUC has recently begun to publish a graph in the Chief Constable's annual report showing that for most years since the troubles began road deaths have exceeded deaths from political violence (RUC, 1995, p.102). These comparisons are misleading as O'Leary (1993: 12-13) has pointed out. Most of the deaths in Washington DC are criminally, not politically, related deaths and most people support the use of the motor car and are aware of the risks. He argues that it is more sensible to relate the total deaths to per capita death-tolls from internal political violence in liberal democracies. On this basis he shows that the conflict between the two communities in Northern Ireland has been intense. It has exceeded the internal political violence of any member state of the European Union and has the highest levels of violence of any liberal democratic state of the post 1948 world.

## The security apparatus

Since 1969 political violence in Northern Ireland has been tackled by four different forces: the Royal Ulster Constabulary, which was formed in 1922 following the setting up of the state; the B Specials, an auxiliary force which was disbanded in 1970 following the recommendations of the Hunt Report (1969); the Ulster Defence Regiment, in essence, a replacement for the B Specials and which was merged into the Royal Irish Regiment (RIR) in 1992; and the British Army, which was introduced into Northern Ireland in 1969. At the outbreak of the troubles the total personnel of the RUC, B specials and the British Army in Northern Ireland was almost 11,600.

Four years later the numbers had tripled to 33,000 and the numbers have remained at over 30,000 throughout the period. This works out as 200 army or police personnel for every 10,000 people in Northern Ireland.

Ever since the creation of the Northern Ireland state the composition of the security forces has been a contentious issue (Farrell 1983). When the RUC was established 21 per cent were Catholic, but the proportion has been steadily declining. By the 1930s it had dropped to 17 per cent and by the start of the troubles in 1969 to 11 per cent. The Catholic composition of the RUC now stands at some 8 per cent. The composition of the B Specials was even more contentious with most members being Protestant, a pattern which was repeated in the UDR and the RIR. The policy of the primacy of the police introduced by Merlyn Rees in 1976, known as Ulsterisation, led to an expansion of both the RUC and UDR, radically increasing the number of Protestants in the security forces (Hillyard 1997). Policing cannot therefore be seen in isolation from the broader social structure. It has provided important employment opportunities for one section of the community and this will pose a major structural problem following any settlement, due to the need for a drastic reduction in the number of security personnel.

The legislative framework for dealing with political violence was laid down in the Northern Ireland (Emergency Provisions) Act (EPA) 1973 (Boyle et al., 1975; Hadden et al., 1990). The architect was Lord Diplock who was asked to consider 'what arrangements could be made in order to deal more effectively with terrorist organisations...otherwise than with internment' (Diplock Commission, 1972, p.1). Most of his recommendations were accepted and enacted in the EPA, creating a separate system of criminal justice for those involved in political violence compared with those involved in what has become known as 'ordinary decent crime'. As well as retaining the power to re-introduce internment, the EPA provided extensive powers of stop, search and detention for the police and security forces, abolished trial by jury, introduced special rules for the admissibility of evidence and created a number of new offences principally relating to membership of proscribed organisations.

In 1974 in the wake of the Birmingham Bombings the government rushed through the Prevention of Terrorism (Temporary Provisions) Act (PTA) which applied to the whole of Great Britain and Northern Ireland. It contained five main components: it established a system of port controls; provided very broad powers of arrest and detention; gave the Secretary of State the power to issue exclusion orders; introduced a range of new criminal offences and provided for proscription of certain types of organisation (Hillyard 1993). Roy Jenkins, the then Home Secretary, described the powers as draconian and went onto argue that such powers were 'fully justified to meet the present danger'. In Northern Ireland the PTA reinforced the emergency legislation, although until 1987, most arrests were carried out under the EPA. In Britain, the PTA created, as in Northern Ireland, a dual system of criminal justice. Those 'suspected' of being involved in political violence were dealt with by an extraordinary system while the burglar, the violent robber, the rapist and the serial killer - ordinary decent criminals - continued to be arrested and tried under normal criminal procedures.

These two pieces of legislation together formed the platform for the security strategy. Over the years there have been numerous amendments and extensions to both pieces of legislation which have provided the security services with even greater powers and further eroded the normal safeguards in the criminal justice system. At the same time, additional legislation has been introduced to make even more radical changes. For example, in October 1988, Tom King, the Secretary of State for Northern Ireland, announced that there was to be a partial abolition of the right to silence in Northern Ireland. This was provided for in the Criminal Evidence (Northern Ireland) Order. It effectively abolished a defendant's long-standing right to remain silent by permitting adverse inferences to be drawn if he or she exercises that option.

This extraordinary security apparatus has not been able to defeat the violence and bring greater security for everyone living in Ireland and Britain. Despite huge resources it has failed to assert its authority and produce social order. At best it has simply achieved what has been euphemistically called 'an acceptable level of violence' and at worst it has exacerbated the situation by further alienating the Catholic community from the state and reducing any confidence they may have had in the notion of 'the rule of law' (Asmal 1990).

There is, of course, an historical legacy to all of this (see, for example, Townshend, 1983; Farrell, 1986; Palmer, 1988; Hogan & Walker, 1989). Neither the size of the security forces nor the coercive nature of the security legislation is exceptional in Ireland. In the middle of the nineteenth century the size of the garrison in Ireland was double that in Great Britain and the police strength three times that of England and Wales. Moreover, most of the provisions in the emergency legislation can be traced to one or more of the 105 separate Acts of Coercion which were introduced in Ireland between 1800 and 1915. For example, the Protection of Life and Property (Ireland) Act permitted arrest and detention without trial of persons belonging to secret societies. The Prevention of Crimes (Ireland) Act 1882 allowed for the suspension of trial by jury in specific instances and the Criminal Law and Procedure (Ireland) Act 1887 gave powers to declare any association unlawful. After the formation of the Northern Ireland state under the Government of Ireland Act 1920, the Northern Ireland government passed the Civil Authorities (Special Powers) Act (NI) 1922 and the EPA contains similar provisions, including the power of internment.

These historical forms of social control were not isolated responses to periodic bouts of violence, but were products both of the social divisions in Ireland and the colonial relationship which has existed between Britain and Ireland for centuries. Popular protests against many different forms of injustice were commonplace and the demand for national independence never left the political agenda. Much effort, of course, has gone into disguising the long historical roots of both pieces of emergency legislation. For example, the inclusion of the phrase 'Temporary Provisions' in the title of the PTA suggests that it is merely a reactive piece of legislation to the current violence. A more accurate title would be Prevention of Terrorism ('Continuing Provisions') Act to reflect the two hundred history of most of the security legislation in Ireland.

**Problems with the security apparatus**

During the last twenty-five years there have been numerous violations of human rights. The list is extensive (see Foley, 1995). There have been allegations of shoot to kill (Stalker, 1988; Blom-Cooper, 1994); collusion between the security forces and Protestant paramilitary groups (Statewatch, 1993); the use of unnecessary force on the streets, including the use of live rounds; indiscriminate use of CS gas and plastic bullets (Information on Ireland 1987; Hadden et al., 1990); abuse of stop and search powers amounting to harassment of communities and individuals (McVeigh, 1994); abuse of the powers of arrest and detention for the purposes of intelligence gathering (Walsh, 1982; Hillyard, 1993); mistreatment of people while being interrogated in custody (Taylor, 1980); the prolonged use of detention before release without charge; the questionable use of informers and supergrasses (Boyd, 1984; Gifford, 1984; Hillyard and Percy-Smith, 1985; Greer 1995) and the intimidation of lawyers by the police (British Irish Rights Watch, 1994; O'Rawe, 1995). In addition there has been criticism of the following: the abolition of trial by jury (Greer and White, 1986); the partial abolition of the right to silence, the case-hardening of judges in Diplock Courts (Hadden et al., 1990) and the inadequate means of legal redress either through the inquest system (British Irish Rights Watch, 1992) or through the Independent Police Complaints Body (Committee for the Administration of Justice, 1993).

Many of the allegations have been upheld by international organisations. The European Commission and the European Court for Human Rights have issued a number of adverse decisions on the emergency legislation and the behaviour of the security forces in Northern Ireland and elsewhere. Some of the more important include the judgements that the interrogation techniques used at the time of internment constituted 'inhuman and degrading treatment';[1] that suspects held under the seven day power of the PTA violated Article Five because none of the suspects had been brought promptly before a judicial authority;[2] that the shooting dead of three unarmed members of the IRA in Gibraltar constituted unreasonable force[3] and that the failure to allow defendants access to a lawyer violated Article Six, the right to a fair trial.[4]

Amnesty International has issued a wide range of reports drawing attention to its concerns in Northern Ireland. For example, in 1978, it issued a critical report on the treatment of suspects in Castlereagh and Gough detention centres (Amnesty International 1978). It has also been concerned about the alleged shoot-to-kill policy and published an extensive report in 1994 (Amnesty International, 1994). Another international body which has been critical is the United Nations' Human Rights Committee. In 1995 it called for an immediate closure of Castlereagh detention centre and was critical of a number of aspects of the operation of the emergency law including extended periods of detention without charge, the lack of access to legal advisors and entry into private property without judicial warrant. It also expressed concern that notwithstanding the establishment in the United Kingdom of mechanisms for external supervision of investigations of incidents in which the police or military are allegedly involved, especially incidents that result in death or injury, the investigations are still carried out by the police and they lack sufficient credibility (O'Rawe, 1995). Further condemnation of Castlereagh Detention Centre has come from the European Committee for the Prevention of Torture, claiming that it posed a 'significant risk of psychological forms of ill-treatment' (Council of Europe, 1994).

Throughout the whole period, the issue of the status and treatment of prisoners has been a key aspect of the security problem (Rolston and Tomlinson, 1988). What was known as Special Category Status was granted in 1972 to members of paramilitary organisations who had been convicted in the courts and who claimed to have been politically motivated. The Labour Government, however, following the recommendation of the Gardiner Committee (1975) decided to phase it out. This led in 1980 and 1981 to the longest ever collective struggle in prison and the death through hunger strikes of 10 prisoners (Beresford, 1987).

Strip-searching has been another contentious issue. A year after the hunger strikes in 1981 the strip searching of women prisoners became the subject of considerable controversy as extra strip searches were introduced. Remand prisoners making court appearances in Belfast were particularly affected by the change in policy (National Council for Civil Liberties, 1986). In March 1992 the issue was once more on the political agenda when it was reported that the prison authorities, presumably with the support of the Northern Ireland Office, had taken the unprecedented step of strip-searching every woman prisoner in Maghaberry Jail, apart from one who was recovering from an operation (Statewatch, 1992).

A third important prison issue has concerned the transfer of Irish prisoners from Britain to Ireland. There have been numerous complaints about the difficulties which families have experienced in trying to visit their relatives in Britain. On some occasions it appears that the authorities have deliberately prevented a visit by 'ghosting' the prisoner to another jail shortly before the visit was due to take place. Family members were therefore put to considerable expense and much stress to no avail. Critics of current policy argue that Irish prisoners receive a 'double sentence' by not being allowed to serve their sentences in the North or South of Ireland. The British government, however, has opposed the transfer of prisoners and has put forward a range of different arguments, all of which have been challenged (Committee for the Transfer of Irish Prisoners, 1991).

**Denial of the problem**

The Government has refused to acknowledge that there are any problems with the security apparatus. It has used a variety of techniques to support its position. To begin with, it has continued with the practice of establishing 'independent' reviews to confirm the legitimacy and need for emergency legislation. These reviews have been widely proclaimed by the British Government as independent of the state and have been vaunted as neutral and protective procedures, potentially curbing the scope of emergency legislation (Ni Aolain, 1996). Yet they have been far from independent. Each reviewer has been closely associated with the establishment and the terms of reference started with the premise that the legislation was necessary.

Secondly, the Government has tried to add further legitimacy to the security apparatus by the use of Commissioners and Assessors. In 1992 it appointed an Independent Commissioner for the Holding Centres and in 1993 it appointed an Independent Assessor of Military Complaints Procedures. The terms of reference for the former made it explicitly clear that one of the main purposes of the appointment was 'to reassure the public that the police have nothing to hide and that persons detained in the Holding Centres are not being ill-treated or *denied their rights*' (Blom-Cooper, 1994, p.4, italics added). Both pieces of exceptional legislation permit the denial of certain rights in the Holding Centres, the right not to be held for an excessive time period and the right to legal counsel. The establishment of such posts, however successful in preventing ill-treatment, play a part in legitimating the violations of human rights enacted in the emergency legislation.

Thirdly, whenever there have been allegations of violations of human rights, successive governments have been extremely reluctant to establish inquiries and when they have been established, they have done little to encourage confidence in the rule of law. In 25 years of conflict there have been only seven inquiries into specific incidents (British Irish Rights Watch, 1996). Only one, the Widgery Tribunal, was a public enquiry in the sense that it was held in public. It was set up under the Tribunal of Enquires Act 1921 and investigated the shooting dead of 13 people by the British army in Derry in 1972 (Widgery Report, 1972). It exonerated the security forces and led one legal commentator to observe that as a result of the Widgery Report the precious legal asset of a Tribunal of Inquiry] appeared to be greatly impaired (McMahon, 1974). A campaign continues for a fully independent enquiry. The Compton Enquiry (1971) into the allegations of brutality by the security forces on the day of internment reached the conclusion in relation to the interrogation in-depth of 11 individuals that it found no evidence of physical brutality, torture nor brainwashing, a finding which led to widespread criticism. The Bennett Committee (1979) which was established after allegations of ill-treatment of detainees at Castlereagh detention centre was muzzled from the start. Its terms of reference required it only to look at police procedures and practice. It was given no brief to examine the particular allegations. The Stalker Enquiry established to investigate the deaths of six people shot dead by the security forces in 1982 was surrounded in controversy following Stalker's removal and suspension following unfounded allegations that he had been in breach of police discipline in Manchester (Stalker, 1988). Most of the media believed that there was a conspiracy at the highest level (Murphy 1991). As the British Irish Rights Watch (1996, p.3) has concluded, 'all of them [the enquiries] raised more questions than they answered, failed to bring perpetrators to book, and undermined the very public confidence they ought to have reinforced'.

The denial that there is anything wrong with the security apparatus is perhaps seen most strongly in the government's current position on the RUC. In May 1996 it issued a White Paper inappropriately and misleadingly entitled *Foundations for Policing: Proposals for policing structures in Northern Ireland* (1996). It is nothing of the sort and simply reasserts the status quo. The closest it gets to acknowledging that all is not well in the RUC is when it records that much attention has been focused on the views expressed in the report published by the Police Authority, following its own consultation exercise, concerning the RUC's name, badge and uniform. It then goes on to say that the government 'has noted with interest the consultation exercise'. Yet as the findings generally reflected 'a lack of political agreement and no consensus to support legislative change in any of these areas' (para 1.11) it does not propose to introduce any legislation in this area. Instead it 'will reflect on the nature of any political agreements reached in course of the political talks which might impact on these matters'.

Nowhere does the White Paper acknowledge that there are any major problems with the RUC. Throughout it blandly talks about 'the community' without once conceding

Northern Ireland has at least two very divided communities, one of whom has had little confidence in the RUC since its inception and has been particularly critical of it during the last 25 years. It claims that surveys show a large majority of the people in Northern Ireland believe that the RUC already does a good job and reproduces data from the 1995-96 Community Attitudes Survey showing the proportion of Catholics and Protestant in support of the police. The findings, however, contrast with a smaller and more focused study in 1994 by McVeigh (1994). He interviewed 600 eighteen year olds about their contacts with the police and he uncovered a pattern of abuse cutting across religion, class, gender and employment status. He found that 26 per cent of all respondents reported being harassed by the security forces at least once. Nearly half of Catholics compared with some 12 per cent of Protestants said that they had been harassed. Almost 60 per cent of students and 30 per cent of young working class people reported harassment. The survey suggested that 'a substantial section of the next generation of Northern Irish citizens is dissatisfied with the policing service it receives' (McVeigh, 1994).

Further evidence that there are major problems with policing in Northern Ireland comes from as yet an unpublished study by Ellison based on a series of in-depth interviews with Protestant and Catholic officers in the RUC. He found that some Protestant officers harboured deep-seated sectarian attitudes towards their Catholic officers (Breen, 1996).

There are thus major issues concerning both the abuse of human rights and the form, style and composition of the police which the Government seeks to deny in one way or another. This does not facilitate the peace process. At some point these issues will have to be placed upon the political agenda because they go to the heart of the problem. If there is no widespread consensus over the type of policing and the form of law, neither will gain the confidence of the disaffected community and coercion rather than consensus will continue to be part of the landscape of Northern Ireland.

**Developments since the ceasefire**

Since the ceasefire in August 1994 there has been considerable discussion among community groups, political parties and civil rights organisations about the future of policing, the emergency legislation and the possibility of a Bill of Rights and numerous recommendations have been made (Ruane, 1994; British Irish Rights Watch, 1995; Committee for the Administration of Justice, 1995). The British government, however, has not shown the same sense of commitment or urgency. More importantly, it has by its actions and through its various statements, restricted the possibility of radical reform of the security apparatus emerging from the peace process. Very subtly, it has predetermined any outcome by insisting that British models of policing, criminal justice and human rights protection are maintained. There are a number of specific examples.

In June 1995 the Secretary of State for Northern Ireland announced that the government, the RUC and Police Authority for Northern Ireland (PANI) would jointly conduct a fundamental review of policing, which would consider among other matters the future organisation, style and size of the RUC. It was expected that this would be completed by the summer of 1996 with implementation in April 1997. To date this comprehensive review has not seen the light of day. However, the May 1996 White Paper makes it abundantly clear that the government expects the current structure of policing to continue. In a foreword, the Secretary of State for Northern Ireland, Sir Patrick Mayhew, emphasises that the tripartite structure would continue because it was 'overwhelmingly supported' by the responses received - some 54 replies. He then went on to say the operational independence, impartiality and integrity of the police and their freedom from partisan political control would be reinforced.

To consolidate the current structure, the White Paper recommends the adoption in Northern Ireland of the police reforms introduced in England and Wales under the Police and Magistrates' Courts Act 1994. In essence these reforms simply impose a much stricter managerial structure of accountability on the police. In return for control of the budget, the Chief Constable will be required to produce a clear statement of objectives, which in the first instance will be produced by the Secretary of State and then extended by PANI. These objectives will then be monitored by means of performance indicators. In the past the Chief Constable has always had control of operational matters and PANI could exert some influence on the form or style of policing only through control of the budget. With the loss of this control, the position of PANI will be further emasculated.

The unpreparedness of the government to confront even the smallest of changes to the RUC was seen in the sacking in March 1996 of David Cook, the Chair, and Chris Ryder, a board member, of PANI. Politically, neither man could be considered to be remotely supportive of nationalist politics. David Cook, a lawyer, has been a long-time member of the Alliance Party and the first non-unionist Lord Mayor of Belfast. Chris Ryder, a journalist, has written supportive books on both the RUC and the Ulster Defence Regiment (Ryder, 1989, 1991). Yet both were sacked for what were seen as unacceptable views.

The row between the two men and the rest of the authority had been rumbling for some time. The pair had been pressing for two modest changes. The first was to make the authority more open and transparent after years of secrecy when even the name of its Chairman was never published. The second issue concerned symbolism and oaths of allegiance. There are 19 days of the year, including the 12th of July when hundreds of Orange lodges commemorate Protestant King William's defeat of Catholic King James at the Battle of Boyne, on which the RUC code requires that all RUC stations fly the Union flag. It was felt that this practice, particularly on the Twelfth, prejudiced the perception of the modern RUC as an impartial, even-handed and apolitical police service (Ryder, 1996). Similarly, it was felt that the requirement that every member of the RUC should swear an oath of office dating back to 1836, pledging to 'well and truly serve our Sovereign Lady the Queen' and not 'belong to any association, society or confederacy formed for or engaged in any seditious purpose...or in any way disloyal to our Sovereign Lady the Queen' does little, Ryder and Cook argued, to encourage Catholics to join the police.

Their demands were not particularly radical. They asked only that there should be a change in the symbolism and ritual, allied to greater openness, but this was too far for the other members and rather than sack the rest of the Police Authority, the Secretary of State sacked the two reformers after two-thirds of the authority passed a vote of no

confidence in them on 21 February 1996.
Ryder (1996, p. 27) has been very critical of the Secretary of State's decision. He argues that:

> it sends the wrong signal about the possibility of change at a time when the concepts of accommodation, reconciliation and tolerance, which are central to a lasting settlement, need to be rigorously defended. Creating a widely acceptable policing order based on the consent and co-operation of the entire community - and within which divisions and differences are understood, respected and accepted - will be one of the cornerstones of the new tolerant society that must be created if Northern Ireland is to enjoy eventual stability.

Policing is not the only area where the Government appears determined to maintain the status quo. A similar pattern is observable in relation to the exceptional legislation. In December 1995 the government renewed the EPA for a further two years with minor amendments much to the consternation of the Standing Advisory Commission on Human Rights. It strongly criticised the government for not consulting it before publishing the Bill, arguing that the decision ignored the advice of the Advisory Committee and the recommendations of the UN Committee Against Torture, which called for the repeal of emergency legislation for Northern Ireland (Boyle, 1995). In 1996 the government further consolidated the emergency legislation by introducing the highly controversial Prevention of Terrorism (Additional Powers) Act which extends, amends or repeals certain sections of the Prevention of Terrorism Act 1989.

In addition, in January 1996 the Secretary of State announced that he had established a review under Lord Lloyd of Berwick to consider the future of the need for specific counter-terrorism in the UK if the cessation of terrorism in Northern Ireland led to a lasting peace. The review would take into account the continuing threat from other kinds of terrorism and the United Kingdom's obligations under international law. The other member of the review team was Mr Justice Kerr, a Northern Ireland High Court judge. It was therefore very much a British review, making no concession to the minority community in Northern Ireland by having an international member of the team. Moreover, in June 1995, Northern Ireland officials expressed their view to Ni Aolain (1996) that they expected both the EPA and the PTA to be replaced by a single permanent piece of legislation to cover the whole of the United Kingdom. The outcome appeared a foregone conclusion, even though any permanent replacement of emergency legislation is an undisputed violation of international law.

The British government also appears determined to maintain the status quo in the area of the protection of human rights. Here the Government has insisted on the British model of protection. In the ironically entitled document *A Framework for Accountable Government in Northern Ireland* (1995) it is argued that protection of specified civil, political and cultural rights would come about as a result of the consultation process. Then it put a ringfence around any substantial protection arguing that such protection would accord with the constitutional arrangements of the United Kingdom. This is the heart of the problem. The United Kingdom has no constitutional protection of human rights, hence the demand by a range of bodies for at least the incorporation of the European Convention of Human Rights. Others, such as Liberty

(1991) and IPPR (1990) have gone much further and produced Bills of Rights.

Part II of the framework document, *A New Framework for Agreement*, agreed by the British and Irish governments, notes that there is a 'large body of support, transcending the political divide, for the comprehensive protection and guarantee of fundamental human rights'. However, the British government considers the current arrangements sufficient. The document continues that both governments would encourage democratic representatives from both jurisdictions in Ireland to adapt a Charter or Covenant for the protection of the 'fundamental rights of everyone in Ireland'. However, there is no explicit statement that this would be legally binding. On the contrary, the document makes clear that any protection has to be in accordance with each country's constitutional arrangements.

Finally the government has been most reluctant to take any positive steps in relation to prisoners. This is a vitally important security issue at the heart of the peace process. Whereas the Irish government moved quickly and released nine prisoners for Christmas 1994 and a further 12 by Easter 1995, the British Government dragged its heels on both the release of prisoners and the transfer of prisoners from Britain to Northern Ireland. Following the escape of six prisoners from the Whitemoor special security unit in September 1994 security for all maximum security prisoners was significantly tightened and all the IRA prisoners experienced a deterioration in prison conditions and facilities (Statewatch, 1995). In Autumn 1995 the Government announced that the remission rate would be increased from one-third to one-half, but this simply restored the position to what it had been in 1989 and was hardly a major concession.

In all these areas which lie at the heart of the problem in Northern Ireland, the government has clearly set the parameters for any reform and it is difficult to see what flexibility there might be in all-party talks to suggest radical reform of the police, the security legislation or the protection of human rights. The British way of doing things has been quietly consolidated since the ceasefires. This raises the question whether the British government was ever serious about encouraging radical reforms in Northern Ireland which would be broadly acceptable to both communities. All the evidence suggests that it has spent the last two years reinforcing the unionist position. Some nationalists argue that in fact the British government was never interested in making any accommodation to nationalism and simply wanted to stop the violence by producing splits within the nationalist camp. In any event this analysis of the British government's responses on key security issues shows very clearly that it is part of the problem of achieving peace in Northern Ireland. In such a context is there any possibility of the parties in the peace talks reaching a comprehensive settlement including radical reform of the security apparatus which would achieve widespread consensus?

**Prospects for the reform of security**

The prospects do not look hopeful. Sinn Fein, who at the start of the process appeared to believe that some major constitutional change would follow a ceasefire, have been excluded from the process following the decision of the IRA to break the ceasefire and renew its campaign of violence. At the same time the amount of support it receives from the nationalist communities who have enjoyed nearly 18 months of peace must be another factor in the equation.

The Irish government has taken a diametrically opposed position to the British on a number of key aspects. It was always keen to push the process on as quickly as possible. The departure of Reynolds, who had played a virtual brokering role in the peace process, had a major impact on current politics. Bruton, who appears to be taking an increasingly pro-Unionist position, has shifted the balance of power. Moreover, following the breakdown in the ceasefire the Irish government has been left with egg on its face, after placing so much faith in Sinn Fein's ability to deliver. As a result the pan-nationalist alliance of Sinn Fein, the SDLP and the Irish and American governments has been significantly weakened.

The Ulster Unionists and Democratic Unionists have played a clever role and have remained virtually outside of the whole process. They have conceded little and certainly there has been no public indication that they would be prepared to compromise very much in return for a permanent end to the conflict. They appear as resolute as ever to defend their power and position. This position was further strengthened during the peace process due to the decline in the Conservative Government's majority in the House of Commons, prior to election defeat in 1997. The loyalist paramilitaries, in contrast, have shown a much greater willingness to reach some sort of compromise. Their ceasefires have so far held and the personal contacts developed in prison with republicans have no doubt played a part in creating some degree of trust between the two sides. Perhaps the key factor for the paramilitaries on both sides is that it has been their communities, located mainly in deprived working class areas, who have suffered the most from violence and they do not wish to see another generation growing up experiencing nothing but war.

The Labour Party's significant shift towards a more pro-Unionist position under Tony Blair is another important element in the equation. In 1981, the Party adopted the principle of a united Ireland by consent together with the policy that any future Labour Government would act as persuaders of the Unionists. The 1983 election Manifesto spelt out this policy and Kevin McNamara, when he become Labour's front bench spokesperson on Northern Ireland in 1988, proceeded to pursue this policy with commitment. One of Blair's first moves when he became leader in 1994, however, was to replace McNamara. McNamara immediately saw the dangers and wrote to Blair warning him of the consequences:

> It is vital at this extremely sensitive time that we are not seen to alter a policy stance which has been constant since 1981. Our position affects the context in which all the parties in Ireland operate and any shift at this time could be deeply destabilising. Secondly, our policy position is one which will encourage Unionists to negotiate the best possible deal for themselves in the next two to three years. If we shifted policy, Unionists might be encouraged to hold out against any pressure from the Conservatives to compromise - in the belief that we will prove a soft touch (Quoted in Pilger, 1996, p.27).

In March 1996 the Labour Party made another highly significant change in policy when Jack Straw advised the shadow cabinet to drop its opposition to the PTA, a policy which it had followed since 1981 despite the constant refrain from the government that they were supporting terrorism.

Such a configuration of political forces means that the prospects for a solution to the Northern Ireland problem look bleak. The Unionist position has been skilfully consolidated and the pan-nationalist alliance significantly weakened ever since the installation of Bruton in the South and the ending of the ceasefire. The expectations of the minority community for parity of esteem and the abolition of the coercive apparatus look no nearer than they were during the Civil Rights campaign. Certainly, the possibility of major constitutional changes, on which the ceasefire appeared to have been negotiated, is likely to amount to no more than cross-border co-operation in some uncontentious areas such as tourism or electricity supply. This leaves a dangerous mixture of thwarted expectations and political powerlessness; a classic recipe for further violence.

**Notes**

1. European Court of Human Rights, Ireland v. United Kingdom, 18 January 1978.

2. European Court of Human Rights, McCann and Others v. The United Kingdom, 28 October 1994.

3. European Court of Human Rights, McCann and Others v. the United Kingdom, 28 October 1994.

4. European Commission on Human Rights, Murray v. United Kingdom, 27 June 1994. The decision, however, was overturned by the Court.

**References**

Amnesty International (1978), *Report of an Inquiry into Allegations of Ill-treatment in Northern Ireland*, Amnesty International:London.
Amnesty International (1994), *United Kingdom: Political Killings in Northern Ireland*, Amnesty International:London.
Asmal, K. (1990), *If Law is the Enemy...Human Rights in Northern Ireland: Britain's Responsibilities*, The Britain and Ireland Human Rights Project:London.
Bennett Report (1979), *Report of the Committee of Inquiry into Police Interrogation Procedures in Northern Ireland* Cmnd. 7479, HMSO:London.
Beresford, D. (1987), *Ten Dead Men: The Story of the 1981 Irish Hunger Strike*, Grafton:London.
Blom-Cooper, L. (1994), *First Annual (1993) Report of then Independent Commissioner for the Holding Centres*, NIO:Belfast.
Boyd, A. (1984), *The Informers: A Chilling Account of the Supergrasses in Northern*

*Ireland*, Mercier:Dublin.

Boyle, K., Hadden, T., and Hillyard, P. (1975), *Law and State: The Case of Northern Ireland*, Martin Robertson:London.

Boyle, M. (1995), 'Civil Liberties Diary', *Just News*, Vol. 11, No. 1, p. 8.

Breen, S. (1996) 'A Study Depicts a "Them and Us" RUC', *The Irish Times*, 2 November.

British Irish Rights Watch (1992), Current Developments in Inquests in Britain and Ireland. Record of the Proceedings of a Seminar held in London on 27 June 1992.

British Irish Rights Watch (1994), *In defence of the defence*, Fourth Report to the United Nations Special Rapporteur on the Independence of judges and lawyers concerning the attempted intimidation of defence lawyers in Northern Ireland, BIRW: London.

British Irish Rights Watch (1995), Human Rights and the Peace Process. Briefing 26 June 1995.

British Irish Rights Watch (1996) *Response to the Lord Chancellor's Consultation Exercise on Public Inquiries*, BIRW:London.

Committee for the Administration of Justice (1993), *A Fresh Look at Complaints Against the Police*, CAJ:Belfast.

Committee for the Administration of Justice (1995), *No Emergency, No Emergency Law: Emergency Legislation related to Northern Ireland - the case for Repeal*, CAJ: Belfast.

Committee for the Transfer of Irish Prisoners(1991),*Double Sentence*,CTIP: Dublin.

Compton Report(1971),*Report of the Enquiry into Allegations against the Security Forces of Physical Brutality in Northern Ireland arising out of the Events on 9th August 1971* Cmnd. 4823, HMSO:London.

Council of Europe (1994), *Report to the Government of the United Kingdom on the visit to Northern Ireland carried out by the European Committee for the Prevention of Torture and Inhuman and Degrading Treatment or Punishment from 20 to 29 July 1993* CPT/Inf (94) 17, Council of Europe:Strasbourg.

Diplock Commission (1972), *Report of the Commission to Consider Legal Procedures to Deal with Terrorist Activities in Northern Ireland* Cmnd. 5185, HMSO:London.

Farrell, M. (1983), *Arming the Protestants: The formation of the Ulster Special Constabulary and the Royal Ulster Constabulary, 1920-27*, Pluto:London.

Farrell, M. (1986), *The Apparatus of Repression*, Field Day:Derry.

Foley, C. (1995), *Northern Ireland: Human Rights and the Peace Dividend*, Liberty: London.

Gardiner Report (1975), *Report of a Committee to consider, in the context of civil liberties and human rights, measures to deal with terrorism in Northern Ireland* Cmnd. 5847, HMSO:London.

Gifford, T. (1984), *Supergrasses: The use of accomplice evidence in Northern Ireland*, Cobden Trust:London.

Greer, S. (1995), *Supergrasses: A Study in Anti-Terrorist Law Enforcement in Northern Ireland*, Oxford University Press:Oxford.

Greer, S. C. and White, A. (1986), *Abolishing the Diplock Courts*, Cobden Trust:

London.
Hadden, T., Boyle, K., and Hillyard, P. (1990), *Ten Years on in Northern Ireland*, Cobden Trust:London.
Hillyard, P. (1993), *Suspect Community: People's Experience of the Prevention of Terrorism Acts in Britain*, Pluto:London.
Hillyard, P. (1997), 'Policing Divided Societies: Trends in Northern Ireland and Britain',in Francis, P., Davies, P. and Jupp, J. (eds), *Policing Futures: The Police, Law Enforcement and the Twenty First Century*, London: Macmillan Press.
Hillyard, P., and Percy-Smith, J. (1985), 'Converting Terrorists: Supergrasses in Northern Ireland', *Journal of Law and Society*, Vol. 11, pp. 335-55.
HM Government (1995), *Frameworks for the Future*, Belfast:HMSO.
Hogan, G. and Walker, C. (1989), *Political Violence and the Law in Ireland*, Manchester University Press: Manchester.
Hunt Report (1969), *The Advisory Committee on Police in Northern Ireland* Cmnd. 535, HMSO: London.
Information on Ireland (1987), *They shoot children; the use of rubber and plastic bullets in the North of Ireland*, IoI: London.
Institute for Public Policy Research (1990), *A British Bill of Rights*, IPPR:London.
Liberty (1991), *A People's Charter, Liberty's Bill of Rights: A Consultation Document*, Liberty:London.
McMahon, B. M. E. (1974), 'The Impaired Asset: A Legal Commentary On the Report of the Widgery Tribunal', *The Human Context*, Vol. 6, pp. 681-99.
McVeigh, R. (1994), *"It's Part of Life here." The Security Forces and Harassment in Northern Ireland*, CAJ:Belfast.
Murphy, D. (1991), *The Stalker Affair and the Press*, Unwin Hyman:London.
National Council for Civil Liberties (1986), *Strip Searching: An Inquiry into the strip searching of women remand prisoners at Armagh Prison between 1982 and 1985*, London: National Council for Civil Liberties.
Ni Aolain, F. (1996), 'The Fortification of an Emergency Regime', Albany Law Review, Vol. 59, No. 4, pp.1353-87.
Northern Ireland Office (1996), *Foundations for Policing: Proposals for policing structures in Northern Ireland*, Cmnd. 3249, HMSO:Belfast.
O'Leary, B. and McGarry, J. (1993), *The Politics of Antagonism: Understanding Northern Ireland*, Athlone Press:London.
O'Rawe, M. (1995), 'United Nations' Human Rights Committee', *Just News*, Vol. 10, No. 1, pp. 4-5.
Palmer, S. (1988), *Police and Protest in England and Ireland 1780-1850*, Cambridge University Press:New York.
Pilger, J. (1996), 'Ireland's Hard Labour', *New Statesman and Society*, 1 March.
Rolston, B. and Tomlinson, M. (1988), 'The Challenge Within: Prisons and Propaganda in Northern Ireland', in Tomlinson, M., Varley, T. and McCullagh, C. (eds), *Whose Law & Order? Aspects of Crime and Social Control in Irish Society*, Sociological Association of Ireland: Dublin.
Ruane, C. (ed.) (1994), *Policing in a New Society*, Centre for Research and Documentation and Belfast Community Forum on Policing:Belfast.

RUC (1990), *The Chief Constable's Annual Report 1989*, HMSO:Belfast.
RUC (1995), *The Chief Constable's Annual Report 1994*, HMSO:Belfast.
Ryder, C. (1989), *The RUC: A Force Under Fire*, Methuen:London.
Ryder, C. (1991), *The Ulster Defence Regiment: An Instrument of Peace?*, Methuen: London.
Ryder, C. (1996), 'Secret RUC Rituals Behind My Sacking', *The Observer*, 10 March.
Stalker, J. (1988), *Stalker*, Penguin:London.
Statewatch. (1992), 'Mass Strip Search At Maghaberry', *Statewatch*, 2:3, May-June, pp. 9-10.
Statewatch (1993), 'Collusion and Britain's Irish Policy', *Statewatch*, 3:4, July-August. pp. 12-13.
Statewatch (1995), 'Northern Ireland: Prisoners and the Peace Process', *Statewatch*, 5:2, March-April, pp. 18-19.
Sutton, M. (1994), *An Index of Deaths From the Conflict in Northern Ireland, 1969-1993*, Beyond the Pale:Belfast.
Taylor, P. (1980), *Beating the Terrorists? Interrogation in Omagh, Gough and Castlereagh*, Harmondsworth: Penguin.
Townshend, C. (1983), *Political Violence in Ireland: Government and Resistance since 1848*, Clarendon:Oxford.
Walsh, D.P.J. (1982), 'Arrest and Interrogation: Northern Ireland 1981', *Journal of Law and Society*, Vol. 9, pp. 37-62.
Widgery Report (1972), *Report of the Tribunal Appointed to inquire into the events on Sunday, 30th January 1972, which led to loss of life in connection with the procession in Londonderry on that day by the Rt. Hon. Lord Widgery, O.B.E., T.D.*, H.C. 220, HMSO:London.

# 9 Education: A panacea for our sectarian ills?

*Kevin Rooney*

Community relations work in Northern Ireland faces a silent crisis, one the government seems barely aware of and which it has no strategy to tackle. Education for Mutual Understanding (EMU) and Cultural Heritage - introduced in 1992 to encourage respect between Catholic and Protestant children and promote non-violent ways of resolving conflict, is clearly failing (Paul McGill, quoted in *Education Guardian*, 16 September 1996, p.4).

The above quote appeared less than two months after the 'siege of Drumcree'. When one considers the sectarian tensions unleashed by the confrontation at Drumcree church yard and on the nearby Catholic Garvaghy Road, it is perhaps unsurprising that many agree with the assessment that community relations work in Northern Ireland is failing. Sectarian tensions provoked by the Orange Order marches came dangerously close to spiralling out of control in many parts of the six counties. Armagh, Bellaghy, Derry, Downpatrick, Dunloy, Keady, Newry, Newtownbutler, Pomeroy, Roslea, Strabane and various interfaces in Belfast and elsewhere saw sectarian confrontations over Orange parades reduce Catholic-Protestant relations to a new low.

McGill appears correct when he laments the poor state of community relations in the aftermath of the 1996 marching season. What is questionable is his linking of community relations and education. He automatically assumes education to be a panacea for our sectarian ills. More specifically, McGill sees integrated Education for Mutual Understanding between Catholics and Protestants as a way of solving the conflict. Ray Mullan, a representative of the Northern Ireland Community Relations Council (NICRC) shares a similar belief that education is the hope for Northern Ireland, while at the same time calling for a more co-ordinated approach between education and community relations policies, in arguing that 'nobody is taking control and nobody is showing leadership. It has come down to the Department of Education. It is their responsibility to make EMU work' (*Education Guardian*, 16 September 1996).

The idea that education is a major contributor to conflict resolution has become an article of faith among the Northern Irish educational establishment and within the community relations industry. One month before the events at Drumcree, the University of Ulster hosted a conference on the theme 'Education for Mutual Understanding and Democratic Participation'. The conference brought together a wide range of academics and practitioners to discuss the role of education in building bridges between Catholics and Protestants and assisting in conflict resolution. None of the speakers or participants raised any dissenting voices to question the significant role given to education in conflict resolution. This chapter takes a critical look at the educational policies designed to assist in conflict resolution. The first part of the chapter traces the origin and development of education as a sphere for assisting in conflict resolution, exploring in particular the development of Integrated Education, Education for Mutual Understanding (EMU) and Cultural Heritage. The latter half of the chapter weighs up the various arguments and evidence put forward to support the idea that the educational sphere can assist in conflict resolution.

## The early days

Since the inception of the Northern Ireland state in 1921 religious segregation has been the distinctive characteristic of the education system. In other words, the vast majority of Protestants attended Protestant only (also known as 'controlled') schools; likewise most Catholics attended Catholic only (or 'maintained') schools. Church control of Catholic schools is fiercely guarded and defended by the Catholic Church, which see schools as an essential ingredient in developing a Catholic ethos within every individual Catholic child. Protestant schools do not normally view church control as such an important issue.

Religion and cultural segregation is bound up with the history of conflict between Britain and Ireland stretching back hundreds of years. On occasions education was placed at the centre of struggle between Catholic Ireland and Protestant England. Until the late eighteenth century the Catholic population was banned from formal education by the penal laws, a set of laws established by Britain in order to promote British control throughout Ireland. Although the penal laws were abolished in the early 1800s, shortly after the Act of Union in 1801, they emphasised a trend that has continued to this day, namely religiously segregated education. With the creation of the Northern Ireland state in 1921, segregation between schools continued and if anything was reinforced, as the various churches scrambled for influence and control. It was these particularist interests which shaped education provision for the next 70 years and more (see Akenson, 1973; Dunn, 1990).

With the outbreak of renewed conflict in 1969 attention began to be drawn to the role of the churches in exacerbating or healing divisions. In particular the role of segregated education was increasingly viewed by some as a contributory factor to the very polarised community relations that existed in the early 1970s. By the mid-1970s a number of government sponsored research initiatives looking into the role of education and its relationship to the conflict had been carried out by Northern Ireland academics (Malone, 1973). Many towns had become demarcated into separate Catholic and Protestant areas. This separation was especially pronounced in working-class districts of Belfast. Increasingly, the lack of contact between Catholics and

Protestants came to be seen as a major factor in the continued conflict. A school of thought developed which argued for more contact between Catholic and Protestant children as a way of overcoming sectarian division. A theory of conflict resolution developed rapidly upon the assumption that the conflict in Northern Ireland was a clash between two different religious groups, one Catholic nationalist, the other Protestant unionist (Wilson and Tyrell, 1995, pp. 230-41).

Beginning with the diagnosis that the root of problem was ignorance of the identity of others, the prescription was that children of all religious persuasions needed to be educated together at an early age. As a result they would be able to respect each others culture and faith. For community relations advocates, integrated education, or at the very least increased contact between Catholic and Protestant school children, became the key to breaking the cycle of violence.

**Integrated education**

The impetus behind the push for integrated education comes from the belief that the traditional school system has reinforced divisions between Catholics and Protestants. What is required therefore is religiously mixed schooling in order to overcome mutual suspicions. Integrated education can be defined as bringing together in one school, pupils, staff, and governors drawn in roughly equal numbers from both Protestant and Catholic traditions. Its aims and objectives are quite clear. While its supporters would not claim that religiously mixed education is the answer to Northern Ireland's problems, they do see integrated education as having a part to play in pushing back sectarianism and creating the basis for a more tolerant society. Such education should assist in 'cultivating the individual's self-respect and therefore respect for the other people and other cultures. Integrated Education means bringing children up to live as adults in a pluralist society, recognising what they hold in common as well as what separates them and accepting both (Northern Ireland Council for Integrated Education, 1996b, p.4).

The roots of integrated education in the North can be traced back to the outbreak of conflict. The present integrated education movement came into being with the advent of the 'Troubles'. It expanded in the late 1970s, as an increasing number of parents from all sections of the community saw integrated education as a way to assist Northern Ireland out of the political impasse. This first group of supporters became known as All Children Together. Other groups such as the Belfast Trust for Integrated Education came into being as the campaign for mixed schools developed. In the late 1970s parents from different parts of the community approached existing non-denominational schools, controlled by the Northern Ireland Education and Library Boards, asking them to consider changing their structures and ethos to become 'more welcoming to parents of all religions and none' (NICIE, 1996b, p.1). Frustrated by the lack of response the parents decided to act on their own. They set up a second level school in 1981 which became Lagan College. Although the establishment of the College met with muted criticism in some quarters, media coverage was extensive and usually favourable. Perhaps the supportive media interest was boosted as a result of the hunger strike by Republican prisoners which occurred in that year. As each hunger striker died and republican areas erupted in violence, community relations plummeted. The opening of Northern Ireland's first integrated school appeared to offer a glimmer of hope at a time of acute crisis.

By 1988 a further seven integrated schools had been established. As the integrated movement gained momentum a control body and umbrella organisation was developed to act as a focal point. This new forum became known as the Northern Ireland Council for Integrated Education (NICIE). 1989 was to be a pivotal year for advocates of mixed schooling. Not only was NICIE set up, but the British government, through the Education Reform Order, provided for Grant Maintained Integrated Status legislation to encourage and facilitate the development of integrated schools. The legislation established funding for recurrent expenditure such as teachers' salaries, books and equipment from day one and funding for capital expenditure, such as the cost of buildings normally after a period of three years. By 1996 there were 32 integrated schools across Northern Ireland, with a further three planned for 1997 (NICIE 1996a).

Integrated schools are now a permanent and expanding part of the educational landscape. Increasingly their intake has involved children from the most working-class and deprived areas of the province and can now be said to reflect a true cross section of the community. Entitlement to free school meals is often used to indicate social class. An average of 27 per cent of children in Northern Ireland are eligible for free school meals. In integrated schools the average is 25 per cent, with some schools having as high as 47 per cent of their pupils entitled to free meals. These figures expose the myth that integrated education is an overwhelmingly middle-class practice. Although the number of integrated schools is still dwarfed by the maintained and controlled sectors, integrated schools are tolerated and in many instances supported by the majority of the population.

Attacks on the practice of integrated education are a rarity today and are confined to the odd maverick cleric or Free Presbyterian minister. The attacks which do occur tend to be defences of the segregated system rather than critiques of integrated education itself. For example, a series of letters in the nationalist Belfast morning paper *The Irish News*, arguing for and against integrated schools were notable for their conciliatory tone. The debate was sparked off by a well known Catholic priest, Fr. Denis Faul, when he urged parents to refrain from sending their children to mixed schools (*Irish News*, 29 September 1996). His argument was that under canon law Catholic parents must send their children to maintained schools. This contention rested upon the invocation of canon law, not on the deficiencies of integrated education. In the ensuing debate between supporters and critics of integrated education not one of those who were critical of integrated education remotely questioned the premise on which integrated rests, namely that it has a contribution to make in improving community relations by virtue of the fact that Catholic and Protestant children are taught together in the same classroom.

Occasionally, the value of integrated education is challenged on the grounds that it cannot mask wider limitations. McAleese (1996) argues that the transmission of sectarianism is clearly rooted in the home and in the community, and its locus is essentially in the family. On integrated education she argues that 'carts appears before horses' in the sense that sectarianism needs to be tackled in home environments as the first step. She also thinks that supporters of integrated education fail to see the 'intrinsic value of Catholic education', suggesting that forgiveness amongst Catholics and the marginalisation of the 'men of violence' have arisen from the Catholic school system. Under this critique, the aim behind integrated education is misplaced and perhaps out of date. Opposition to violence and the value of Christian forgiveness are instilled into children within the Catholic schooling system.

## EMU and Cultural Heritage

Although integrated education has received a largely favourable press, it should be remembered that only 2 per cent of pupils attend these schools. The number may be growing, but attendees are likely to remain a small minority for the foreseeable future. This is one reason why attention has shifted to EMU as a more widespread means of building bridges and overcoming division and conflict. To understand the importance of EMU and the related Cultural Heritage programme, they must be placed in the context of the ongoing community relations and conflict resolution initiatives within education in Northern Ireland. Before investigating their history and origins a precise definition and rationale is required.

The Northern Ireland Council for Curriculum, Examinations and Assessments (NICCEA) define Education for Mutual Understanding and Cultural Heritage as helping pupils to develop positive values and mutually respectful relationships and to appreciate human differences of all kinds, including culture, disability, ethnicity, politics and religion. EMU and Cultural Heritage are also designed to allow pupils to deal constructively with conflict. Cultural Heritage involves helping pupils to develop an understanding of their own way of life and that of others by providing opportunities to consider the many influences on culture and to appreciate the shared and distinct cultural traditions within Northern Ireland. While encouragement of a sense of belonging to one's own cultural background is provided, alongside respect and value for other cultures. Pupils are asked to consider perceptions by others of their own identity. The programmes are designed to cut across curricular boundaries and also have implication for school ethos, the pastoral care system, the schools's disciplinary policy, extra-curricular activities and relationships with the school and beyond.

*The origins and role of EMU and Cultural Heritage*

Since the outbreak of the conflict in 1969 the British government has introduced a range of community relations initiatives aimed at containing, if not ending, the violence. It is fair to conclude that up until the mid-1980s most of these measures were of a fairly disparate and largely incoherent nature. Interestingly though, when the Community Relations Ministry was closed in the mid-1970s it was the Department of Education in Northern Ireland which was handed the major responsibility for supporting the voluntary sectors, as well as schools and community relations programmes (Griffiths, 1974, p.16). In the late 1980s a framework began to be set in place which was to provide the foundations of a much clearer and coherent community relations policy. At the core of the new policy was the determination to increase contact between Catholics and Protestants, thereby hopefully quelling the animosity between them.

The Central Community Relations Unit (CCRU) was established in 1987 as a unit within the Central Secretariat of the Northern Ireland Civil Service. In 1990 the Community Relations Council (NICRC) was set up with government assistance. The CCRU now provides the backbone of community relations work in the North. In short, its task is to assist in the development of community relations work at whatever level possible throughout Northern Ireland (see Fraser and Fitzduff, 1991; Fitzduff, 1989; NICRC, 1994, 1995).[1] With the new structure in place and a commitment to encourage greater contact between Catholics and Protestants generally, the emphasis on contact between young unionists and nationalists has taken on added significance. Under the Education Reform Order (1989) the government:

1 Adopted a commitment to support initiatives towards the development of planned integrated schools.

2 Provided that EMU would form a compulsory cross-curricular theme in the new common curriculum, (though with no direct assessment of individual pupils as part of EMU).

3 Established Cultural Heritage, a second cross curricular theme linked to community relations, as part of the common curriculum.

4 Placed a statutory responsibility on school governors to report annually to parents on steps taken to promote EMU. This is the only aspect of the Northern Ireland curriculum which has this reporting requirement.

5 Implemented a statutory requirement to include EMU and Cultural Heritage in the curriculum of all schools from 1992. Financial support is also provided by the government, via the Department of Education in Northern Ireland, to promote cross-community contact between schools.

For proponents of community relations, issues of culture and history are seen as divisive. Biased presentation of history has led some young people to harbour an intense hatred of the 'other side' and in some instances for this to have led them to join paramilitary organisations (see Morgan, 1989; for a rebuttal of this theory, see Ryan, 1994). By making both EMU and Cultural Heritage a compulsory element within the curriculum they believe it will play an important part in promoting reconciliation. So what has been the effect of EMU and Cultural Heritage? Has its implementation in Northern Ireland's schools helped the cause of community relations? Has EMU turned students away from sectarian attitudes?

*Assessing the impact of EMU and Cultural Heritage*

From the material published to date it appears that the jury is still out on these questions. Alan Smith has made two observations in relation to its success or otherwise. The first point is that the period between implementation in 1992 and its impact on schools is still relatively short and provides limited opportunity to consider how effective it has been. Secondly, as EMU finds its place within the curriculum teachers perceptions of it differ. They are uncertain if EMU is solely related to increasing harmony between Catholics and Protestants or whether it should be interpreted more widely, including more universal aspects, such as gender relations, human rights and ethnic diversity in an international context. Despite this reservation he believes that 'in the short term, however it appears that most schools will rely heavily on a strategy which focuses narrowly on generating more inter-school contact between Catholic and Protestant pupils' (Smith, 1995, p.174).

Given the relatively short time span between the implementation of EMU and Smith's analysis of its impact he was perhaps understandably reluctant to be too judgemental about the performance and role of EMU. However, with the publication of the report *Education for Mutual Understanding: The initial Statutory Years* in the second half of 1996, we can begin to get a clearer picture of the effect of EMU to date. The authors argue that EMU requires stronger and more precise definition within the curriculum if it is to contribute to the improvement of community relations in Northern Ireland. They go on to make a number of recommendations:

1 The amalgamation of EMU and Cultural Heritage (pp.11-13).

2 The development of more specific guidance which highlights concepts such as human rights, civic responsibility, democracy and justice, and explores their relevance to contemporary society in Northern Ireland (pp.14-20).

3 The development of strategies which help teachers and pupils address more challenging controversial issues related to the conflict in Northern Ireland (pp.20-22).

4 The development of strategies within schools which address the fragmentation and lack of coherent planning for EMU across subjects and age groups (pp.22-25).

They also note that some schools have taken a minimalist approach to the application of EMU. Although the authors are still cautious in delivering a definitive verdict on EMU's impact to date two things stand out from their report. Firstly, some technical and organisational modifications are required to make the system more coherent. Secondly and more importantly, although they note some criticisms of EMU (pp. 7-8) these negative elements are seen as mere teething problems. There is no questioning of the view that the underlying assumptions of EMU are sound. In fact the authors suggest that EMU may have helped shape the political landscape of Northern Ireland and contributed to the peace process.

[T]here is some evidence to suggest that government support for Education for Mutual Understanding, along with a range of other community relations initiatives, has helped change the discourse in Northern Ireland by introducing a language which allows people to express their support for cultural pluralism and political dialogue rather than sectarianism and political violence (Smith and Robinson, 1996, p.82).

Where once the view that education could play a part in conflict resolution was one amongst a number of views, today it appears to be the major view. Almost everyone in Northern Ireland accepts the view that EMU is the way forward. In 1997 one would be hard stretched to find a negative comment about EMU and the role of education in contributing to community relations more generally. Increasingly, reference to the prospects for the peace process is not complete without a reference to the role of the educational sphere.

The idea that the educational sphere can be the arena for conflict resolution is not a completely new idea. It is more the case that it has taken on a greater significance in recent years. For example, when the problem in Northern Ireland is defined as a cultural one, as a clash of two competing identities, the solution is sought in education. However when the problem is defined structurally, as was more often the case before the peace process, many people argued that the solution was to be found in institutional reform or constitutional change. It is the change in focus from structural inequalities to personal attitudes which has allowed the proposed educational initiatives to predominate. Once the problem is largely interpreted as a cultural one it follows that the prescription must be an injection of cultural tolerance, hence the plethora of community relations initiatives founded on the basis of celebrating diversity and pluralism, particularly though not exclusively in education. If we can only understand each other a little more, the theory runs, then perhaps we can find an answer to our problems. This appears to be a common sentiment amongst the community relations industry today, a sentiment articulated by Dominic Murray who found:

[a] high level of mutual ignorance existing about schools attended by either major religious/cultural group...This ignorance is in no way confined to the educational domain. Indeed it can be argued that the very existence of a general lack of knowledge between the major cultural groups in Northern Ireland contributes significantly to the suspicion and intolerance which exists. Segregated schools, however, may contribute to and reinforce this separatism in society as a whole. It may be that the cultural experiences undergone by children in such schools have an effect on their attitudes in later life (Murray, 1985, pp.10-11).

Murray was arguing that cultural ignorance may be a *contributory* factor to the conflict. More recently, other writers have identified cultural ignorance and intolerance as the *major* factor in the conflict (see for example, Foster, 1989). Today the balance of opinion is heavily weighted in favour of the 'cultural conflict theory'. If we understand this point then we can begin to understand the importance attached to integrated education, Cultural Heritage and EMU as ways of overcoming cultural divisions between the 'two traditions' and thus of overcoming the conflict (Osborne, 1987).

## Education not the panacea

Advocates of the theory that education, particularly EMU and Cultural Heritage, are changing the political discourse in Northern Ireland for the better have yet to provide evidence which proves the existence of this link. The evidence from Northern Ireland appears to suggest a very different conclusion. Rather than sectarianism being on the decrease it appears to be more entrenched than at any other time in the last 28 years. True, the amount of violence has decreased, but it is dangerous to equate this with a corresponding decline in sectarian attitudes. A recent survey on the situation in Northern Ireland has claimed that '[e]veryone agrees that division between the two communities is getting worse' (Hadden et al, 1996, p.3).

All of the indicators point to the fact that community relations are at a very low ebb. Sectarianism is flourishing in Northern Ireland precisely at the very time when the various educational initiatives launched a few years ago would have been expected to have delivered some positive results, no matter how limited. It is worth repeating that not only has there been no reduction in community divisions, but community relations have deteriorated at the same time as various community relations programmes have expanded. The answer to the question posed earlier of whether the implementation of EMU and Cultural Heritage in Northern Ireland's schools has helped the cause of community relations appears to be negative. Time is drifting for those supporters of EMU and Cultural Heritage who plead that a more long term view is required before assessing its success or failure. This claim begs the question, exactly how long is required before we can evaluate EMU?

The cycle of sectarianism tends to suggest that the emphasis on education as a way of building bridges between the two communities has not succeeded. The burning of Orange halls, Catholic churches and Catholic schools, the tit-for-tat boycotts of Protestant and Catholic businesses and the heightened tensions over the Orange parades make a mockery of claims that community relations may be on an upward curve. On the contrary, the Protestant pickets outside a Catholic church in Harryville, Ballymena provide an example of a worrying new development in sectarianism. Rather than giving various educational and conflict resolution initiatives more time to work in diminishing sectarian and community tensions, one should perhaps instead examine the ideological basis on which they are premised in the first instance. At the root of EMU and Cultural Heritage is the implication that the conflict persists simply because people lack the cultural tolerance and maturity to live at peace with each other. In other words the various conflict resolution initiatives in operation today are rooted in a cultural interpretation of conflict. The basic premise is that a conflict like that in Northern Ireland is caused by misunderstanding or an inability to communicate. The solution must be for the various branches of the community relations industry to teach the combatants how to communicate with each other, with a view to overcoming their mutual suspicions. It is true that some educationalists and community relations proponents acknowledge the importance of structural factors (see for example, Smith, 1995; Fitzduff, 1995). Nonetheless they appear to represent a minority.

## Cultural identity or structural inequality? Identifying the right question

The cultural view of the conflict tends to point to the sharp and bitter religious divide and examples of sectarianism and religious intolerance. Is it possible that conflict resolution theorists have identified the wrong question? Instead of cultural difference existing at the roots of the conflict perhaps one would do better to examine the structural differences that exist at the heart of Northern Ireland's troubles. It may be the case that the cultural pluralist position mistakes the cultural expressions and manifestations of the conflict for its deep causes.

It subjectivises the conflict and supposes that a change of ideas and perceptions will resolve it. It ignores the structural basis. Even descriptively, the cultural approach is mistaken. Northern Irish culture deviates little from mainstream western culture on such issues as myth, nationalism, religion, compromise and violence...in other words, ordinary liberal democratic concerns produce conflict in the structural context of Northern Ireland (Ruane and Todd, 1991, pp. 39-40).

For stucturalists the roots of the conflict lie in actual social relationships not in perceptions. For them the conflict is ultimately about conflicting interests not conflicting ideas. The claim of Ruane and Todd that liberal democratic concerns produce conflict runs counter to much of contemporary thinking on Northern Ireland, which views the province as a 'place apart'. The North is viewed as somewhere that is steeped in ancient hatreds, a site of conflict which is a hangover from a premodern era. It is often pointed out that levels of religious affiliation and church attendance in Northern Ireland are the second highest in Europe, exceeded only in the Republic of Ireland. Often this is used to suggest that the people of Northern Ireland are living in a more conservative pre-modern society.

Cairns has compared attitudes to the issues of welfare, law and order and political protest in Northern Ireland with those elsewhere in Britain. On a range of different questions on these three issues there was very little divergence between Northern Ireland and the rest of Britain. On the questions where there were marked differences, there is little to indicate that the attitudes of people in Northern Ireland are pre-modern.[2] The differences appear to suggest that attitudes are shaped by experiences. In Northern Ireland, which has the highest rate of unemployment in Britain, people adopt a more sympathetic attitude to the plight of the unemployed. The differences certainly do not suggest that Northern Ireland is a pre-modern society. On the issue of the death penalty they display a more enlightened attitude (Cairns, 1991, pp.142-56).

The idea that people in Northern Ireland are intolerant and insular in their *attitudes* does not stand up to scrutiny either. In their analysis of attitudes to cross-community contact, Gallagher and Dunn found that in many ways Catholics and Protestants led separate existences. There was little intermarriage, high levels of residential segregation and, as we have already seen, primary and secondary education is highly segregated. Yet whilst there was little cross-community mixing, there were high levels of professed support for cross community mixing. Catholics were generally more open to mixing, but a majority of Protestants expressed tolerant views on cross-community mixing. It does seem reasonable to suggest that the reason there has been little opposition to EMU, Cultural Heritage and integrated schools is because people in Northern Ireland are favourably disposed towards mixing. The predominant attitude appears to be one of tolerance rather than intolerance towards people from the other main community (Gallagher and Dunn, 1991, pp.7-20).

Ruane and Todd have suggested that culture is a site of conflict not because of cultural intolerance, but because of structural inequalities. They point out that cultures do not appear out of thin air. Catholics and Protestants had their own schools, religious organisations, newspapers and cultural associations under Stormont, but Protestants also 'controlled the public sphere, the state apparatuses, the industrial and financial sectors of the economy, the broadcasting media, higher education - and imbued them with a ethos which served further to reinforce their culture' (Ruane and Todd, 1996, p.198).

This dominance has been radically reduced with the introduction of direct rule, but the Protestant middle class still hold a disproportionately powerful position in Northern Irish society. It is the unequal distribution of power in society which acts as a source of conflict rather than individual attitudes. Put simply, Catholics have an expectation that the state is run in the interests of others. Catholics and Protestants display tolerance towards individuals from the other main 'cultural tradition' This tolerance is not evident when it comes to the question of the exercise of power in Northern Ireland.

Initiatives like EMU and Cultural Heritage which promote tolerance and the celebration of cultural difference attempt to circumvent divisive issues like the constitutional position of the province. In doing so they avoid the question of the structural inequality rather than challenge it. Whether intentionally or not, the promotion of mutual tolerance and the celebration of cultural difference is built on the assumption that different identities can never be transformed. The idea is to tolerate differences rather than transcend them. In itself there is nothing dangerous about this idea, but in the context of Northern Ireland, a society which has deep structural inequalities, there is the danger that it obscures the underlying inequalities. Speaking on the ambiguity of multiculturalism and the ensuing problem for tackling racism Kenan Malik has noted that 'as the discourse of culture has recast the concept of race in a new form, so multi-culturalism represents not a means to an equal society, but an alternative to one, where inequality has given way to the toleration of difference and indeed of inequality' (Malik, 1996, p.170).

There is nothing inherently progressive about cultural diversity. The language of cultural diversity is not only employed by liberal anti-sectarians in attempts to promote cross community tolerance. In the summer of 1996 it was often invoked in defence of controversial Orange parades. Responding to opposition to the Apprentice Boys march on Derry's walls, Apprentice Boys insisted upon the rights of all to assert their traditions and culture. The idea that the dispensing of culture and tradition would lead to a bland world is completely consistent with the promotion of cultural diversity. In not taking account of the underlying structural inequalities in society the promotion of cultural diversity and focus on attitudes runs the risk of presenting society as one of two divided communities, whose inter-relations need to be continually regulated by a few enlightened experts.

## Conclusion

In many respects the origins of EMU, Cultural Heritage and integrated education lie in the sincere attempt to overcome the conflict and heal community divisions, a very worthwhile goal. Yet however well intentioned, the emphasis on attitudes only serves to obscure where the real problem lies. One cannot escape the fact that severe structural inequality remains in Northern Ireland. Direct British involvement has reduced some of the structural imbalances between the two communities. Most of the blatantly discriminatory practices have been stopped through a mixture of legislation and changes in the administration of the state, but there is no doubt that a deeper level of structural inequality remains. The local security forces remain predominantly Protestant and breaches of civil liberties continue to occur. In other words the nationalist sense of grievance is not simply a perception, but based on real experiences. The classroom teacher will have difficulty implementing EMU and nurturing respect for difference while basic inequalities remain (Smith, 1995, p.183).

It is clear that the conflict in Northern Ireland springs from a clash over competing sovereignties and a lack of equality. The elevation of culture and people's ignorance of the 'other', as a major source of division, at best avoids the underlying problem of structural inequalities and at its worst blames the people who are most disadvantaged by those inequalities for their own situation. No amount of exhortations in the classroom to understand the 'other' culture will do anything to improve the problem of structural inequalities and thus remove the source of the division. In fact, as demonstrated by the controversy over Orange parades in the summer of 1996, the elevation of cultural difference only serves to reinforce division.

Increasing sectarianism, highlighted by marching confrontations, boycotts, church pickets and burnings raises serious questions about the effectiveness of EMU, Cultural Heritage and other initiatives aimed at improving community relations in Northern Ireland. Put simply, it appears that the ideological assumptions which underpin conflict resolution theories with educational policy in Northern Ireland are both flawed and dangerous. Not only is the structural element underestimated, but the constant emphasis on cultural difference may actually cement and reinforce division. Perhaps teachers should stick to education and let the politicians find a political way forward. In its present form education is not a panacea for our sectarian ills.

## Note

1. The status of the NICRC and its relationship to other branches of the community relations industry is not straightforward. Even members of the NICRC differ in their description of the Council. To some, it is a quango, to others a registered charity. Although the CCRU is a government body which co-ordinates funding in the field of community relations, it also assists in the promotion of legislation. The NICRC has specific responsibility for promoting community relations through working with non-governmental organisations, the voluntary sector and cultural groups. The NICRC also ties in quite closely with the Department of Education who have major responsibility for promoting EMU. It is also noticeable that expenditure on community relations in

Northern Ireland has continued to grow, despite cuts in other areas. Add to this the considerable amounts of money coming in from the European Union and it would be no exaggeration to say that community relations is one of the very few booming industries in Northern Ireland (see Hinds, 1995).

**References**

Adams, G. (1986), *The Politics of Irish Freedom*, Brandon:Dingle.

Akenson, D. H. (1973), *Education and Enmity: the control of schooling in Northern Ireland 1920-50*, David and Charles:Newton Abbot.

Cairns, E. (1991), 'Is Northern Ireland a conservative society?', in Stringer, P. and Robinson, G. (eds) *Social Attitudes in Northern Ireland, 1990-91*, Blackstaff: Belfast.

Darby, J. and Dunn, S. (1987), 'Separated schools: the research evidence', in Osborne, R.D., Cormack, R.J and Millar, R.L. (eds), *Education and Policy in Northern Ireland*, Policy Research Institute:Belfast.

Dunn, S. (1990), 'A History of Education in Northern Ireland since 1920', Standing Advisory Commission on Human Rights, *Fifteenth Report*, HMSO:London.

Dunn, S. (ed.) (1995), *Facets of the Conflict in Northern Ireland*, Macmillan:London.

Fitzduff, M. (1989), *Typology of Community Relations Work and Contextual Necessities*, Policy Planning and Research Unit:Belfast.

Foster, R., (1989) 'Varieties of Irishness', in Crozier, M. (ed.), *Cultural Traditions in Northern Ireland: Varieties of Irishness*, Institute of Irish Studies:Belfast.

Frazer, H. and Fitzduff, M. (1991), *Improving Community Relations*, NICRC:Belfast.

Gallagher,A.M. and Dunn,S.(1991),'Community relations in Northern Ireland: attitudes to contact and integration', in Stringer, P. and Robinson, G. (eds), *Social Attitudes in Northern Ireland 1990-91*, Blackstaff:Belfast.

Griffiths, H. (1974), 'Community Development in Northern Ireland: a case study in agency conflict', Occasional Papers in Social Administration, University of Ulster: Coleraine.

Hadden, T., Irwin, C. and Boal, F. (1996) 'Separation or Sharing? The People's Choice', *Fortnight*, supplement, No. 356.

Hinds, J., (1995), 'A guide to community relations funding', *Journal*, No. 10, Community Relations Council.

Hume, J. (1990), 'Europe of the Regions', in Kearney, R. (ed.), *Across the Frontiers*, Wolfhound: Dublin.

Malik, K. (1996), *The Meaning of Race*, Macmillan:London.

Malone, J. (1973), 'Schools and Community Relations', *The Northern Teacher*, Vol. 11, No. 1, pp. 7-14.

McAleese, M. (1996), 'Interview', *Reality*, Redemptorist Order of Ireland, Maynooth.

Melaugh, M. (1995), 'Majority-Minority Differentials: Unemployment, Housing and Health', in Dunn, S. (ed.), *Facets of the Conflict in Northern Ireland*, Macmillan: London.

Murray, D. (1985), *Worlds Apart: Segregated Schools in Northern Ireland*,

Appletree: Belfast.
Northern Ireland Council for Integrated Education (NICIE) (1996a), *Developments in Integrated Education, incorporating Annual Report 1995-96*, NICIE: Belfast.
NICIE (1996b), *Integrated Education in Northern Ireland*, NICIE: Belfast.
Northern Ireland Community Relations Council (NICRC) (1994), *Annual Report*, NICRC: Belfast.
NICRC (1995), *Annual Report*, NICRC: Belfast.
O'Tuathaigh, G. (1991), 'The Irish-Ireland Idea: Rationale and Relevance', in Longley, E. (ed.), *Cultures in Ireland: Division or Diversity?*, Institute of Irish Studies.
Robinson, A. and Smith, A.(1992), *Education for Mutual Understanding: Perceptions and Policy*, University of Ulster: Coleraine.
Ruane, J. and Todd, J. (1991), '"Why can't you get along with each other?" Culture, Structure and the Northern Ireland conflict', in Hughes, E. (ed.), *Culture and Politics in Northern Ireland*, Open University Press: Milton Keynes.
Ruane, J. and Todd, J. (1996), *The Dynamics of Conflict in Northern Ireland: Power, conflict and emancipation*, Cambridge University Press: Cambridge.
Ryan, M. (1994), *War and Peace in Ireland: Britain and the IRA in the New World Order*, Pluto: London.
Smith, A., (1995), 'Education and the Conflict in Northern Ireland', in Dunn, S. (ed), *Facets of the Conflict in Northern Ireland*, Macmillan:London.
Stringer & Robinson,(1991) *Social Attitudes in Northern Ireland 1990-91*, Blackstaff, Belfast.
Wilson & Tyrell, (1995) 'Institutions for Conciliation and Mediation', Dunn (ed), *Facets of the Conflict in Northern Ireland*, Macmillan, London.

# 10 The economics of the peace process

*Pete Shirlow*

Throughout the conflict in Northern Ireland, economists, the business community and political representatives, from both the British and Irish states, vigorously argued that political violence retarded the socio-economic development of the Northern Irish economy, due to the instability and uncertainty caused by intimidation, murder and civil disorder (Gorecki, 1995). The most commonly pursued thesis was that the protracted and intense nature of conflict diverted valuable public and private resources into military expenditure as opposed to more productive social and private investment. Therefore, within weeks of the paramilitary ceasefires the cessation of political violence was acknowledged as an event which signified the withdrawal of impediments which had blocked the utility and direction of the economy and had hindered the promotion of economic growth, socio-economic well-being and extended material prosperity.

However, in a society condemned by sectarian disputation and cultural competition the economy has and continues to be an instrument for political contestation and social control (Shirlow and McGovern, 1996). Debates concerning the economy have been an evident part of ideological division which in turn aid the reproduction of sectarian asperity. As such it is has always been difficult to separate complaints about economic discrimination and political and cultural oppression, which emanate from both communities (McGarry and O'Leary, 1995). Certainly, the direction the economy was to take in peacetime produced alternative perspectives from the pro-Irish and pro-British communities. For Seamus Mallon, of the Social Democratic and Labour Party, the critical economic issue is equality:

> The most certain political fact is this: the nationalist community in the North of Ireland will never again accept a position where they are second-class citizens in their own land. Whatever the differences among them, there is a common resolve that never again will they accept the status of a subordinate and abused minority formerly assigned to us by the combined weight of the British government and the Unionist majority (Mallon, 1994, p.38).

John Hume leader of the Social Democratic and Labour Party, view of the Unionist community was more forceful than his counterpart when he stated that the Unionist mind-set based largely in the Protestant population of Northern Ireland...encourages widespread discrimination and conflict but is unsustainable' (1994 p.4).

In republican discourse emphasis has been given to the need to end British rule and to terminate the life of what is perceived as an unjust and undemocratic Northern Irish state (McGovern and Shirlow, 1997). As recently noted in the pages of An Phoblacht:

> It is often assumed, both by the media and many politicians in Ireland (North and South) that inequality against Catholics has been reduced, and that discrimination can be accounted for by historical factors rather than current practices. As such many argue that the political and human rights significance of discrimination has diminished...This is an example of how propaganda and self-imposed censorship has led to a serious distortion of reality. We all know that discrimination exists and is part and parcel of British oppression (An Phoblacht, 1994, p.14).

For pro-union academics such as Paddy Roche, the argument has been that in relation to a re-unified Ireland that Irish nationalist 'reluctance to confront economic reality has been recently intensified by...self-delusion' (1994, p.8). Overall, since the current controversy concerning the political economy of Northern Ireland broke a few years ago pro-Union thinkers entered the fray with unusual vehemence (Coulter, 1996). Pro-Union thinkers have appeared to believe that the instrumental advantages of the constitutional and statutory status quo are so profound that they are irrefutable. If anything pro-Union intellectuals have clearly felt that in progressing the economic status and validity of the Union that they are at last adopting the advancement of their key political asset. The Cadogan Group, in particular, aims to demolish the case for a united Ireland by examining the economic consequences of the removal of the British subvention (Cadogan Group, 1992). They stress the removal of the Westminster subvention would mean that:

> strains would arise from any attempt to make the residents of low income southern counties subsidise the living standards of their more affluent northern neighbours. Equally, the majority of northern residents are unlikely to welcome a reduction in living standards as the cost of a unification to which they were ideologically opposed (Cadogan Group, 1992, p.34).

Given the depth and significance of these competing views and the distribution of material resources it is not surprising that the demarcation which exists between the pro-British and pro-Irish communities is played out in a range of socio-cultural arenas which include habituation, production, consumption and residence. Although the conflict and sectarian divisions which permeate Irish society cannot be rooted in direct economic explanations which focus on the abstraction of inequality, deprivation and economic opportunism, due to the centrality and importance of national identities and the future constitutional status of Northern Ireland, it is still the case that the economy is a site within which sectarian discord is articulated. As such socio-economic conditions have indirectly encroached upon the conflict in terms of the character, objective and dominion of sectarianised politics (Shirlow and McGovern, 1996). The economy continues to be a weapon used to support, renew and reproduce the mode of political operation and cultural contestation which was evident before peacetime. If anything the cessation of violence has clearly indicated the depth of astringency and acrimony that exist between the pro-British and pro-Irish communities.

In addressing the concerns that the 'peace process' does not provide the structure for inclusive dialogue and democratic participation and that the economy is being used as an alternative although less violent arena of conflict and contestation, this chapter examines the nature and character of contemporary readings of the economy and their effect upon debates related to socio-economic conditions. The primary aim of the analysis presented is to provide an understanding of the sterility of the debates regarding socio-economic conditions and to provide an alternative platform of inquiry on which reasoned political debates could be advanced. As such this chapter has three objectives; firstly, to identify how the direction and regulation of the economy and the notion of a 'peace dividend' has taken a distinct ideological form; secondly, to profile the socio-economic impediments which blight the Northern Irish economy; thirdly, to produce an alternative framework of analysis.

**Framework documents and materialist explanations**

According to the Joint Framework Documents (JFD) one of the key challenges for a peaceful settlement is the active reconstruction of the region's economic base, rather than the use of public expenditure to compensate for Northern Ireland's terminal economic decline. There is already an enormous anticipation that the cessation of violence will be followed by tangible and corporeal improvements in the economic well-being of both communities, leading to major improvements in terms of the physical environment, infrastructure and the provision of employment. This expectation has been fuelled by high profile announcements of economic aid and a genuine willingness by the international community to assist in the building of peace. As such the main thrusts of the JFD are closer co-operation between the two states, support for North-South trade and the full protection of specified civil, political, social and culture rights as the basis of an envisaged settlement.

Unfortunately the peace settlement outlined in the JFD is clearly not designed to break the grip of sectarianism over Irish society. It proposes and supports mutual acceptance of ideals and principles which in themselves block the evolution and utility of democratic politics based upon an alternative to ethno-nationalist discourses. If anything the 'peace process' is a scheme for managing sectarianism and is based upon a sectarian stalemate between the pro-British and pro-Irish sections of Northern Ireland's population.

The most striking feature of the JFD is that it clearly determines what can and could be achieved, but does not actually locate or elucidate on the mechanisms capable of achieving certain goals and long-sought political and economic stability. As such its political, cultural and economic principles are essentialist and aspirational in a broad sense, but are also cleverly contrived in other ways in order to perpetuate the political dominance of both states in alliance with the business elites and middle-income populations of Ireland-both north and south. As such, the JFD like so much of the rhetoric attached to the period of paramilitary inactivity, has been aspirational, coded and filled with ideological gratuities and enticements (Hazelkorn and Patterson, 1995; Purdie, 1991).

Beyond the articulation of material progression, no significant structures or models of economic development which would resolve income inequality, social marginalisation and the social dislocation caused by some of the worst socio-economic conditions in the European Union (EU) have been advanced. As such, beyond the myth that economic structures would be democratised through the support of inclusive and participatory frameworks, those who have benefited most from the vast bulk of investment, drawn in parallel to support the transition through peace, are private investors and the upper and middle income classes. As such the economy was not to become an arena in which significant dividends either in terms of material benefits or democratic accountability were to accrue to the most socially deprived sections of Northern Irish society (Tomlinson, 1995).

Undoubtedly some of the most optimistic discussions of the peacetime economy and its future direction focused upon the probability of a significant 'peace dividend'. In particular, this has been viewed in the context of distended mobile capital investment and financial aid from international sources such as the US and EU. Unfortunately, of the estimated £360 million provided by the peace divided which was to come from the US, British Exchequer and EU funds, only around 9 per cent has been targeted for community development initiatives.

Accordingly, community initiatives which would aid not only those who are in desperate need, but also those very neighbourhoods which have been ravaged by twenty five years of war, were effectively relegated behind private investment strategies. As is evident from the distribution of these funds the vast bulk went to an elite business class who already enjoy the highest rates of disposable income in the UK and who are probably the most subsidised business class in western Europe. As noted by Smith in relation to the distribution of these funds, 'the monied mandarins were still at the apex of that system and still in control. It was in many ways a revelation that the administration of power and the distribution of wealth had been affected very little over twenty five years of war' (Smith, 1995, p.11).

Clearly, there is a disproportionate amount of omnipotence which is exercised by the business class over Northern Irish society and its socio-economic affairs. In effect the funding provided through the 'peace dividend' has tended to stream to those who can manipulate the opportunities created by the ceasefires due to the influence they have over the state fundholders and distributors. Somewhat ironically, those who had been unjustly affected by the allocation or war, intimidation and suffering, were provided, during the period of peace, with an unequal distribution of the 'peace dividend' and the material opportunities that were presented. In relation to this John Major's address to the Institute of Directors at Stormont in 1994 clearly stated that:

> ...peace will give a massive boost to Northern Ireland's economy. Equally, the chance of more prosperity, more jobs, better security for families, must be the most powerful incentive for peace. I know that the business community is already

preparing for new opportunities. So is the Government in partnership with you.

Thus we are presented with the economy as a catalyst not only for prosperity, but for the continuation of peace itself and the guarantee of security through economic growth. Moreover, the obvious dependency of the government upon the business elite in the overall plan of maintaining peace is part of an overall stratagem aimed at building class alliances which marginalise those whose poverty, social alienation and political hostility is to be dismissed and virtually excluded. Such an alliance which virtually dismisses the crucial role of the paramilitaries and the socially marginalised sections of the population is clearly undemocratic and unaccountable. Furthermore, the notion that a strong economy will secure peace is wholly illusionary. Any examination of the body politic of Northern Ireland indicates that political power is highly fragmented and that peace means more than higher wages, augmented North-South trade and successful boardroom dealings.

Of course John Major is not the only individual to pursue the materialist argument that economic well-being can condition the conflict and its eventual resolution. Bill Clinton stated at the first Trade and Investment Conference in Washington that 'the creation of jobs in Northern Ireland is an extremely important factor in the peace process equation. There is a direct correlation between unemployment and the incidence of violence' (interview in Omnibus, 1994, p.22). Clinton's supposition that job creation will somehow remove political antagonism is undoubtedly unrealistic as it is based on the simplistic notion that conflict in Northern Ireland is based upon differences in material well-being between sections of the population. Such a materialist reading of the conflict has been advanced in many quarters and has tended to support the notion that the rational self-interest of the individual influences political identity and that material differences conditions conflict itself. Such a perspective has been continually articulated by state and government representatives (McGarry and O'Leary, 1995).

In the materialist cognition of conflict it has been argued that each community is fighting to remove, gain or maintain economic control and/or inequality (Chomney, 1995). A more collateral explanation is that economic co-operation and trade, as outlined in the JFD, will provide economic growth followed by a more equitable distribution of resources which will remove socio-cultural antagonisms and claims of injustice and discrimination. As critically noted by McGarry and O'Leary 'materialist interpretations also suggest benign prognoses about the prospects for conflict resolution' (1995, p.267). However, given the confines of conventional economic analysis and its failure to fully comprehend the background of capitalist restructuring, the erosion of social protection and the mismanagement of welfare structures, there is evidently no clear strategic vision of how perceived benefits can be realised and equally important how a mechanism to deliver such benefits can be directed to areas of most need.

In relation to the materialist analysis, it is important to stress that issues concerning employment, unemployment and social dislocation are not at the heart of the peace process, as it is clear that opposition between the pro-Irish and pro-British communities is centred upon the present and future constitutional status of Northern Ireland. It is also manifest that the Irish Republican Army's decision to call a ceasefire was not based upon an expected 'peace dividend' centred upon job creation and extended material prosperity (Anderson and Goodman, 1995). However, within the sectarian construct in which Northern Irish society is positioned it is obvious that socio-economic issues and perceptions concerning economic well-being are part of the socio-political fabric of political debate, identity and animosity.

**Conventionalist economics and social exclusion**

Increased external investment, it is believed, will allow a more equitable distribution of employment, as external investors tend to implement fair employment legislation more vigorously than their indigenous counterparts. Although true in some cases the permanence of territorial and residential divisions means that the location of companies in any given location tends to mean that labour markets tend to still be drawn from either Catholic or Protestant areas (Shuttleworth and Shirlow, 1996). Moreover, the claim that external investors create net jobs gains is also somewhat misleading. Throughout the 1980s and early 1990s the external sector merely produced one job for every job lost elsewhere in the economy. Furthermore, these companies tended to create a significant number of jobs which are part-time or short term in character.

The essentialist notion that improved north-south trade and possible joint-collaboration by both states over investment and infrastructural improvement and that it encompasses nationalist aspirations which can be 'separated from the project of territorial claim over the island of Ireland' is unacceptable to both Irish Republicans and Unionists (Tomlinson, 1995, p.15). One only has to view Unionist hostility to the quasi-institutionalised co-operation between Bord Failte and the Northern Ireland Tourist Board to comprehend how such relatively benign arrangements produce profound political repercussions.

If anything the whole direction of increased North-South co-operation laid out in the JFD, whether economic or political, merely indicates to Republicans that at the constitutional level there is no indication of a removal of British sovereignty in Northern Ireland. For Unionists the same document provides succour for the notion that economic co-operation is a distinct process of rolling integration (Teague, 1993). It may well be the case that the direction the economy is moving in and the ideological confrontations that it is creating are not producing the expected outcome of cross-community and cross-border co-operation beyond the boundaries of the business elites and middle income groups.

In terms of the policies promoted by the Irish and British states the Northern economy is to be tied to an energetic promotion of conventional economic development strategies. Unfortunately, the multiple crises facing the underemployed, low paid and unemployed have produced few coherent or critical responses from the majority of elected or state representatives examining the limitations of perpetuating conventionalist and growth-led strategies which promote highly unequal economic growth strategies (for a conventionalist analysis see Barnett, 1995; Carter, 1995; O'Donnell, 1995).

Since the ceasefires the main characteristic of development policies has been the doctrine and trust placed upon neo-liberal economics and a materialist ideology which upholds the ideals of free enterprise and free trade. The consequence of sustaining such an economic model has been the advancement of a restrained and overtly ahistorical perception of economic development which not only expatriates social issues but also foregoes a valid examination of important cultural and political mechanisms (Northern Ireland Council for Voluntary Action, 1996; Peet, 1991). Clearly, the complex issues of discrimination, boycotting and social truncation are not central issues within the ongoing strategy of economic regeneration. The exclusion of such factors is so significant that it undermines the relevance of the conventionalist mode of peacetime economic-led regeneration. In a society in which such issues are a distinct part of everyday political and cultural representation their omission further indicates the sterility and lack of imagination which is slowly destroying the actual process itself.

For peripheral regions, such as Northern Ireland, the capacity to perform positively within this new profoundly competitive mode of industrial organisation is impeded by the fact that the Northern Irish economy is so rearward in terms of its dynamics, character and ability that it neither contains the productive capital or political power necessary to compete equitably. In internal terms the uneven development of the Northern Irish economy is demarcated by protracted socio-economic marginalisation due to the combined growth of poverty, underemployment and an inequitable distribution of social opportunity. The pursuit of a development model which is still tied to free market policies has and will continually fail to resolve distributional conflicts (Shirlow, 1995).

Furthermore, the failure of the policies, aimed at re-constructing the Northern Irish economy, to re-distribute wealth more equitably will only reproduce a host of unsavoury social conditions. Therefore, it seems somewhat ironic that the government equates job creation with conflict resolution, but continues to support conventionalist growth-led strategies of economic renewal which perpetuate the very social marginalisation and alienation which they are supposedly intent upon removing. Clearly, this is not irony but instead such a situation indicates the dominance of conventionalist economic planning and the tunnel vision which permeates government sponsored strategies.

The indigenous-controlled manufacturing base, which is supposed to lead the economy out of its morass, is continuously impaired by a lack of innovation, high-levels of over-specialisation in disintegrating low-value added sectors, reduced levels of accumulation, grant dependence and a loss of industrial competitiveness. The combination of these structural impediments has continually retarded the development of an indigenous-controlled economy centred upon market-led innovation and self-reliant productive systems.

Furthermore, the failure of indigenous-controlled industry to emulate a more successful model of development, centred upon flexible automation and the full integration of research and development, condemns Northern Ireland to a peripheral role which is incapable of challenging the uneven distribution of technical and social progress within the EU. The hollowing out of Northern Ireland's economy is not merely based upon a continual process of de-industrialisation but is also reinforced by an emergent technological paradigm centred upon dynamic efficiency, skill profile alterations, the nature of commercial capital investment strategies and adhesion into the global economy (Lipietz, 1986). As new technologies become the motive and carrier force of economic expansion, especially such technologies as microelectronics, telecommunications, data processing, optical technologies, robotics, renewable energy sources and biotechnology, the inability of the Northern Irish economy to generate such technologically-led industries is a significant impediment in itself. If anything a mastery of such technologies is critical to the perpetuation of continued growth and structural competitiveness (Teague, 1993). Yet few firms in Northern Ireland are likely to possess the capital, skills and knowledge needed for basic research and for product and process development. As such, the structural inadaptability between the indigenous and externally controlled sectors and the prominence of out-dated neo-liberal growth strategies which are pursued by policy makers and conventional economists, framed around cost minimisation, are generally invalid and wholly inappropriate in relation to the type of post-Fordist accumulation strategies which are being applied elsewhere (Shirlow, 1995).

Post-Industrial flexibility also raises anxieties about the prevailing nature of employment and labour market segmentation within Northern Ireland.[1] Flexible labour modes, deindustrialisation and the advancement of an observable service class have each modified the symmetry of local labour markets throughout Northern Ireland and in so doing have assembled an inequitable dispersal of material affluence and social welfare (O'Hearn, 1993). Preceding labour market alliances are also being eroded through transformations within the gender division of labour, underemployment the growth of inactivity, the deskilling of productive labourers and the accentuation of educational requisites by employers. This alteration and modification of traditional labour market structures has, in turn, created an expressive disjunction between middle income technical and professional employees and a low income employment sector whose wage rates and employment conditions have declined dramatically (Smith, 1991). The segmented nature of emerging labour markets indicates not only a polarisation in employment and wage conditions but also an increasing gap in social rank and socio-economic opportunity (Shuttleworth and Shirlow, 1996).

If anything, the middle and upper income groups of Northern Ireland now enjoy the benefits of increased consumption opportunities and relative job security. The recent growth in the financial services sector and the nature of technical upgrading among externally-controlled companies have provided employment opportunities for third level graduates and technically trained staff. In Northern Ireland the benefits of economic policy have been disproportionately controlled by the middle and upper income groups whose skill levels and educational training are closely tied to contemporary labour recruitment structures. Middle income and higher income groups have also benefited from post-Fordist consumption patterns and investment opportunities within the tourism, retail and entertainment sectors.

What is clearly evident is that the systemic distortions created by post-industrial alterations in labour market structures have not been addressed by contemporary policy making structures either before or since the ceasefires. In Northern Ireland it is patently observable that the contemporary nature of institutional governance is incapable of overriding the vagaries of inequitable strategies or economic development. What we are left with is a general failure by policy makers and conventional economists to concede that the extent to which new productive techniques and labour market structures could or will alter unequal levels of participation is both constrained and ultimately limited. It is clear that the development policies being promoted during peacetime are nothing more than aspirational in that they continuously presume that the protracted support of conventional economic growth structures will somehow instinctively generate widespread socio-economic benefits. As such the development of productive and social forces is continually being tied to a distinct demarcation of class interests and opportunities. Without any effective challenge against the positivist and inverted focus being implemented to reconstruct the Northern Irish economy, it is unsurprising that it remains a site of sectarian competition, but also an arena which can be mobilised by the British and to a lesser extent the Irish state as an instrument of social and political control (Munck, 1993).

The emergence of a post-Industrial economy, flexible labour markets, de-industrialisation and extended income inequality, has been guided not only by what are commonplace socio-economic shifts, but also by a purposeful manipulation of the class structure in order to alter the socio-political fabric of Northern Ireland. In terms of Northern Ireland's social structure, two broad trends have been most evident. First is the growth of white collar employment and second a rise in unemployment, low-paid employment and underemployment among an increasingly marginalised low income class (Cebulla and Smith, 1995). In relation to the former it has been obvious that the British state has ensured, throughout the conflict, the reproduction of sufficient outlets for professional and administrative employment and investment opportunities, even though such investment and state-directed support strategies are wholly unprofitable and stand in stark contradiction to the monetarist mode of accumulation evident throughout the rest of the UK (Gaffikin and Morrisey, 1990).

**Regulating an economy at war: regulating an economy at peace**

In western societies states intervene within the economy in order to regulate the market, compensate economic failure and advance structures of growth (Murtagh, 1993). Moreover, most states also adjusts and inure wage earners to the perpetuation of capitalist production through a mix of workplace and social regulation (Teague, 1993). The regulation of labour in relation to the medium of capitalist production, in Northern Ireland as elsewhere, has centred upon various mechanisms of social authority, material inducement, education, vocational training and the mobilisation of social forces. However, Northern Ireland is somewhat unique in that, for the British and to a lesser extent the Irish state, the regulation of the economy has been concerned with more than the resolution of accumulatory crises and antagonisms (Lipietz, 1986).

The economy has in itself become an arena within which the British state can pursue not only strategies of socio-political control, but also the discourse and promoting of political 'normalisation'. In relation to this the Government continually reiterate that they have 'no selfish, strategic or economic interest in Northern Ireland'. In overall terms the evolution of the economy is conditioned by continued deindustrialisation and by the British state's adoption of economic strategies designed to 'manage' armed socio-cultural conflict (Cebulla and Smith, 1995). To no small degree these two elements of recondite and consuming economic alteration and a long term political crisis that has centred on the very existence of the Northern Irish state have been very much interwoven and have made the governance of Northern Ireland both economically and politically exceptional (Rowthorn and Wayne, 1988).

The ideological goal of state regulation of the economy has been to dilute Unionist hegemony and to recruit Catholics into the realm of social power in order to provide new socio-political relationships in which divided loyalties are supplanted by shared material concerns. Moreover, the perpetuation and extension of material prosperity and sustenance by the British state has been conditioned by the desire to create a middle and upper income class who will act as a buffer between the state and the traditional working class loyalist and republican communities whose political hostility is acknowledged as generally uncontrollable (Smith, 1996).

As such and since the inception of direct rule, the burden placed upon the British state has been to elaborate a set of socio-regulatory customs which will restrain the contestation of its overall legitimacy (Tomlinson, 1995). This has been pursued through a policy of socio-political normalisation and the adoption of socio-political practices whose primary goal is to construct a set of social relationships which, it is hoped, will surpass certain sectarian hostilities and supply socio-economic 'normality' (Shirlow and McGovern, 1996; Cebulla and Smith, 1995). Moreover, the primary aim of state intervention has been to regulate and/or restrain political antagonisms as well as accommodate new socio-economic mechanisms of political hegemony.

Although, sectarian asperity is still manifest among all social classes there is an ever growing body of evidence which maintains the hypothesis that the upper and middle income group, irrespective of religious association, are inclined towards similar lifestyles and consumerist pursuits which are non-antagonistic. In particular the emanation of a numerically significant group of upper and middle income Catholics attests that there is a process of social mobility which supports a mode of socio-cultural realignment with the British state. This condition has led McCann to emphasise that 'in business, commerce and the professions there is no disadvantage in being a Catholic' (1994, p.52).

Furthermore, the emanation of current class forces is impacting upon the homogeneity of a Catholic population not only segmented by discordant material experiences, but also by an upper and middle income Catholic group which is arrogating a subtle reconciliation with the British state. As O'Connor notes: 'the perception that British direct rulers have none of the discriminatory instincts of Unionist government is more enthusiastically expressed among Catholic civil servants and lawyers than it is in unemployment blackspots like Strabane...' (1994, p.18).

Among upper and middle income Protestants there has been a process of embracing and openly tolerating variant all-Ireland institutions. The business community, in particular, is eager to elevate cross-border trade, company coalitions and the exchange of industrial know-how (Felderly, 1994). In regard to the antecedent epoch of Unionist hegemony the British state has sought to reconstruct the arrangement of the political connections of upper and middle income groups through re-designing the spatial loci of contested political identities (O'Connor, 1994; O'Toole, 1994).

The consolidation of upper and middle income forms of solidarity which are cross-community in character is supported by the state as a form of conflict resolution which will stimulate integrated schooling and a more tolerant political agenda which may incorporate joint-sovereignty or an arrangement for power sharing. It is correspondingly the reason of progressing cross-border reconciliation which will aid such political goals through re-locating economic activity with the objective of acquiring and expanding the productive dimensions and market opportunities of an all-Ireland economy (Baker, 1983). In overall terms the superintendence of investment capital and resources, the conception of alternative patterns of labour market regulation and the pattern of regulating production and consumption, while unmistakably responding to more general influences, has also been regulated by the desire to re-define the statutory dominance of the state.

Therefore the state in response to a relatively undynamic business elite, who have been reluctant to invest within the Northern Irish economy, has undertaken the role as a capital-risk provider. It continually provides relatively large amounts of capital and resources for enterprise development which are deemed financially hazardous (Porter and O'Hearn, 1996). Such state-led risk taking has produced a regime of soft subsidies for the corporate sector and has allowed private investors to produce distended, corpulent and inflated profits. The irony is that such a development was facilitated by a Conservative Government which aimed to produce neo-liberal economic policies elsewhere in the UK economy. In terms of political representation the elite class has, due to such benevolence, developed lobbying and capital securing skills which have virtually removed the need to engage in more common modes of political activity. As such they are becoming a depoliticised class, due to the major subsidies which maintain their accumulatory and consumption demands. Therefore, such soft subsidies create an atmosphere not only of dependency, which depletes the competitive incisiveness of the private sectors but it also leads to a mutual dependence between the state and the business and middle income classes (Cormack et al., 1993).

However, the British state has not devoted the same energy or commitment to those on low incomes. This has been due to a policy and form of containment based upon spatial and ideological considerations. Spatially, socio-cultural antagonisms were to be restrained, whenever possible, within certain low income arenas. Ideologically, the predicament created by conflict was to be contained among those who, it was surreptitiously perceived, could not exceed inter-communal conflict, those whom one previous Secretary of State allegedly referred to as the 'the political Neanderthals, the very people who only understand policing and not compassion' (Felderly, 1994: 32).

As the state has striven to safeguard and advance the position of the upper and middle income groups it has applied inferior attention to the preservation of inherited labour market structures. The erosion of which has impacted heavily upon the material well-being of the low income classes. For this group, particularly between 1971-1995, labour market conditions have become extremely inhospitable. A 42.7 per cent growth in non-earner families, a three-fold increase in poverty, a 32.2 per cent decline in income, and a rise in unemployment from 4.3 per cent to 14.2 per cent are all evidence of extensive social dislocation (Borooah, 1993; Shuttleworth and Shirlow, 1996; Teague, 1993). Furthermore, nearly a third of the jobs produced, between 1990 and 1995, were professional, managerial or administrative positions. During the same period access by religion to such positions was nearly equal, in terms of population size, and included a significant 32.8 per cent growth in Catholic representation since the mid-1970s. However, in terms of education and class background survey evidence has indicated that around 72 per cent of successful applicants, for such positions, had third level degrees and came from upper and middle class backgrounds (data supplied by Fair Employment Commission, 1996).

The result of these contemporary labour demand structures is a inclination to federate non-sectarian middle class solidarity while at the same time estranging sections of both the Catholic and Protestant working class (O'Connor, 1994). For many working class Catholics, the benefits accruing from twenty five years of struggle, in which, they could legitimately argue, they have borne the brunt of suffering, are passing them by (Rowthorn and Wayne, 1988). On the other hand, for many working class Protestants their inability to gain access to worthwhile employment within the new labour markets is not accepted as the result of economic re-construction, but of a Protestant middle class that has forsaken them and a Catholic population who are in socio-economic terms in the ascendant. In the often unpleasant and desolate space produced by these twin processes of alienation and social marginalisation the nature of contemporary loyalism and republicanism is being forged, reconstituted and reproduced (Anderson and Goodman, 1995; Rolston, 1995: Tomlinson, 1993).

It has always been evident that the use of funds to generate employment in low incomes areas was designed to placate the non-republican and non-loyalist groups within those arenas. This has been achieved through state alliances with the churches, the Social Democratic and Labour Party and the vetting of individuals with paramilitary connections. This policy of investment was also until very recently guided by a desire to advance funds even if projects were unfeasible, non-profitable and unsustainable. As such funds were used, by the state, in order to be seen to be concerned about the issues confronting areas of high unemployment and social alienation. In relation to state sponsored investment in Belfast, the Audit Office (1996) has charged that the provision of funds was seriously inadequate in that the fund providers did not exercise proper control over the use of public funds. Grants, it has been claimed, were paid out without any written conditions. There was, it has been alleged, no process to track grants and applications were not means tested. It was also found that many projects were awarded funding without any appraisal or assessment of their worth. If anything these early ventures were part of a depoliticising exercise in which the state wished to present itself as politically neutral, interventionist and compassionate despite the obvious cost implications.

For the low income Catholic group the relative abundance of funding from the state sector and a raft of statistics which record their inferior socio-economic status and the everyday realities of widespread social exclusion clearly influences the character and sustenance of Sinn Fein and the politics of re-unification (Bean, 1996). Since partition, the secondary status of this community and the inability to gain widespread social mobility has inspirited the belief that as a community they have been ghettoised and abused by the economic dominance of the Unionist community and by the political activities of the British state. It is not surprising that republicans, due to a deterioration in social conditions, view Northern Ireland as little more that a sectarian statelet (McGovern and Shirlow, 1997). In reality they are, like their low income

Protestants, condemned by a lack of skills or talents which are at present being mobilised within the labour market, especially in relation to securing well-paid employment. As such the low income Catholic group is not reconciled with or prepared to accept the Northern Ireland state because they are, as they were previously, visibly excluded from engaging in social mobility and/or employment opportunities. As such the materialist arguments and conventionalist economic strategies adopted since the ceasefire are unlikely to affect such individuals and may indeed highlight that even during peacetime they still remain isolated and socially excluded. Of course the same is true of a Protestant working class who are also now largely excluded from the benefits received prior to and since the ceasefires.

In terms of traditional class alignments, the regulation of the economy and civil society has furthered a shift from a hegemonic and industrial form of state regulated sectarianism towards a post-industrial structure. The orchestration of this transformation has been ordained by a British state who have striven to ensure social mobility for the upper and middle income Catholic groups, while at the same time pushing their Protestant counterparts away from their previous hegemonic hold. The central aim of this strategy is to fasten the upper and middle income groups so firmly to British state funds that they cannot operate or reproduce their material well-being without recourse to that very state. The expectation is that these groups will ultimately owe fidelity to the subvention, which underwrites their material position, and not to perpetuating traditional socio-religious hostilities. For the low income classes, the manipulation of material resources has produced few benefits. Therefore, it is not surprising that traditional sectarian hostilities are now discernibly located and replayed among a low income class embroiled in what is increasingly an intra-class war (McCann, 1995). What links and delimits the multifarious elements which constitute the politics of 'normalisation', is the state's primary desire to present itself as the sole site of legitimate authority. It does this by characterising Northern Ireland as an 'orderly' liberal democratic regime beset by the irregularity of an atavistic sectarian war and incongruous political concerns. It should also be remembered, however, that the aim is to provide an environment conducive to the operation of a capitalist economy.

While the politics of 'normalisation' can, and sometimes (as in the case with anti-discrimination legislation) does entail the advancement of policies and strategies which may be observed as 'positive', their implementation and ideological goals do not necessarily conform with or produce a rational society in which social relations no longer influence the manner of socio-cultural antagonism and hostility. The peace process and its dividend can be viewed in such a manner. The illusion is one of progress, equality and social advancement. The reality, however, is of unjust class alignments and the perpetuation of the very social and productive relationships which produce, stimulate and engender social unevenness and a sense among those who are socially alienated that, whether there is peace or war, virtually nothing is going to change. If anything, the adoption and inclusion of low income communities within the reconstruction of the Northern Irish economy would have produced a confidence in the process of peace building and negotiation.

## Conclusion

Of course peacetime has been paralleled by a range of civil disturbances which have been influenced by events at Drumcree and the exclusion of Sinn Fein from the peace talks. The violent events around Drumcree and the subsequent boycotting of shops in particular have had, it is contended, a significant and negative effect upon the economy. It has been alleged that these events stimulated a downturn in tourism and enquiries to the Industrial Development Board from mobile capital investors. In relation to these events the head of the Northern Irish Tourist Board, John Bailey, denounced those who would destroy the prospects of economic success. This line of argument has emanated from both the British and Irish governments and has had popular appeal in the local press. However, to argue that violence is wrong because it hinders economic develop clearly exposes the complete failure to examine more crucial issues which are impeding the actual peace process itself. If anything, such deliberations merely highlight that the two states and their representatives know what the symptoms of division are, but do not fully comprehend the causes. In such a situation it is all the easier to demonise and condemn than truly explore and examine more fruitful avenues of inquiry and conflict resolution.

Furthermore, the removal of the gun from Irish politics, whether temporary or permanent, has permitted the re-emergence of classic forms of sectarian opposition and conflict. The boycotting of businesses, the burning of homes and disputes over marching clearly indicate that even the removal of extreme forms of violence does not remove or impede the actual nature of sectarianised conflict. As is the case with the economy it to has become an arena within which to play out the hostilities which will not be removed by the peace process.

In terms of the economy what is needed is the creation of a Commission for Economic Reconstruction and Social Inclusion. The aim of this commission would be to:

1 Plan co-ordinate and integrate new initiatives.
2 Manage and direct adjustments in the economy.
3 Ensure that development benefits areas of most need.
4 Provide meaningful consultation and participation mechanisms.

Clearly there is a need for a new approach, involving a much more focused and targeted direction, greater emphasis on participation by communities and avoiding unnecessary layers of duplication and bureaucracy. A combination of macro policies to stimulate the general economic environment, meso developments strategies to upgrade the productive base of such a weak region and socially-inclusive micro initiatives to tackle unemployment at the local level is regarded as the necessary approach to a successful economy. As such any settlement would not only remove economic ambiguity, but would also allow the blueprint for policies which reflect a more determined political and cultural vision of what the economy should strive to achieve. This should also help ensure that support can be mobilised for successful implementation of the policy. Moreover, a democratic economy has to revise the balance of economic power in order to alleviate poverty and reduce inequality.

In regenerating the economy it is vitally important that the benefits of success are spread throughout each community. Other issues should concern policing, the rehabilitation of prisoners, victim support schemes, the retraining of displaced workers and the removal of political vetting in relation to community employment schemes. Unless economic regeneration provides jobs and hope to the unemployed, these people will not interconnect with the peace process. Any programme for reconstruction should have clear criteria, including active community involvement, priority for areas of highest deprivation, cross-border and border-region projects, new programmes for community development, a major programme to tackle long-term unemployment and special programmes aimed at those who have suffered directly from violence. More attention should be should also be paid to the promotion of mutual trust at the grassroots level. Unless this occurs any accommodation among political elites would be based on insecure foundations. In effect, while we all want a durable peace, are we ready for it in a cultural and political sense?

**Notes**

1. The debate concerning post-industrial flexibility has focused on work and employment relations. Two forms of flexibility are identified. Functional flexibility deals specifically with the organisation of work and the capacity of a firm to adjust the tasks undertaken by productive and technical workers in response to demand and technology alterations. Numerical flexibility refers to the capability of a firm to alter employment and wage levels. The emergence of such distinct forms of flexibility has also been tied to new production techniques and workplace structures centred upon core and peripheral workforces.

2. The other major factor which keeps the Northern Ireland economy from terminal collapse is the large injection of public money or 'subvention' from the British exchequer. In 1993 the subvention was estimated to be worth approximately £3.5 billion, or 35.8 per cent, of Northern Ireland's GDP. The level of state subvention and the direction of public-sector driven growth clearly indicates the pressure on the British government (given the continuation throughout the 1980s of socio-political conflict) to maintain a modicum of social stability (Cebulla and Smith, 1995).

**References**

Anderson, J. and Goodman, J. (1995), 'Euro-Regionalism: National Conflict and Development', in Shirlow, P (ed.) *Development Ireland: Contemporary Issues*, Pluto: London.
Baker, D.G. (1983), Race, Ethnicity and Power: A Comparative Study, Routledge: London.
Barnett, R. (1995), 'Economic implications of Peace' *Through Peace to Prosperity*, Northern Ireland Economic Council:Belfast, No. 3, pp. 48-56.
Bean, K. (1996), The New Departure, *Causeway*, No. 6, pp. 202-13.

Borooah, V.K. (1993), 'Northern Ireland-Typology of a Regional Economy', in Teague, P. (ed.) *The Economy of Northern Ireland: Perspectives for Structural Change*, Lawrence and Wishart:London.

Carter, C. (1995), 'Economic implications of Peace' *Through Peace to Prosperity*, Northern Ireland Economic Council:Belfast, No. 3, pp. 85-91.

Cebulla, A. and Smith, J. (1995), 'Industrial Collapse and the Post Fordist Overdetermination of Belfast', in Shirlow, P (ed.) *Development Ireland: Contemporary Issues*, Pluto: London.

Chomney, D. (1995), 'To Develop or not to Develop'. Paper presented to the Political Economy Unit: Belfast.

Cormack, R.J., Gallagher, A.M. and Osborne, R.D. (1993), *Fair Enough? Religion and the 1991 Census*, Fair Employment Commission: Belfast.

Felderly, E. (1994), *Fight for it. Or get out*. Conflict: Ontario.

Gaffikin, F. and Morrissey, M. (1990), *Northern Ireland: The Thatcher Years*, Zed: London.

Gorecki, P. (1995), 'Economic implications of Peace', *Through Peace to Prosperity*, Northern Ireland Economic Council:Belfast, No. 3, pp. 10-34.

Hazelkorn, E. and Patterson, H. (1995), 'The New Politics of the Irish Republic', *New Left Review*, No. 211, pp. 49-71.

Lipietz, A. (1986), *Mirages and Miracles*. New Left:London.

McCann, E. (1995), *War and an Irish town* 2nd edn, Pluto:London.

McGarry, J and O'Leary, B. (1995), *Explaining Northern Ireland*, Oxford:Blackwell.

McGovern, M. and Shirlow, P. (1997), 'Sectarianism, Regulation and the Northern Ireland Conflict', *Reclus: Journal de L'Espace Geographique*, No. 37, pp. 13-32.

Munck, R. (1993), The Irish Economy: Results and Prospects, Pluto:London.

Murtagh, B. (1993), Planning and Ethnic Space in Belfast, University of Ulster Press: Coleraine.

Northern Ireland Council of Voluntary Associations (1996), *The Donisson Report*. NICVA: Belfast.

O'Connor, F. (1993), *In Search of a State: Catholics in Northern Ireland*, Blackstaff: Belfast.

O'Dowd, L. (1980), 'Shaping and Re-shaping the Orange State: An Introductory Analysis', in O'Dowd, L., Rolston, B. and Tomlinson, M. (1980), *Northern Ireland: Between Civil Rights and Civil War*, CSE: London.

O'Donnell, R. (1995), 'Economic implications of Peace', *Through Peace to Prosperity*, Northern Ireland Economic Council:Belfast, No. 3, pp. 35-47.

O'Hearn, D. (1993), 'Global Competition, Europe and Irish Peripherality', *The Economic and Social Review*, Vol. 24, No. 2, pp. 169-97.

O'Toole, F. (1994), 'Floating unity on a tide of people', *The Guardian*, 23 February 1994.

Peet, R. (1991), *Global Capitalism*, Routledge:London.

Porter, S. and O'Hearn, D. (1995), 'New Left Podsnappery: The British Left and Ireland', *New Left Review*, No. 212, pp. 66-86.

Rolston, B. (1995), 'Selling Tourism in a Country at War', *Race and Class*, Vol. 37, No. 1, pp. 41-51.

Rowthorn, B. and Wayne, N. (1988), *Northern Ireland: The Political Economy of Conflict*, Polity:Oxford.

Shirlow, P. (1995), Contemporary Development Issues in Ireland in Shirlow, P. (ed.) *Development Ireland: Contemporary Issues*, Pluto:London.

Shirlow, P. and McGovern, M. (1996), 'Sectarianism, socio-economic competition and the political economy of Ulster Loyalism', *Antipode*, No. 82, pp. 123-47.

Shirlow, P. and Shuttleworth, I. (1994), The Fear of Employment, *Parliamentary Brief*, Vol. 3, No. 3.

Shuttleworth, I. and Shirlow, P. (1996), 'Vacancies, access to employment and the unemployed' in McLaughlin, E. (ed.) *Policy Aspects of Employment Equality*, SACHR: Belfast.

Smith, J. (1991), 'Industrial Development and the unmaking of the Irish working class', in Hutton, S. and Stewart, P. (eds), *Ireland's Histories*, Routledge:London.

Teague, P. (1993), 'Discrimination and Fair Employment in Northern Ireland', in Teague, P. (ed.) *The Economy of Northern Ireland: Perspectives for Structural Change*, Lawrence and Wishart:London.

Tomlinson, M. (1995), 'Can Britain leave Ireland? The political economy of war and peace' *Race and Class*, Vol. 37, No. 1, pp. 1-22.

# 11 The Northern Ireland peace process: A gender issue?

Rachel Ward

## Introduction

The search for a peaceful solution to the seemingly intractable problems in Northern Ireland has been ongoing since the time of the civil rights marches in the 1960s. The contemporary peace process can be dated back to the talks between Hume and Adams, the outcome of which was a peace initiative taken by the then Taoiseach, Albert Reynolds and used as a basis for talks with John Major, which resulted in the Downing Street Declaration of 15 December 1993. This was followed in 1994 by the IRA ceasefire and the subsequent Combined Loyalist Military Command (CLMC) ceasefire. Despite the end of both, the former after 18 months and the latter unofficially, the term 'peace process' has remained. The process has been a combination of politics at the constitutional level and at the grassroots, with the latter being a groundswell of initiatives from individuals and community and women's groups. An example of the latter development was the Opsahl Commission of 1992 which took soundings from a variety of interested parties regarding solutions to the problems of Northern Ireland (Pollak, 1993). However, constitutional politics have dominated the peace process. At that level, there is much lower female representation, ensuring that the influence of women has been muted.

That the peace process has on occasion appeared an exercise in futility has, according to one perspective, been due to the fact that women have not had a greater say in its development. Scuh a view sees women as peacemakers, while the majority of men have a narrow, sectarian outlook and so do not look at the broader issues. In their experience of working in community and women's groups, women have developed valuable skills which could be used in formal politics. They have also made an important contribution to the peace process in their own right, by building bridges across the community divide based on the common problems faced by those from working class backgrounds. The latter two points are valid ones, but the argument that women *qua* women can make a difference to the peace process because they are more inclined towards peace than men, is questionable. It should be noted that this view is not normally stated explicitly, but is revealed by reading between the lines. The Northern Ireland Women's Coalition (NIWC) was established just 6 weeks before the May 1996 election to 'all-party' talks. One of its key aims was to ensure that women were elected, but it had no clear policies and refused to be drawn on the border issue. This implies that simply by the presence of women, a different perspective will be brought to the debate. In an interview with two NIWC members, one of them, Annie Quinn, argues that 'if this Women's Coalition had happened 20 years ago, we wouldn't have 3000 killed.'(Sharrock, 1996, p.7). A survey conducted by Miller et al. found that 45 per cent of female and 32 per cent of male respondents were of the view that 'things would improve if there were more women in public office.' (Miller et al., 1996, p.158).

A direct link is made between gender and the peace process. The abuse of women for sectarian reasons, which, *in extremis*, resulted in the murder of Margaret Wright and Anne Marie Smyth is seen as part of a pattern of the subordination of women. The needs of women who have suffered during the years of conflict are in danger of being overlooked because of their status. Accordingly, McWilliams argues: 'Central to any peace settlement, therefore should be the reworking of power relations between men and women, including restoration of some sanctions against men's violence and controls upon it.' (1994, p.25). Following this line of thinking, women are the victims, passive in the face of male abuse, so a peace settlement should ensure that 'female passivity' is elevated over 'male aggression'. According to Women Together for Peace, women should use their natural propensity towards peacemaking to influence the peace process. Women are '...less aggressive. They are more likely to seek agreement. They should exert their influence over men.'(Anne Carr, quoted by Breen, 1996, p.6).

This chapter is based on upon a number of semi-structured interviews with women, mainly from Belfast, who are involved in politics either at the community level in women's groups, or within political parties. The chapter examines the notion that women, by virtue of their gender, can make a difference to the peace process. In consideration of this notion, two questions are raised. The first asks how much impact have women made on the peace process? The extent to which women have been involved in the peace process either from within political parties or community and women's groups will be examined. The second question asks whether women *qua* women can influence the peace process; are they 'natural peacemakers'? This is followed by a consideration of the NIWC in light of the issues raised by these questions.

**The impact of women on the peace process**

The persistent low level of female representation in politics in Northern Ireland has been well documented (Wilford et al., 1993; Roulston, 1996; Ward, M., 1995; Morgan and Fraser, 1995). Recent studies have shown an upward trend in female candidates and women elected (Miller et al., 1996). However, the peace forum election in May 1996 demonstrated that in numerical terms no significant progress has been made. Only 13.6 per cent of those elected were women (*The Guardian*, 1 June

151

1996, pp.8-9). Since 1993, the number of women elected to local councils has been in the region of 12 per cent. In Belfast City Council there are currently 6 women councillors out of a total of 51 (12 per cent) of which 3 are SDLP, 2 SF and 1 UUP. In contrast, Manchester has 27 per cent, Liverpool 34 per cent, Bristol has 28 per cent and Westminster has 30 per cent.[1]

Women's political activity is predominately from within their communities, as members of community groups, women's groups and political parties. A number of women councillors said that they had been active in the community for years before standing for election. Community activism is seen as a platform into politics, for those who want to take that path. Women 'cut their teeth' in community politics. They develop the confidence and the skills necessary for them to survive in the male bastion of City Hall. Community activism is also considered an important contribution to the peace process. It has provided havens away from the troubles and the pressures of living in deprived and marginalised areas. Bridges have been built across the community divide from these organisations, by such mechanisms as the twinning Catholic and Protestant women's groups, devices which have helped to break down prejudices born of ignorance of the 'other' community. (Dunne, 1996, p.14). These women's efforts received high profile recognition when President Clinton and the First Lady visited Northern Ireland on 30 November 1995. Hilary Clinton spent time with women from the community organisations. This, however, was the source of some resentment amongst women in political parties as '...not one woman from a political party was invited to meet Hilary Clinton - it was all women from community groups...since the peace process women in political parties have been forgotten about' (SDLP).[2]

The contribution of women at the grassroots of political activity was acknowledged by the Opsahl Commission. The commissioners were 'profoundly heartened by the resilience of spirit and creativity shown by many of the people who appeared at our hearings, notably the women.' (Pollak, 1993, p.4). In arguing that women's community activism should be 'recognized and supported' and that the problem of under-representation in formal politics should be addressed, the Commission contended: 'While there is no simple relationship between women's political participation and the resolution of the conflict, the experience of women's involvement in local community groups suggests that they could have an important contribution to make in the search for a political and constitutional settlement'. (Pollak, 1993, p.85).

The Opsahl Commission report notes that some people were suspicious and considered them to be 'outsiders'. Among this group were 'republican-minded people from West Belfast' (Pollak, 1993, p.3). This is not to say though that discussions regarding the future of Northern Ireland were not taking place within such sections of society. An example is 'Clar na mBan', a group which formed in 1992 for discussion 'around the future of women in the context of Irish national unity.' (Clar na mBan, 1994, p.3). Following the Hume-Adams talks and the Downing Street Declaration of December 1993, the group decided to hold a conference in 1994 which they called 'Women's Agenda for Peace', to counter the sense of marginalisation from the ongoing political process. There was concern about the fact that women were not mentioned in the Downing Street Declaration. At the conference, Oonagh Marron proclaimed that it was 'time to send a message to those negotiating on our behalf that this time around our support will not be unconditional; never again will we collude with the exclusion of people, with the denial of their rights. (Clar na mBan, 1994, p.9).

Other, similar, warnings were issued. Carol Coulter declared:

there is a danger that, whatever settlement or peace deal is concluded, that it would seek to undermine and ultimately to close down that kind of democratic community development and organisation which has become so important here in the North, and which is now also taking off in communities throughout the South as well, which bear no allegiance to the existing political system and which in fact are a reflection of the exclusion of the women and the poor and the marginalised from the system (Clar na mBan, 1994, p.12).

There was a sense that the peace process had been dominated by a small number of men which meant that the people of Northern Ireland, men and women, had been excluded. A second conference was held in 1996. Speakers highlighted such points as the need to '...take control of the process...', '...to think about the economic situation...and to listen for soundings that Protestant and loyalist women are making too.' and that 'peace and reconciliation in Ireland must involve everybody.' (Zell, 1996, p.14-16).

Some initiatives by women aimed at fostering peace in Northern Ireland have been the focus of much media attention. The Peace People provide an early example of women taking a high profile in promoting a message of peace. They were formed in August 1976, after 3 children were killed and their mother badly injured by a car whose driver had been shot dead at the wheel by the British Army. Mairead Corrigan, the aunt of the children, expressed her feelings on television and Betty Williams gathered signatures from Protestant and Catholic women who wanted an end to the violence. The first protest on the day after the funeral drew 10,000 people who were mostly women. The following three months saw over 150,000 people on marches and demonstrations (Brock-Utne, 1985, p.47). The two women leaders were awarded the Nobel Peace Prize in 1977, but Williams decided to keep the money for herself, an example which Corrigan followed, leading to a split in the organisation.

The work of the Peace People was arguably very noble; they brought large numbers of people out onto the streets to show they wanted an end to violence. However they were criticised by republicans for failing to condemn violence on the part of the British Army. One could also question the effectiveness of these displays in the long term because they avoid the conundrum of how peace can actually be achieved. Similar demonstrations were made under the auspices of Women Together for Peace, after the end of the IRA ceasefire in February 1996. They organised demonstrations during which they held white doves to signify their desire for the peace process to continue. Another example of a woman taking a high profile in the interests of peace was the visit to Northern Ireland by the President of the Republic of Ireland, Mary Robinson, in June 1993. This was deemed controversial because the President went to a Republican area of Belfast and shook Gerry Adams by the hand. This action was symbolic of the view that for any solution to be found, Sinn Fein need to be included in negotiations.

The interviewees were asked whether they felt women had made any impact on the peace process either through political parties or in community groups. There was no overall agreement that this was the case. A woman from the SDLP asserted: 'It's like everything in our party. You have the influence that you want to have. If you push you have your voice heard...I really couldn't see that as a gender issue within the party.' Following from this sentiment, a woman from the Progressive Unionist Party (PUP) stated: 'I would say the men in the PUP are as much for the peace process as the women are. There's no difference'. The similarity of attitude would be reflected in policy decisions. The respondent from Sinn Fein felt that there was a 'big influence' due to the level of involvement that women have in the party: '...more and more women are coming up through the structures...at Republican Family meetings which are held to sound out the grass-roots opinion regarding major decisions, it's...usually women who go...and are very outspoken...'. Women Into Politics (WIP) pointed to the 'correlation' between the peace process and the '...increase in women's community development...There was incredible pressure on the ground from prisoners' groups and different community groups telling the leadership that something had to be done', while the Shankill Women's Centre (SWC) was far more negative: 'The peace process hasn't developed; it is fundamentally flawed because Sinn Fein aren't at the table.' Women Together for Peace (WTFP) described the peace process as '...a bottom up movement - the prisoners had a lot to do with it as the women were holding the fort'.

The respondents from political parties were asked what had motivated them to join and whether they felt that women had any influence within their party. The woman from the PUP said that she had joined because it was an alternative to traditional green and orange politics and that if a woman was put forward it was because she was the best person for the job; '...it's definitely not tokenism.' The NIWC representative joined because it was a 'challenge' and because no other party represented her views. In discussing the influence that women have within their party, the woman from the SDLP said: 'it's a political party and like all politics you have got to fight for your seat - there's no man going to stand back and say 'it's yours dear, take it'. The woman from Sinn Fein joined because of her republican and working class background and felt that women in the party were quite influential. She highlighted the fact that three-quarters of the Belfast leadership are women. The woman from the Ulster Unionist Party (UUP) had been a member for 30 years. She felt that women were now coming to the fore in the party and gave the example of the forum elections, whilst admitting: 'When it came to rank us the two men came first. I don't know whether that was because the majority of delegates would have picked men or whether the men had been involved longer and more actively in politics. One of them had been at the old Stormont.

This last point leads one to question whether the UUP and other parties who ranked their women candidates third or fourth on the list were serious about having women representatives in the forum and the talks, or whether it was an exercise in tokenism and a means of countering any criticism, not least from the NIWC. Does the fact that women are being ranked at all in the male dominated sphere of constitutional politics mean that they have influenced the agenda? Concerns regarding the equal representation of women and the importance of broader issues such as health and education, which tend to be termed 'women's issues', have been given some attention. The SDLP, Sinn Fein and the UUP have women's sections and the Alliance Party has a spokesperson on women's issues. Sinn Fein and the SDLP operate a policy of positive discrimination with regard to positions of responsibility within the parties. Along with the Alliance Party they have 'positive action' including 'training and development courses, designed to encourage women to stand for both party and elected offices.', while the UUP has an 'exhortatory strategy' (Miller et al., p.176). With regard to policy, whilst all the major parties endorse equal rights for women, only the Alliance Party (APNI) and Sinn Fein have produced substantial policy documents devoted to 'women's issues'.'(Miller et al., p.179). At the grassroots level, arguably the activism of women has contributed to the pressure from below on the constitutional parties to keep the peace process going, although this would be difficult to quantify.

**Has the impact made by women on the peace process been due to the fact that they are women?**

Much is made of the ability of women to connect across the community divide, through women's groups getting together to lobby jointly for funding, or women from different political parties meeting to discuss common problems. Yet the ability to discuss common problems does not mean that women will be as willing to address constitutional issues in such a conciliatory manner. It should also be noted that such endeavours by women are not a new phenomenon; they would occur even if there was no conflict, as political and economic marginalisation are not a symptom of that conflict, although they may exaggerate effects. Are women better able to compromise; are they 'natural' peacemakers? If there were more women involved in politics would there necessarily be a different perspective on the situation in Northern Ireland? These questions received a mixed response. The majority of interviewees felt that women were better at compromising than men because of the challenges that they have to face on a daily basis.

> Because they are the primary carers, they have had to compromise themselves, whereas men have never had to compromise on anything. I think its generally women that take the first moves and are prepared to listen (WTFP).

> We are more willing to compromise because we look at the economic issues and...what's best for our kids, so we're looking at it with a totally different emotion from males. On the constitutional issues, I feel that we would definitely be better. We don't use word play and beat around the bush; we get direct to the point and get the issues out on the table and debate them wholly (NIWC).

It was acknowledged that 'women' are in no sense a homogeneous entity:

> Not all women are the same; women are terrorists as well...Overall I would say that women are the peacemakers. You would hope that if there were more women there

would be more dialogue because you can see common threads and they have worked together over the years across the communities. The issue of the border is a problem, but that could be talked about. The male politicians have to be dogmatic and against everything to keep the blood boiling. (Women's Information Group (WIN)).

There was a tendency towards generalisations:

I would say that women are more the peacemakers than men because it's men that cause all the wars. Women are more willing to listen to the other side. Men seem sometimes to have a very blinkered point of view. I'm thinking about Paisley when I say that (PUP).

Women look at things from a different perspective. As long as everybody gets something out of this then is that not more important than one person losing? (SDLP).

The underlying assumption seems to be: feminine - good; masculine - bad. If more women are to assert themselves and put themselves forward so that they have a say in the political process, surely it will mean standing up for certain principles and perhaps being aggressive in their negotiating style? Finding accommodation with someone who is diametrically opposed to you does not mean capitulation, which is what could happen if what are seen as traditionally male qualities are not taken on and used positively. Viewing women as somehow being better than men because of a perceived propensity towards caring and nurturing has dangerous implications, in that 'the feminist critique of acquisitive, aggressive masculine values provides the perfect language in which the powers that be can hope to persuade us to reconcile ourselves to the lower horizons and more homely ambitions traditionally associated with a woman's view of the world' (Hume, 1996, p.5).

In the context of Northern Ireland this can be interpreted as the abandonment of principle in order to maintain a 'peace' which would be simply the absence of war, with the fundamental issues of contention glossed over. The perception that the conflict in Ireland is simply because two sections of society and particularly the men thereof, are unable to agree how that society should be organised, absolves the British government of responsibility, and in the setting of the current peace process, gives it the role of neutral arbiter.

One respondent highlighted the problem in viewing women as 'natural' peacemakers:

I think its a really dangerous theory and its a kind of subversion of feminism: bringing out our passive, caring side. Certainly the women that I work with and myself too, we have strong beliefs, strong views and strong politics. I wouldn't be prepared to just suppress those in order to be caring, compromising and conciliatory. What I am prepared to do is put them on the table and say this is what I feel, this is what I think and this is what I want. Now you put what you want on the table and let's see if there's an overlap here that we can work out that we could both live with. That is different (Women's Support Network (WSN)).

Having questioned the notion that women are natural peacemakers, are there any actions by women *qua* women which have made an impact on the peace process? Has the focus on 'women's issues' helped broaden political discussion? It was noted earlier that women from different backgrounds connect over common problems. The interviewees were asked whether they felt that this was a platform for peace. Before answering this, many reacted against the term 'women's issues' because they felt that such issues should be the concern of the whole community. An example response was: 'I hate that phrase 'women's issues' because really they're community issues. The reason they're called 'women's issues' is because women put them forward and they affect women. It kind of marginalises them...' (SWC). Other women stressed the commonality of issues:'Yes, most talks around these sorts of issues have been going on for a long time - this is where people from different religions find their commonality...I myself would find I would have more in common with Sinn Fein than with, say, DUP stuck up in leafy land' (PUP). 'Definitely, everybody in Northern Ireland has a common interest...problems in a Protestant community are the same problems in a Catholic community.' (NIWC).

A less optimistic response was:

I think its been a problem for the Northern Ireland Women's Rights Movement as it was, that it stayed focused on those types of issues and refused to discuss the wider political issues. For me that's a denial of reality...I don't know if you could build peace on that, but it's one of the things that has to be done...if you want to resolve differences, you start from your similarities (SF).

Even more negative was:

This idea of peace is absolutely ridiculous. You can't have peace until you have just and democratic structures...People have to define the peace that they want and in order to do that they have to acknowledge what has prevented that peace. That is the real job to be done either by our politicians or by our agencies or the opinion makers of this state (WSN).

You'll never have peace here unless people are ready. People, especially in the Unionist community, who are quite liberal don't acknowledge past injustices because they believe that in acknowledging them they have some responsibility to them and they are not ready for that yet (WIP).

In essence, the focus on women's issues and the work that women have done in their communities has highlighted commonalities, but there is still the fundamental constitutional question to be addressed. With regard to the latter, groups such as the Women's Support Network and Women Into Politics are working to debate how differing aspirations can be accommodated, but the wider impact of this at the present time can be likened to dropping a very small stone in the middle of a very large pond.

However their endeavours are a step in the right direction.

## The Northern Ireland Women's Coalition

Frustration with the prevailing absence of women's voices was a big factor in the formation of the NIWC. One interviewee described the NIWC as a 'catalyst' in changing the gender balance of the political sphere. It certainly has raised the profile of women in politics and all respondents indicated that this was a positive factor, whether or not they supported the NIWC overall. The NIWC manifesto, which reflects the hurried nature of its establishment, states that it brings together women 'from all walks of life. They are Protestant and Catholic, unionist and nationalist, republican and loyalist.' The elections themselves netted the NIWC only 1.03 per cent of the vote, but this was enough to realise one of their stated aims; 'to get at least two women to All Party Talks.' (NIWC, 1996a, p.1). The manifesto promises that the NIWC will bring a fresh approach to political negotiations to achieve a 'workable solution' compared to the traditional political parties with their 'fixed agendas' (NIWC, 1996a, p.2). It advocates inclusion of all elected parties at the negotiations; the equal right of women to be included in those negotiations, and 'a pluralist society based on respect and equality for all.' (NIWC, 1996a, p.3). Included in this latter principle is the call for a review of policing, the criminal justice system and the position of prisoners. The Women's Coalition has received much criticism from women's groups and political parties for the undemocratic nature of its formation and the fact that it is unclear for whom and on what it actually stands. For example, the West Belfast Women's Network issued a statement signed by 30 feminists which declared: 'We do not believe that our interests as women in this society can be guaranteed by voting for women candidates simply because they are women.' (see O'Reilly in *An Phoblacht/Republican News*, 13 June 1996). Writing in defence of the Women's Coalition, Annie Campbell stated: 'The very initiative that we in the coalition are taking is a microcosm of what needs to be accomplished in the talks. No exclusions. All views respected. Working for an agreed accommodation.' (1996, p.7).

In July 1996, the NIWC published a statement on its progress which outlined the objectives which had been realised. These were:

> putting pressure on political parties to actively seek and address women's views and to select women candidates; demonstrating that women were available to contest elections and to train women in electoral politics; fielding candidates who would directly address women and getting Women's Coalition representatives elected; raising the level of public debate and awareness about women in politics and encouraging media attention on the issue and demonstrating the contribution that women have made, and can make, to politics, peace and progress (NIWC, 1996b, p.1).

Here are two NIWC members at the multi-party talks and there was a great deal of media interest in the Coalition. However, pressure on political parties to actively seek and address women's views and to select women candidates has been an ongoing concern of the women members of political parties. The media coverage leading up to the elections in May could leave one with the impression that women were totally excluded from politics. One respondent felt 'very angry that suddenly the whole media discovered women in politics, as if women did not exist before Monica McWilliams and Pearl Sagar came forward. They didn't do one serious interview with any woman from any political party throughout the campaign; it was a trendy headline grabbing thing to do' (SDLP).

An article about the NIWC noted: 'Given that women account for over half the electorate...the Women's Coalition looks well-placed to see its two top-ranked candidates, Monica McWilliams and Pearl Sagar, win their seats.' (Sharrock, 1996, p.6). This assumes that the women of Northern Ireland would be falling over themselves to vote for a woman to represent them at the talks. The reality was that the majority of the electorate voted, not along gender lines, but for the party which best represented their political views. An individual's gender is but one aspect of his or her political make-up; class, age, religion, and ethnicity are all contributory factors.

The electoral system adopted meant that the top ten parties each got two seats at the talks. Consequently, the UUP with 24.17 per cent and the SDLP with 21.36 per cent are sitting alongside the NIWC with only 1.03 per cent. This is blatantly undemocratic. The voting indicated that the NIWC represent an extremely small minority of the electorate. Brendan O'Neill argued that the electoral process was gerrymandered to the extent that 'no-one is represented, not even the political parties themselves. As a result an organisation like the Women's Coalition can waltz on into the talks, claim the moral high-ground as the 'representatives' of a beleaguered minority and set a new agenda (O'Neill, 1996).

The NIWC manifesto asserted that '...a vote for the Northern Ireland Women's Coalition is a vote for the equal right of women to be involved in that political discussion.' (NIWC, 1996a, p.2). Interviewees were asked whether they felt that the NIWC was a solution to the gender imbalance within politics and whether women should be involved *qua* women. The responses were generally quite negative, but favourable aspects of the NIWC campaign were acknowledged: 'It's like the Green Party - they have no impact. The useful thing is it makes women more acceptable in politics so it may improve the ability of women to enter politics.' (UUP).

> I think what the formulation of the NIWC did was it put the focus on women and that was good, but you still have to keep up the pressure...There's a lot of lip service being paid...Men put the onus on women to get into political parties, but it's like an empty invitation if they aren't prepared to change (SWC).

> We said that women should have equality and we do have as much right. I don't think it's enough being women and I don't think any of us stood on a platform saying that...Being women we've a right to be heard and what we are saying is we've as many skills as men. You can't just stick women in because they're women - that would be silly (NIWC).

The latter statement appears to contradict one quoted in the previous section, which said that women are more willing than men to compromise and would be better at debating constitutional questions. Others were quite vitriolic in their responses:

there were 5 NIWC women standing in my area, which I thought was hypocritical because they were standing women against women...these people that stand on the outside and think they know what they're talking about have had a big shock. When they went into the forum, I know that one of the DUP councillors said to them: 'Could you girls sit down and keep your mouths shut - you don't know what you're talking about.' (SDLP).

Women struggled for so many years to get equality and men aren't allowed to join their party. Where's the equality for men there?...What's going to happen when the constitutional question comes up? How are they going to debate that with other parties? They don't even have policies, they work on each issue as it arises! (PUP).

I don't think its enough just to say "we're representing women", because they don't represent all women...as republican women they would prioritise the peace process first rather than voting for women. There's no point in voting for women when we don't know what they're going to say (SF).

It's the calibre and politics of the women that's important...We didn't feel that the Coalition was doing anything different than the boys had been doing for a long, long time. They were colluding with that system...They were asking women to split their identities and that was the overwhelming basis on which the Network decided not to get involved. In our work it's important that a woman's total identity is respected (WSN).

An article in 'Women's News' quotes Pearl Sagar asking 'What is so wrong with going in to the table with an open mind?', in response to a challenge about the NIWC's lack of a stance on the constitutional issue. (Carolan, 1996, p.17). There are two problems with this approach. Firstly, is it possible to go anywhere with an 'open mind'? Sagar is from a working class Protestant background, so when it comes down to fundamental issues, if the majority of Coalition members decide that Northern Ireland should unite with the Republic, what would her reaction be? Secondly, how can one hope to negotiate without having a position to negotiate from? The Coalition's political principles include: 'political inclusiveness', 'equity' and 'respect for human rights', which are important, but the talks are about negotiating a peace settlement, which ultimately means finding a way of organising society which will not affront the identities of the unionists, loyalists, nationalists and republicans. The NIWC believe that they can move the debate on from the longstanding intractable positions of the traditional political parties by 'nurturing the talks' (NIWC, 1996b, p. 2) and by focusing on the 'bread and butter' issues which have been the impetus behind community activism and links between the communities. The limitations of this approach have already been outlined. Furthermore, is there really anything new in what the NIWC are trying to do, apart from raising the profile of women in politics? Under the heading 'New Thinking', the manifesto stressed the importance of 'local and international investment' for 'social and economic development'. (NIWC, 1996b, p.3). Traditional parties, such as the SDLP whose membership is 47 per cent women,[3] have been active in encouraging investment in Northern Ireland. The SDLP have also taken on a nurturing role in trying to maintain dialogue during the peace process.

## Conclusion

The Northern Ireland peace process is not a gender issue. It has highlighted the prevailing inequalities between men and women in the political process which need to be addressed. This does not mean to say that a person's gender gives them a natural right to be in power positions. Instead, what needs to be tackled is the notion that certain attributes are innately male or female. It is within all of us to be assertive and aggressive, and such qualities are essential in this sphere.

The women who have been involved in the peace process have had to become more assertive in order to get funding for their community projects or to make their voices heard in their political parties. The women working in the communities have demonstrated that there are areas of commonality, which is an important contribution to finding accommodation. Issues which have been ghettoised as 'women's issues' are really important community issues which the work of women politicians and community workers is giving a higher profile. Continuing pressure from women within political parties and from community groups will see a change in the gender balance, but this will be a slow process.

Women in Northern Ireland have had some influence on the political agenda because they are taken more seriously by the political parties in terms of policies and the encouragement of increased numbers of women representatives. The NIWC may have helped to facilitate women into positions of influence within their respective parties because of the heightened focus on the gender imbalance. However, that women should receive a higher profile is the only point around which there is any consensus.

While some women are peacemakers, other women are quite the opposite and would refuse to compromise. It is not enough to just want peace in the minimalist form of the absence of war. The debate which needs to take place regarding how a genuine peace can be achieved requires the input of skilled negotiators, male and female.

## Acknowledgements

The author would like to thank the European Studies Research Institute at the University of Salford for its generous funding of the fieldwork for this chapter.

## Notes

1. Data supplied by individual councils.
2. Many interviewees did not wish to be named. Accordingly, they are identified only by party affiliation, although they are speaking in individual capacities.
3. Personal correspondence with Gerry Cosgrove, SDLP administrator, 10 June 1996.

## References

Breen S, (1996), 'Fear has returned', *The Guardian Supplement*, 29 February.

Brock-Utne, B, (1985), *Educating for Peace: A Feminist Perspective*, Pergamon: London.

Campbell A. (1996), 'Women's Coalition - right of reply', *An Phoblacht/Republican News*, 4 July.

Carolan, F. (1996), 'Women on the move: The Women's Coalition', *Women's News*, No. 79, June/July.

Clar na mBan(1994),*Women's Agenda for Peace:Conference Report*, Clar na mBan: Belfast.

Dunne, M. (1996), 'United we stand', *Everywoman*, July.

Hume, M. (1996), 'What's wrong with masculinity?', *Living Marxism*, May, pp. 4-5.

Miller, R.L., Wilford, R. and Donoghue, F. (1996), *Women and Political Participation in Northern Ireland*, Avebury: Aldershot.

Morgan,V.and Fraser,G,(1995),'Women and the Northern Ireland Conflict: Experiences and Responses', in Dunn, S. (ed.), *Facets of the Conflict in Northern Ireland*, Macmillan: London

NIWC, (1996a), *Manifesto*, NIWC: Belfast.

NIWC, (1996b), *Statement of Aims*, NIWC: Belfast.

O'Neill B, (1996), 'Democracy is not about the majority', *Living Marxism*, September, pp. 17-19.

O'Reilly R, (1996), 'Women's Coalition - what's the agenda?', *An Phoblacht/Republican News*, 13 June.

O'Rourke P, (1996), 'The Peace People', *An Phoblacht/Republican News*, 8 August.

Pollak, A. (ed.) (1993), *A Citizens' Inquiry: The Opsahl Report on Northern Ireland*, Lilliput: Dublin.

Roulston, C. (1996), 'Equal Opportunities for Women', in Aughey, A. and Morrow, D. (eds.) *Northern Ireland Politics*, Longman:Harlow.

Sharrock, D. (1996), 'Brave New World', *The Guardian Supplement*, 27 May.

Ward M, (1995), *Unmanageable Revolutionaries: women and Irish nationalism*, Pluto: London.

Wilford, R. et al, (1993), 'In Their Own Voices: Women Councillors in Northern Ireland', *Public Administration*, Vol. 71, pp. 341-55.

Zell, A. (1996), 'Women's Agenda for the Future', *Women's News*, No. 79, June/July.

# Part Four
# CONCLUSION

# 12 Conclusion

*Chris Gilligan and Jon Tonge*

The primary aim of this book was to provide a substantial discussion of themes within the peace process. Although it was not an attempt to produce a catechistic question and answer session, the book nonetheless sought to address four key issues. Firstly, why did a peace process develop? Secondly, what were the major themes within the process? Thirdly, what have been the major difficulties? Finally and most tentatively, what are the future prospects for the peace process?

In respect of the first question, it is evident that a peace process developed due to changes in republicanism, which sought new allies and accepted a twenty-six county state speaking on behalf of a thirty-two county nation. No longer did republicans see themselves as sole 'liberators' of Ireland. The extent to which this does indeed constitute the death of republicanism, as Mark Ryan has argued, depends upon the extent to which the winning of new friends has been accompanied by the abandonment of old ambitions. The discussion of changing republican agendas highlighted how the emphasis upon parity of esteem and inclusive dialogue amounted to a creed of 'new reformism' seemingly at odds with traditional republican objectives. Unquestionably the acceptance of the once 'neo-colonial' southern state; emphasis upon parity of esteem and search for inclusive dialogue represent a new form of republicanism. What needs to be determined is whether this shifting republicanism is based upon revised ends or means. The desire for inclusion in all-party talks may offer a chance to articulate 'republican objectives', but do those objectives any longer amount to genuine republicanism?

Perhaps less evident, but of equal importance, are the changes in the British government's approach, from one of conflict resolution to conflict management. Without intergovernmentalism, the search by republicans for inclusive dialogue would not have developed. The new approach of the British government has been to work closely with the government of the Republic of Ireland to divert republicans from a military stategy towards a seeming cul-de-sac of indeterminant negotiation.

This leads us to the second question; what have been the major themes of the peace process? The move to conflict management from conflict resolution has been reflected in new approaches, language and institutional structures. On the side of Irish nationalism this can be seen in the construction of the pan-nationalist alliance, a development in which republicans played a central role. Given the similarity of parts of the historical analysis of both constitutional nationalists and militant republicans (a point made by Mark McGovern) this development might not be seen as entirely surprising. Cross-border cooperation was now seen as the motor of change designed to facilitate Irish unity. Its development can be seen in the broader context of the general diminution of the concept of absolute sovereignty and the more specific issue of British promotion of the idea that sovereignty over Northern Ireland is conditional. As with much else in the peace process, cross-borderism was not developed on a bottom-up basis. Its promotion within existing and embryonic institutions formed part of the overall pattern of top-down intergovernmentalism which has characterised political activity in Northern Ireland. A recurring theme within the book has been the marginalisation of both the unionist and nationalist communities beyond the promise of an ultimate say in the formal outcome of a process from which they have largely been excluded. This stands in stark contrast to all the talk of inclusion. The peace process promised the inclusion of a range of voices, including those of women, loyalist paramilitaries, young people, the victims of the conflict and, conditional on an IRA ceasefire, republicans. Yet this inclusion has been at the expense of the majority of unionists and nationalists in the province.

The major difficulty in answering the third question is the tension between the desire for a resolution of the conflict with a successful outcome and the reality of an approach based on conflict management. This introduces two levels to the analysis; at a broad level the issue of the possibility of reconciling nationalist and unionist aspirations and at a more mundane level the resolution of the day-to-day issues arising from the peace process. Even if issues like decommissioning of weapons and Orange parades could be resolved, it was evident that problems could only be postponed without confirmation of changed republican thinking on the future role of unionists. The republican movement oscillated between rejection of the northern majority consent principle and vague notions of covenantship with unionists. The peace process appears to be based on the postponement of this question. The minor issues which needed to be negotiated have been numerous. The lack of movement on the issues of policing and prisoners has been one of the issues which has slowed the peace process. Hillyard emphasised in his chapter the value of confidence-building measures to be developed at the outset of any 'son of peace process'. Whilst critics of the RUC are themselves split between reformers and abolitionists, it may be difficult to achieve any substantive changes in this area.

A further problem, that of consent for parades, was rooted in the theme of parity of esteem. Although the manifestation of such tussles may be violent confrontation, the desire for parity of esteem is not necessarily a barrier to a peace process. Arguably, it is an ambition arising from a tacit recognition of the existing constitutional position in Northern Ireland. The seeming revival of sectarianism has perhaps undermined the efforts of programmes such as Education for Mutual Understanding, subject of Rooney's critical assessment in chapter nine. Such programmes tend to be predicated upon the assumption that ignorance of the other community needs to be overcome. Yet it is at least arguable that the most knowledgeable actors in the conflict are fervent republicans or loyalists. Their political convictions and prescriptions are unlikely to change in the event of a revamped teaching of culture in schools. Unless the tension between the desire for change and the fear of change can be reconciled the peace process is likely to be turbulent.

Finally, what future is there for the peace process? Many of the conditions upon which it was predicated have not disappeared. The themes of intergovernmentalism, cross-borderism and parity of esteem are likely to remain. Indeed a limited political process endured beyond the breakdown of the IRA ceasefire. To be sustained, this political process needed to be based on more than the ambiguities and prevarication of the 1993-96 model, which may well have floundered even if they had progressed towards all-party talks. The intergovernmental approach found in the Downing Street Declaration and Framework Documents used republican language whilst affirming unionist positions; it spoke of the need for inclusion whilst excluding most of the population; affirmed the exclusivity of sovereignty whilst undermining that idea and advanced cross-borderism whilst attempting ringfencing. That such masterpieces of ambiguity achieved even eighteen months of peace might be seen as remarkable. On the other hand it can be viewed as an exemplar of a peace process, in which ambiguity appears to be the central approach.

One reason the peace process appeared to stumble was the short-termism of the (ultimately highly futile) avoidance of an early general election by the Conservative Government in the mid-1990s. This perhaps explains why it showed little enthusiasm in selling the Framework Documents to reluctant unionists. It also indicates that conflict-management was of greater priority that conflict-resolution. Definitive accounts of the role of the British Government between 1993-96 are awaited. The 1997 general election and local elections in Northern Ireland did little other than to confirm the continuing political rise of Sinn Fein and the steady overall growth of the nationalist vote. Sinn Fein's support within the nationalist community reached unprecedented levels and the Party's overall share of the vote in the reached 16.9 per cent, a new record. The significance of this may be to confirm the hegemony of political rather than military approaches within republicanism. Yet this dominance, whilst justifying Sinn Fein's promotion of its 'peace strategy' cannot be entirely assured.

The size of Sinn Fein's vote owed at least something to a sympathy factor engendered by Sinn Fein's exclusion from talks. Two questions are begged. Firstly, will Sinn Fein's abandonment of an 'ourselves alone' approach finally lead to inclusive dialogue with a new British Government? Secondly and perhaps more importantly, has the Party agreed a minimum negotiating position within inclusive talks? The previously non-negotiable issue of the border has now been incorporated within a broader package of demands sought by Sinn Fein, some of which are more reformist than revolutionary in essence. Options such as joint authority, pooling of sovereignty, or even the status quo, with Britain as a persuader to Unionists, appear to be realistic negotiating positions. The rhetorical and actual pursuits of absolute sovereignty might yet be abandoned. Any continuing peace process will test the strength of republican and loyalist vetoes over change.